BUILDING YOUR
BUSINESS PLAN

Small Business Management Series
Rick Stephan Hayes, Editor

BUILDING YOUR BUSINESS PLAN

A Step-by-Step Approach

Harold J. McLaughlin

A Ronald Press Publication

JOHN WILEY & SONS

New York   Chichester   Brisbane   Toronto   Singapore

Library of Congress Cataloging in Publication Data:
McLaughlin, Harold J. (Harold Joseph), 1932–
    Building your business plan.

    (Small business management series, ISSN 0737-7290)
    "A Ronald Press publication."
    Bibliography: p.
    Includes index.
    1. Corporate planning. I. Title. II. Series.
HD30.28.M385   1984   658.4'012   84-11938
ISBN 0-471-88358-1

Printed in the United States of America

10 9 8 7 6 5 4 3 2

To
my beloved wife,
Bev
whose patience
many times
outlasted my own

PREFACE

This book is the result of over two years of research in business planning, carried out through the preparation of business plans for employers and clients. It was written because of the need for published information in this important area of business planning.

I believe that effective business planning is essential for the life and health of any business, whether it is a newly formed or an ongoing enterprise. Factual data are needed in order for investors and executive management to reach intelligent decisions concerning the funding of a new company or the approval of a new budget. These data are usually presented as one year, three year, or five year business plans.

Business plans should include (but not be limited to) a company's charter and goals for the product or service being considered. Market and market share data are also a vital part of the plan, including information on the market size, growth rate, industry pricing policies, competition, and competitive market shares. Detailed department plans are also required to outline goals, projects and project timing, personnel requirements, and, of course, costs. Financial data must be included to show the overall expected costs to achieve the stated goals, and certainly no plan would be complete without a mention of expected profits and return on investment.

Informed with these facts (or estimates), decision makers can better determine if they should fund or deny funding to a company, budget, or program.

It is the purpose of this book to bring together many of the fundamentals of the business plan and by a step-by-step approach, using examples and a case study to show how they can be presented for more effective results.

vii

I sincerely hope that this work will help those who are in a
business planning position to prepare more meaningful plans for
others who must reach the crucial and often agonizing financial
decisions.

HAROLD J. MCLAUGHLIN

San Jose, California
October 1984

CONTENTS

1

COMPANY ORGANIZATION AND PRODUCT/SERVICE DEFINITION

The purpose of this book is to bring together the fundamentals of the business plan to show by a-step-by-step approach and a case study how they can be applied for more effective results. As the title implies, the sequence of chapters parallels the steps that would be followed in planning a new company or in preparing a one-, three- or five-year business plan. It begins with a company's charter, which defines its purpose and goals, and ends with a suggested plan outline, designed for the most effective presentation.

In each chapter, one aspect of a single case study illustrates the topic under discussion. The case study, an actual business plan written by the author for a start-up (new) company, is supplemented by examples taken from competitive companies where additional illustration is appropriate. In the case study and supportive examples, the companies and people are real, but all names have been changed to protect the individuals' privacy.

The business plan case study involves two companies that manufacture products used by other manufacturing firms. Of these two, the primary firm is Creative Manufacturing, Incorporated. It is a start-up company whose chartered purpose is to design, manufacture, and market advanced-technology widgets for the OEM (original equipment manufacturer) market.

At this point some definitions are in order. A widget is a gadget.

It could be anything, which is fine for purposes of this book because it permits readers to interpret a widget as one of their own
products or services.

Creative Manufacturing, Inc., will serve the OEM market with
its products. *OEM companies manufacture or assemble a product or products that are marketed to end users* who put them to
practical use.

Diversified Manufacturing Corporation, the other company associated with Creative Manufacturing, Incorporated, is not part
of this case study. Diversified Manufacturing's corporate charter
is to design, manufacture, and market complete widget systems
for end users. Here, a complete widget system is one that incor-
porates a widget as one of the major subassemblies of the final
product. For example, a widget system could be a power lawn-
mower in which the gasoline engine is the widget, and the end
user is the person who uses it to cut the lawn.

Diversified's annual sales revenues are more than 10 million
dollars a year. The company is also *vertically integrated*, which
means it manufactures most of its widget system components,
including the widget itself.

Diversified tried unsuccessfully to sell its widgets to the OEM
market. Its failure was not due to product quality or price, but
rather to a lack of corporate commitment. Selling widgets (which
at times were scarce) to the OEM sector created a conflict of interest that interfered with the firm's primary business of selling
widget systems. When widgets were scarce, Diversified found itself confronted with a decision to either sell a widget to an OEM
customer or install it in a system to sell to an end user for higher
revenue. The company usually opted to satisfy the end user. As
a consequence, the OEM customer which got short-changed could
not satisfy its own customer requirements. OEMs cannot build
products and a business on suppliers who cannot meet their
contractual commitments. As a result of its erratic deliveries, Diversified was unable to attract a following of OEM customers.

A few key employees, recognizing an opportunity in the OEM
market for the Diversified widget, decided to form a new company, whose product base would be the Diversified advanced

widget. In exchange for the right to use the advanced widget, Diversified became an equity partner in Creative Manufacturing, Incorporated.

Following Diversified's approval of this concept, Creative Manufacturing, Inc., prepared a business plan as its first step to obtain financing. Funds were sought from the venture capital investment community rather than through debt financing. Venture capitalists are firms or individuals who provide start-up capital, or seed money as it is sometimes called, in exchange for an equity position in the venture under consideration. They also provide additional operating capital for new firms that have spent their initial funding. In return, venture capitalists receive additional equity ownership in the firm they are assisting. Debt financing usually takes the form of a bank loan that must be repaid at a specific rate of interest over an agreed-upon period of time.

Creative Manufacturing's business plan comprises the case study throughout this book. It was presented to the investment community in a slightly different format than presented here, but the context is the same, as discussed in more detail in later chapters.

The necessary elements of an effective business plan include: the charter, management, the product, the market plan, department plans, financial plans, and knowledge of how to put it all together. A good plan takes time to put together. It can take as short as a few weeks if all data are available. More probably, it will take many months, or even a year or more for a complex start-up company. But whatever it takes, take the time to do it right the first time! A good plan will be worth it.

DEFINING THE CHARTER

Defining a charter is one of the most important steps in forming a new business or planning a new budget for an existing business. A charter is nothing more than well-thought-out and clearly defined statements as to who you are, what you expect to accomplish, how it's to be done, and by whom. Its statements are based on the five *ws, who, what, why, where* and *when.*

Who?   Who are you?

The proper answer is, logically enough, your company, division, or department name. It often helps if the company name is representative of your product or service. From here on, the questions are more difficult and require much thought.

What?   What is your purpose for being?

What are your products or services?

What markets are you going to penetrate?

What market share do you expect to capture?

What profit margins do you expect to achieve?

What time period will these accomplishments be achieved in?

To properly answer these questions, you must know in detail exactly what it is you are going after, such as the ice-cream-consuming public between the ages of 8 and 16, or the subcompact automobile tire market, or the OEM widget market for end user widget systems. Perhaps it is your goal to capture a 10 percent market share with a 20 percent pretax profit during the first year of operation and a 15 percent market share with a 22 percent pretax profit during the second year. Whatever it is, be explicit.

Why?   Why are you going to be?

In our capitalistic society, the conventional answer is to earn a profit. If you are motivated by benevolence, it may be to improve the lot of humanity through the development of a new and better widget. Whatever your purpose, it should be clearly understood by you, your team, your investors, and your bankers. In other words, enter or continue your business with your eyes wide open.

Where?   Where are you going to sell your product or service? Locally?

Regionally?

Nationally?

Worldwide?

Location is important because it defines your resource requirements and how they will be deployed. One type of resource is needed to sell ice cream bars in a local park with a peddle-powered, dry-ice-cooled vehicle. Vastly different resources are needed to sell the same product citywide with a fleet of "Good Humor" trucks.

It is the same with OEM widget manufacturers. One set of resources is required to be a supplier to small, regional, widget system manufacturers that may require limited quantities of your product. A different set of resources is required to supply high-volume product quantities to a large, multimillion dollar widget system manufacturer that sells its product to a nationwide or worldwide market. Making calculations about this range of choice is part of knowing where you are going to market your product.

When?   When are your going to set up shop?

Next week?

One, two, or three weeks after you receive financing?

After you receive clearance from government agencies?

Timing is important. Are you getting on the bandwagon during the upswing of a new product cycle or the downslope of an existing one? Selling ice cream bars has a product cycle measured in decades. High-technology computer products have a life cycle of about two to five years, depending on the product. Widgets, for the purpose of this discussion, are somewhere in the middle of these two extremes.

Timing affects how the market will be approached: aggressively, as with a new product in a market with few competitors; or cautiously, as in the twilight of a product's life cycle whose dwindling market is heavily populated with competitors, all scrambling for a "fair share."

Timing is all-important when you are considering the construction of a new facility to house your new enterprise, especially in cases where our enviromentally conscious bureaucracies are involved. It can sometimes take two to five years to obtain the necessary permits to begin a new project. Will the opportunity have passed when authorization is given? Whens are not to be taken lightly.

Figure 1.1 is the charter for Creative Manufacturing, Incorporated. Notice that it contains all of the five *ws*. Some are buried in implicit statements, but they are there.

Who.   Creative Manufacturing, Incorporated Charter

What/Where.   License from Diversified Manufacturing Corporation its advanced-model widget for manufacture and sale into the OEM marketplace.

Who.   Diversified Manufacturing Corporation will be an equity participant in Creative Manufacturing, Incorporated, in exchange for a manufacturing and marketing license for its advanced model widget

What/Why.   Creative Manufacturing, Incorporated, will give the widget product design increased efficiency and other design improvements as may be required by market demand.

What/When.   Achieve a 10 percent market share of the OEM advanced-widget market within four years and 15 percent during the fifth year.

Achieve a 39 percent margin on the advanced widget product during the first quarter of the first year of operation.

Earn pretax profits of 18 percent on sales beginning the fourth quarter of year two and continuing through the fifth year at this level.

Provide a positive cash flow beginning in the first quarter of year three.

Produce a net return on investment of 1250 percent by the end of year five.

Expand the product line into other widget models, as market demand and profits permit.

FIGURE 1.1.   An annotated charter

ORGANIZATIONAL DESIGN

The successful organization must be designed to serve the needs of the entire company and/or department.

A manufacturing firm will be organized differently than one whose product is a service. The organization of an engineering department will differ from a manufacturing or marketing department. Though all are different, they still must serve the needs of everyone to get the job done efficiently and harmoniously.

An organizational structure should define all functions and how they relate to one another. How far is this principle observed in the organization of Creative Manufacturing, Incorporated? Creative Manufacturing's organizational chart is illustrated in Figure 1.2. It is a classical organization for a small manufacturing firm, containing five key roles, president, and vice-presidents of Engineering, Manufacturing, Marketing/Sales, and Finance and Administration.

Chief Executive Officer (CEO) and/or President

The chief executive officer (CEO), the president in this example, determines the direction of the company and sets the policies for all other functions (roles) to follow. If a company is a privately held firm (not a public corporation), the CEO is responsible to the owners. If the CEO has a majority ownership of at least 51 percent, then he (or she) is responsible only to himself. If the corporation is publicly held, then the CEO is responsible to the board of directors, who are in turn responsible to the stockhold-

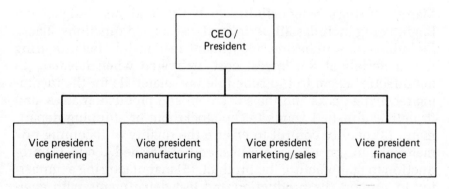

FIGURE 1.2.   Creative manufacturing organizational chart

ers. If the direction and policies set by the CEO are unpopular or ineffective, the board of directors have the power to replace him.

Engineering

It is engineering's primary responsibility to design the company's products, to produce drawings and specifications that will enable others to manufacture them. Once a product is designed, the design must be maintained throughout its life by sustaining engineers. The job of a sustaining engineer ranges from correcting inevitable design shortcomings to cost reduction (in order to maximize profit and keep pace with inflation).

Engineering is also responsible for designing a company's follow-on product, which could be an old product with new features or a completely new one. Product direction, however, is the responsibility of the marketing department, and Engineering should follow its dictates. Too often in immaturely managed companies, a technically educated CEO or engineering manager will design what he or she thinks is the latest and best widget and invest in its manufacture, only to find that it has no market or that it is too expensive for the market that exists. Engineering must take its cues from Marketing, otherwise it could lead the company, unintentionally, down the path to bankruptcy.

Manufacturing

Manufacturing's responsibility to build products designed by Engineering includes all peripheral, associated functions. These include (1) a purchasing department responsible for procuring raw materials at the lowest cost, delivered when needed, (2) manufacturing control to schedule raw materials for the incoming receiving docks and the stockroom and production areas, and to deliver finished goods to the stockroom or shipping department, (3) quality control to ensure the quality of incoming raw materials, in process assemblies, and of finished goods, (4) production to manufacture the product, (5) manufacturing engineering to support the production and test departments with engineering services for the design and redesign of the product, tooling, or test equipment. Manufacturing often has the additional responsibility of facility maintenance.

Marketing/Sales

Marketing/Sales determines what products are needed to satisfy market demand within the company's charter. It also sells all offered products. This broad mandate may entail the following functions:

1. Market research to determine market needs, trends, and competition.

2. Advertising/promotion to make the market aware of and interested in the company's product and its capabilities.

3. Product management to serve as a liaison between the sales, engineering, and manufacturing departments within the company. The liaison function can also provide a factory link with the customer. Product management helps shape the company's product according to market needs. It also ensures that all departments are working together to meet the company's goals for the product and helps to satisfy customers needs with proper factory support.

4. Sales administration to maintain customer order records, generate factory work orders, and ensure that work orders serve the interests of both the customer and company as intended. Reporting on the status of orders, order backlogs, and shipments in an additional aspect of sales administration.

5. Customer service repairs malfunctioning products, either at the company factory or at a customer's site.

6. Sales sells the company's product according to established quotas and prices.

Not meeting sales quotas in either direction, above or below, can be detrimental to the company, its employees, and the customer. On the one hand, underselling may cause an inventory buildup both in raw materials and finished goods. In addition to being expensive at today's high cost of money, inventory buildup can also cause employee layoffs. The result is reduced company profits and possible loss of jobs for employees. If, on the other hand, a product is oversold, it can cause inventory shortages and late deliveries to the customer. To avoid late deliveries, premium prices for raw materials may have to be paid. If employee overtime is required to increase production, the net result is reduced profits and possible customer dissatisfaction.

Finance and Administration

As a company's watchdog, Finance and Administration monitors the amount of money spent, where it was spent, and for what purpose. Actual performance is monitored against planned performance in the areas of sales, costs, expenses, and profits. Performance results are given to the company executives to enable them to make wiser decisions to better run the company.

Finance and Administration also assists in the preparation of business and financial plans and in financial reporting, as may be required by law. Payroll is also its responsibility. Indeed, it pays all bills (accounts payable) and receives and banks all customer payments (accounts receivable). A detailed discussion of this and other departments' plans, including charters, job descriptions, and budgets, will appear in later chapters.

MANAGEMENT TEAM

Who fills the five key executive roles is the most important decision made in the life of any company. As in the selection of a baseball or football team, the right selection of players produces a winning team. The wrong selection produces a disaster. The difference is that in business you are playing (or gambling) with other people's money, or worse yet, your own!

Besides the profit motive, investors all have one thing in common. They are risk avoiders. Whether they are backing a new company or refinancing an established firm, they try to minimize risk as much as possible. Investors want to be assured that they will recover their investment with a reasonable profit at minimum risk. If they can not be so assured, then they will choose alternative, relatively risk-free investments such as U.S. government T bills, money market funds, or high-yield savings accounts.

One way investors minimize risk is to select a management team whose members are, or have been, successful in the type of business under consideration. Investors want management team members with a track record of success. Without that necessary ingredient, funding will be difficult, if not impossible.

During the 1950s and early 1960s, venture capitalists invested heavily in electronics, computers, and other high-technology companies that combined good product ideas with immature management. Their founders were frequently superb technologists or engineers but poor business men. The result was a large number of business failures, with corresponding losses to their investors. The one-time "darling" of the investment community became an unwanted stepchild. Venture capital financing for new Atari-type ventures all but dried up for approximately 10 years.

The boom of the late 1970s once again made technology companies an attractive investment, but with a big difference. Past experiences brought wisdom. Technologists either acquired the necessary business acumen, or they made sure that their people possessed it. And so did the investors.

Today venture capitalists will invest in a company with a first-rate team and a second-rate product. They will usually avoid a company with a second-rate team and a first-rate product. In their opinion, the former has a greater chance of success than the latter.

The word team has been used throughout this discussion in earnest. Any member of management can be a superb individualist and excel in his or her own area. But, unless each can relate to the others, the company is headed for disaster. Honest differences of opinion are necessary and healthy. Basic personality differences are not.

From the investors' point of view, the ideal situation is to provide financial support to a company whose key team members have worked together successfully in the past. This combination minimizes their risks.

In light of investors' concerns, presenting your management team's background to potential investors in the best possible light is important. Investors require a personal profile for each management member that highlights his (or her) training and experience, where he has been and for how long, and above all, his accomplishments. Lengthy, ambiguous resumes that obscure the facts must be avoided. A personal profile of Creative Manufacturing's president, Mr. Joseph Smith, is shown in Figure 1.3. It is in an acceptable format that highlights his qualifications and accomplishments.

In summary, the importance of careful selection of a company's key team members cannot be overemphasized. To maximize a company's chances for success and minimize its risks of failure, each team member should be experienced and successful. As a group they should work well together. Additionally, their qualifications must be presented succinctly and accurately in a business plan to receive favorable consideration.

PRODUCT DESCRIPTION

A business plan should include a product description, written so that others can understand it without an interpreter. Keep industry "buzz" words to an absolute minimum. Buzz words might do great things for your ego, but they do nothing for the person whose attention you are trying to capture. Write the product description with your audience in mind.

If your plan is for an immediate supervisor, chances are good that he or she will be familiar with many industry buzz words and phrases. If it is for a company president or a financial analyst, fewer buzz words and phrases will be understood. Bankers and venture capitalists will understand fewer still. Presidents, financial analysts, bankers, and venture capitalists only want a general understanding of the product, what it does, and how it does it.

Diversified Manufacturing Corporation

Vice-president, Widget Engineering and Development: Four years with the company reporting to the president. Mr. Smith was responsible for the development of Diversified's widget product family. During his last two years with the firm, he was assigned the additional responsibility for marketing the company's widget products to the OEM market. Under Mr. Smith's stewardship, sales of the company's OEM widget products increased by 150 percent.

Acme Manufacturing, Inc.

Cofounder and president. Four years with the company reporting to the board of directors. He successfully developed and introduced to the OEM market a line of widget collection stations that were compatible with the industry's major manufacturer for these products. He later negotiated the sale of the company for a net return on investment of 700 percent to each investor.

Widgets, Inc.

Director of Product Development. Five years with the company reporting to the vice-president of Engineering. He was responsible for the development of a family of industry-compatible widgets that took the company from start-up to over 80 million dollars in sales in five years. He was one of seven company founders.

Additional Experience

Ten years of additional experience in the widget industry with four of its leading manufacturers. Mr. Smith's responsibility within these companies steadily increased from that of a graduate design engineer to the director of Engineering.

FIGURE 1.3. Profile of President Joseph Smith

Writing with self-restraint may be deflating to the ego of a creative, enthusiastic engineer or scientist who feels he has created the best widget on earth. But the hard fact is, presidents, financial analysts, bankers, and venture capitalists are concerned with costs, profits, and return on investment. Companies with products that are not understood in these terms by those who must pay for them are usually not funded.

TABLE 1.1   Creative Manufacturing, Inc., Widget II Specifications

Number of widgets	3 or 4
Number of data pistons	500
Valves per surface	11,000
DUPS per valve	20,000
DUP capacity	160 million
DUP density	6200 per inch
DUP cell time	100 microseconds
Widgee rotation speed	3600 rpm
Widgee rotational time	17.0 milliseconds
DUP transfer rate	10,000 per second
Full valve position time	55 milliseconds
Average valve position time	30 milliseconds
Single-valve position time	6 milliseconds
Valve position error rate	1 in one million
Mean time between failure (MTBF)	6000 hours
Mean time to repair (MTTR)	1 hour
Air filters	0.3 micron HPA type

Electrical

DC power requirements

+9   volts at 3 amps
−9   volts at 2 amps
+18 volts at 4 amps
−18 volts at 4 amps

AC power for optional DC supply

115, 220, 240 volts
+10%–15%, single phase,
60 Hertz at 350 watts

Physical

Dimensions	19 in.(w) × 7 in.(h) × 28 in.(d)
Weight	100 pounds

Environmental

Operating temperature	+ 15°C to +41° C
Operating humidity	10%–80% without condensation

A product description should be as short and definitive as possible—one or two pages at the most and comprised of short, informative statements. Entries do not have to be complete sentences, only complete enough to convey the message. They should be typed with double spacing for easier reading.

If the product is manufactured, as is Creative Manufacturing's advanced widget, the best place to begin is with a detailed engineering product specification. This normally dense and lengthy document must be reduced to one or two pages of meaningful data written in understandable English. To do so, first read through the product specification to determine what it is, what it does, how it does it, what makes it unique, and other outstanding features.

Product uniqueness is sometimes good, and other times bad. What is good is that there are few or no competitors. Product uniqueness can be a disadvantage, however, particularly with an OEM product. An OEM is always concerned if there is only one supplier, especially if the item in question is the key component in the OEM's product. There is a natural concern that the supplier's raw materials may be interrupted. Its employees may go on strike, or worse, the firm may go out of business. A second source is always good insurance. Besides, it keeps suppliers competitive and honest. These issues should guide you as you choose whether to emphasize your product's uniqueness.

Table 1.1, a summary specification for Creative Manufacturing's advanced widget, is the result of reducing many pages of detailed engineering data into two pages of information that adequately describes the product.

In summary, when preparing a product description for a business plan, you should keep it simple, short, and definitive. Know your audience, and write it for them. Avoid (or keep to a minimum) the jargon of your specialized industry.

2

MARKET ANALYSIS AND MARKET PLANNING: AN ESSENTIAL REQUIREMENT

A thorough market analysis and market plan are essential for beginning a new venture or deciding whether an existing one should be terminated or expanded. Many businesses and programs have failed because the importance of these steps was underestimated. The market research, analysis, and plan should be conducted by a qualified company employee or departmental official or by an experienced third party. The most important point is that it be finished before a decision is made to proceed.

Investors can provide the financing. The principals can invest time, money, and energy. Facilities can be built and equipped and personnel hired and trained. Yet it can all be lost if there isn't a market to support the product.

Repeated business failures, which can be attributed to a lack of market research and planning, occurred in many of the shopping centers in the author's home city of San Jose, California. Specialty shops have opened and closed on a regular basis. Some failures were undoubtedly due to poor management, others to undercapitalization or poor economic conditions. But many were caused by an inadequate understanding of the market being served.

Many of the products carried by the specialty stores were also offered by large department or discount stores, often located in the same shopping center. The department and discount stores frequently had a distinct price advantage. For the specialty shops, the problem was a lack of competitive knowledge, which only comes from market analysis and planning.

Patently ridiculous examples of poor market planning are locating a Cadillac dealership in the center of a welfare district and opening a Japanese specialty food store in a predominantly Italian neighborhood. But these extreme examples highlight the essential lesson: the importance of knowing the market to be served.

THE PURPOSE OF MARKET ANALYSIS AND PLANNING

The purpose of market analysis and market planning is to thoroughly acquaint yourself with all aspects of your market so that you can formulate a plan to capture a share of it. Additionally, the analytical and planning process will help you to present a convincing case to investors that your product or service has a reasonable chance of surviving profitably in a competitive environment.

Marketing analysis will help you to estimate the size of your market today, next year, and for five years or more into the future. It will help you to identify your current and prospective customers as well as your competitors. It will also help you to select target markets and estimate market share and sales. A market plan will help you to define your overall marketing strategy. Market planning will help you to put together sales projections as well as make you aware of what may be required to achieve them. Market analysis and planning will help you to set prices for your product that the market will support.

Subsequent sections of your business plan will be dependent on your market plan estimates. These estimates will determine the amount, type, and timing of capital, equipment, and human resources. If they are incorrect, the cost in all three of these resources could be very dear.

Product Market

A market analysis begins by asking what is your market. How does your product fulfill a need? Where is your market? Who makes it up, and how does your product fit into the whole scheme of things?

To ask, what is your market? is to attempt a market definition. Does your product supply the primary or after market: the razors or the razor blades, the typewriters or typing paper, pencils or pencil leads? Think it through carefully to define it. The hardest part of solving any problem is the definition of the issue. This also constitutes the first step to a solution. Thus market analysis depends on articulating a useful definition of what the market is, which in turn depends on asking the right questions.

As an example, lets discuss the "simple" razor and razor blade markets. Who uses razors and razor blades and in what quantity? The answer is simple—or is it? People, past the age of puberty, male and female. What is the proportion of males to females? The question is important because males shave every day; at least, most males beyond a certain age. They would therefore use more razor blades, or so it would seem. Have you counted those who wear beards? Also, certain races don't have heavy facial hair growth, and some religious groups do not permit their members to shave facial hair.

Trendy styles are also a factor. Are beards in or out? If they are in, then fewer blades will be required. If they are now in but going out, then the market trend will be, more blades sold next year than this.

Women are a special element in the razor and razor blade market. How often do they shave? And what do they shave? In the United States women shave their underarms as well as their legs. In some countries, they shave only their legs, whereas in others, for reasons of personal choice or cultural proscription, they do not shave at all.

These questions affect consumption and, therefore, demand. Other demand-related questions are: How many shaves does the average male get to a blade: 1, 2, 5, 10? How many shaves does a woman get to a blade if she shaves only her legs or legs and underarms both? Does she get more shaves to the blade or fewer than a man does? Does leg and underarm hair dull a blade faster than facial hair? Does using the blade less frequently, as a woman would, allow it to rust, rendering it unusable after the first or second time and in need of being replaced? The answer, of course, will affect demand.

Demand for blades of a given type will also vary with the type of razor being used. Are disposables preferred by men? By women? Perhaps the safety razor with replaceable blades is the tool of choice. What type of blade is in vogue, single or double edge, cartridge load or individual blade? What is the market percentage of each? And what is the usage for each type? Let's not forget the electric razor. Its use will affect consumption as well as market demand. Then there is the depilatory, which women (and also men) sometimes use to remove hair chemically. If it is popular, it will reduce the demand for razors and blades. What colors attract men and women? If disposable razors, for instance, were offered only in pink, not too many traditionally minded men would buy them.

The whole point of this discussion is to show what questions are involved in defining your market. Are you going to sell razors only, or razors and blades? To men only, or to women also? In the United States, or in other countries as well? Do you know enough about the users of your product and how they will use it? Do you know enough about your product so that you can predict its performance and life under different conditions? Do you understand the importance of gender for product development?

In other words, where is your market? Is it worldwide, national, regional, or local? Who are your customers? Identify them by name and list them in your plan. Your investors will want to know who they are. How much does each customer purchase weekly, monthly, and annually? How much are they willing to pay for your product? How much is your competition charging for a similar product? What is the size and value of your total market in units and in dollars?

Market Fulfillment

One of the keys to success for any business is to find a need— not partially or haphazardly, but completely. Does your product fulfill all requirements of a market need? If you were serving the family sedan market, for example, wouldn't it be absurd to intro-

duce a compact that delivers only 10 miles to the gallon with a
top speed of 180 miles per hour? The targeted customers would
obtain their needed transportation, but many other market needs
would be unsatisfied, particularly in a society that demands fuel
consumption of 40 miles to the gallon and sets a speed limit of
55 miles per hour.

A more realistic transportation example is the electric automobile. In 1983 it fulfilled the market's speed requirements at an
acceptable operating cost but fell short in operating range (100
miles), refueling (recharging) time, which was overnight, and acquisition cost (very expensive). Because it met many but not all
market requirements, it could not be sold in sufficient quantity
to reduce its acquisition cost.

Competition

Competition must be taken seriously. Too much or too little
(sometimes) can be detrimental to you and your market. Too much
creates a market saturated with the product you are offering, which
can lead to price cutting. The result can be reduced profits and
even bankruptcy, with its consequent loss of investment. Too little
competition, particularly with industrial products, can cause
customer rejection. Customers are often afraid that products with
too few suppliers might not be available in the required quantities at the right time and at competitive prices. Continued supply might be jeopardized if a manufacturer is acquired by a competitor or goes out of business.

Know your competition, their products, strengths, weaknesses, capabilities, and limitations. Keep an eye on their prices
and market share. Knowledge is strength and can be acquired
through several methods.

If a company is publicly held, considerable information can
be obtained from its annual and 10K reports, available through
your public library or your stockbroker (see Chapter 5). You may
also write the financial officer of the company and simply ask for
them. An even better source of information is a prospectus, which
is available, by law, when a corporation plans to sell a new stock
issue on the open market. A prospectus must include the com-

pany's sales and earnings. It generally includes each product line sales and profits as well.

If a company is privately held, data are more difficult to obtain. But though it takes some effort, you can get obtain data from competitors, customers, and suppliers. Industry trade journals are another source, as is the business section of your local newspaper, where new products and contracts are frequently announced.

Knowing your competition also means learning as much as possible about their key personnel such as:

1. How do key personnel fit into the organization?

2. What has been their method of operation with former employers?

3. Have they had a history of success? Or failure?

4. If they recently joined the company, does their history with former employers indicate that they will immediately fire the current staff and hire "their own people"? Or will they replace them over a longer period of time? In any event, both actions can be disruptive.

5. Does the Marketing/Sales executive stand firm on established prices, or does that person have a history of price cutting to "buy" the business? This type of strategy will have an effect on your pricing policy.

6. Does the CEO have a history of shipping products of questionable quality at month end to make the monthly shipments look good? This action will jeopardize the company's standing with its customers and makes it vulnerable to competition.

7. Does the manufacturing manager have a history of shipping high- or low-quality products? What is his on-time record? Does the product work when the customer receives it or is it "dead on arrival"? Check the manufacturing's department organization chart. A quality assurance manager who reports to the manufacturing manager rather than on the same level is a dead giveaway for a potential quality problem. It is the corporate equivalent of "hiring the wolves to guard the chickens."

8. Does the engineering manager have a reputation for good,

solid designs, poor designs, or overdesigned, expensive products? A company that is well run in all areas except product designing may sell for awhile, but not for long. If a product it is overdesigned and expensive to build, it usually cannot be sold at a competitive price and at a profit.

9.   Does the financial officer have a history of paying the company's bills on time or stretching them out? After suppliers become aware of this tactic, they will generally increase prices to compensate for their cost of money to finance customers. Suppliers usually give slow-paying customers the same type of delivery priority. This in turn will increase a product's cost, lower its profitability, and jeopardize its delivery schedule.

10.   Does the financial officer have a history of imposing excessively tough credit restrictions on customers? This policy may lose some deserving customers, particularly the small ones. One should not forget that well-run small companies have a tendency to grow and to remember who helped them in their lean years. This is not to say that the financial officer should be lax and extend credit to the undeserving, but reasonable credit policies are part of a strong marketing plan.

Selecting the wrong strategy for dealing with the above issues makes a company vulnerable to competition. Know the character of your competition. Are they opportunistic, or are they in it "for the long haul"? Are their resources sufficient to see them through a product failure or a recession? Are their products good, average, or bad? Answers to these tough questions can help you to formulate your own strategy.

• Two high-technology companies illustrate the difference between firms that are opportunistic and firms that are in it "for the long haul:" Fairchild Camera and Instrument Corporation and IBM (International Business Machines), respectively.

Traditionally, Fairchild was a supplier of semiconductor components of the electronic industry. It saw an opportunity to adapt its products for the consumer electronic watch and video game markets. Even though both consumer products required marketing and manufacturing skills that were unfamiliar to it, it seized on the opportunity to fill a market need with the hope of earning a fair profit. Fairchild did reasonably well while competition was low, but as competition increased, its weaknesses became evident. Sales and profits declined, and the company subsequently withdrew from both markets. Evidently it was not committed to either market over the "long haul."

IBM, on the other hand, manufactures computer systems and office equipment for sale and lease. Sales and leases are only part of the IBM story, however. The company serves its customers by selling "solutions to problems." It is well known for providing excellent service, and customers have grown to respect and rely on it because they know IBM will be around today, tomorrow, and the following year. "Big Blue's" strategy has produced excellent profits year after year. It is certainly in business "for the long haul."

Knowing your competition's resources will help you to formulate your own strategy. If it is well financed, it can generally endure the usual start-up costs to introduce a new product, even if the industry is already crowded. It may also be able to endure the financial strains of a product redesign if the first one does not work or if it is too expensive to build. Additionally your competitor may be able to afford heavy advertising to help it capture a larger market share. An underfinanced company cannot afford the mistakes of a better-financed one, so plan your strategy accordingly.

Pricing

With the expectation of a larger market share, your competitor might execute a price-cutting strategy at the expense of profits. Its ultimate objective may be to recover deferred profits through greater volume acquired from your market share. Sometimes this tactic works, but more often than not, it succeeds only in upsetting the pricing structure of an entire industry. It has a pronounced effect on the policies of your own and other competing companies.

Knowing the competition's products, including its strengths and weaknesses, is necessary for your own survival. You must research them to determine if they meet all of the requirements and specifications demanded by your market. This is sometimes difficult. As an example, in the technology industries, learning to read a product specification is an art. Manufacturers often cloud the meaning of some features to prevent a direct comparison. A feature can mean one thing to one manufacturer and something slightly different to another. Or a feature can be standard equipment with the one manufacturer and optional with another. Research is required to ensure that your products are competitively priced, on a feature by feature basis, with your competition's.

If your competitor's product is a poor performer requiring frequent preventive or corrective maintenance, it will increase the cost of ownership over its useful life. Knowing this fact can be used to gain a competitive edge if handled properly. The initial purchase price oftentimes has little relationship to the actual cost of ownership over the life of a product. If you have an advantage in this area, your customers and prospects should be made aware of it.

If a product does not operate properly over the full range of its advertised specifications, a customer could lose a considerable amount of money in consequential damages. As an example, the process-control computer industry has designed computers that automatically regulate entire factory processes, including steel and paper manufacturing, petroleum cracking, and power generation. Since a single minute of operation is valued in the thousands of dollars, system failure could be very expensive.

One cause for failure might be ambient temperature variations, which are known to vary widely in a factory environment. If any part of the computer system does not meet its operating temperature design objectives, the entire system could fail, and a system failure could interrupt the manufacturing process. The result is lost time and money. Customers have a tendency to remember whose part caused the expensive failure, especially when it is time to reorder.

Suppose your product exceeds an industry's required performance specifications by a wide margin, perhaps because of overdesign. The resultant higher manufacturing costs would limit you to a market segment that needs this overdesign capability.

The military market is an example of a segment that is generally willing to pay for extra capability.

If the increased product performance capability does not cost extra to manufacture, then other competitors may be required to modify their design, adjust their price, or convince their customers that it is not needed.

It is also important to know how your competitor's product is priced. Is it priced at, above, or below fair-market value? And more important, why is it priced the way it is? Are manufacturing costs in line with those of other competitors? If a competitor's costs are higher, it may have to charge more to realize an acceptable profit or sacrifice profit in order to maintain market share. If its manufacturing costs are lower, it may be able to reduce prices in expectation of capturing a larger market share, or charge market price, expect to maintain market share, and realize a higher profit on each unit sold.

The "why" of a competitor's price structure should reflect its overhead for marketing, engineering, and finance and administration. Its pricing policy will be affected by a large advertising budget, which will be apparent from continuing and varied advertisements in industry trade journals; by the expensive cars provided to sales personnel and company executives, and by the plush appearance of its central and field offices. If its prices don't reflect these overhead costs, then the situation will take care of itself within a short time, by bankruptcy perhaps or disenfranchisement by the parent organization, much to the dismay of the investors and employees.

If, on the other hand, your competition is run on a lean budget, this too will be reflected in its pricing policies. Running a lean operation allows more latitude to reduce prices when competition stiffens or during a recession.

Competitive discounts must be considered in your own pricing policies. If your competitor's discounts are based on a learning curve, you must define your experience level to determine if you too can discount prices and by how much. If the competition offers more than one product, perhaps it can offer a dollar volume discount based on the total dollar value of all products purchased over a finite time. With only a single product, discount alternatives are more limited and can affect competitive posture and prices.

Your competitor's minimum acceptable gross margin is a function of its profit objectives and overhead expenses. This will have a definite effect on its pricing and discount schedules as well as your own.

Market Share

Knowing the market share of all suppliers is vital. It is important to know if all of the suppliers combined are satisfying market demand, or if an industry is plagued by order backlog. If an order backlog condition does exist, is output being increased to meet the demand, or is it being held back in expectation of decreased demand?

Another condition affecting market share calculations is a saturated market where each firm competes for a "fair share" of the available market. In a crowded field, what market share remains for a company that is trying to enter the market? If only a small piece or nothing is left, a company must determine how it can capture a percentage of another's share or increase market demand. To successfully compete, a product or service should be unique or favorably priced. Only by knowing the total market, each supplier's share, and the competition's strengths and weaknesses, can a successful strategy be evolved.

In summary, a thorough market study is essential for your success. It should reveal how you fit into the overall picture. It should give a qualitative and quantitative picture of your competition's organization, personnel, operating methods, products, strengths, weaknesses, capabilities, limitations, pricing, discount policies, and market share.

A MARKET ANALYSIS AND PLAN EXAMPLE

An actual market analysis and plan that was prepared for Creative Manufacturing's business plan is appended to this book to show how the concepts discussed in this chapter are organized in practice. It begins with a detailed analysis of the widget systems market, which is where Creative Manufacturing's product will ultimately be used. Because whatever happens in this market will have a very profound effect on Creative Manufacturing's industry, the market analysis does more than give an overall "big picture." It also provides the basic facts at the outset, so the company's leaders can determine the wisdom of entering a related subindustry. It provides data on market size, growth rate, competition, environment, and use and an evaluation of what it will ultimately mean to Creative Manufacturing.

A subdivision of the widget systems market is the widget market. Creative will sell its product here, primarily. The discussion of the market subdivision is followed by a section on the independent widget manufacturers, the types of products they produce, and the industry's growth rate. The analysis concludes with a section on Creative Manufacturing's widget market, segments, types of widgets, market size and growth rate, trends, competition, prices, and, finally, what all of this means to Creative Manufacturing's product. The only topics not included are profiles of the competitive suppliers and their personnel.

What this plan intends to describe is, first, the overall end user market, then the subindustries that serve this market, and finally, to what extent the market will support another manufacturer. How Creative plans to serve the market rounds out the discussion.

The market analysis clearly indicates that there is sufficient growth in the segment of the widget industry to comfortably support another supplier.

APPENDIX
REVIEW OF THE WIDGET SYSTEMS MARKET

Creative Manufacturing, Inc., products will primarily be sold to OEM widget systems assemblers, better known as widget systems houses. These customers integrate widgets into their end products.

Market Data

This section includes widget systems market information on:

Results, expectations, projections, trends.
1974–1982 revenue components.
Growth rate.
Market size by application area.
Competitive environment.
Worldwide OEM/End user market split.
Small-business widget systems market.
Widget use.
What the figures mean to Creative Manufacturing.

The Widget Systems Market

1977 Results.   Worldwide revenues to U.S. manufacturers grew to $2.7 billion in 1977, representing a 44 percent increase over 1976. Unit shipments reached 88,000.

1978 Expectations.   Revenues are expected to increase to $3.7 billion (38 percent increase) and unit shipments 116,000 (32% increase).

1982 Projections. Future revenue growth will continue at a rate of 32 percent a year and reach $11 billion by 1982. Unit shipments will increase to 300,000.

Trends. A downward price trend is coupled with more aggressive, targeted discount policies.

The competition is creating the need for more professional strategic approaches from both a business and marketing viewpoint. This is no longer a technology-driven business.

The entry of new companies points to the competitive threat at the high end of the product lines; uncertainty lurks at the low end, owing to the inevitable encroachment of the microwidget suppliers (See figs. 2.1 and 2.2).

Market Size by Application
(OEM and End User Widget Systems)

Automation and Control Systems. 52.2 percent of industry 1979 unit shipments; 53.1 percent by 1982.

Involves the use of small widgets in an environment where the widget system is secondary to the function being performed.

Application examples range from machine tools to traffic lights to patient monitoring and instrument testing, cases where the widget system is incidental to the product.

Commercial Auto Transaction. 29.5 percent of industry 1979 unit shipments; 32.3 percent by 1982.

Small widget systems perform the functions of larger, general-purpose widget systems, but for smaller business entities in a more dedicated fashion.

Application examples range from large widget system replacement to auto transaction devices, such as point-of-sale devices.

Problem-Solving Application. 12.3 percent of industry 1979 unit shipments; 8.5 percent by 1982.

The user designates the application and arranges for its implementation. The widget system is sold as a tool to the end user for whatever purpose is desired. The burden is on the user to produce the required application.

Application examples range from military technology to automated instruction to engineering research applications.

Large Widget System Support.   6 percent of industry 1979 unit shipments; 6.1 percent by 1982.

Widget systems are incorporated into some product used in the data processing and/or communications environment.

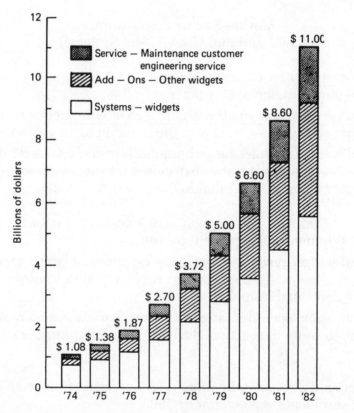

FIGURE 2.1.   Widget system market revenue components, 1974–1982

Applications include communications and intelligent switchers.

Competitive Environment: 1977 Results

Four U.S. suppliers generated 70 percent of worldwide revenues. ITC in its first full year of doing business achieved a 2.7 percent market share. The Model/I remains a spark on the horizon but has not yet achieved its anticipated market share.

None of the international suppliers ranks in the top 20, which generated 96 percent of worldwide revenues and 90 percent of unit shipments. Suppliers and market shares are shown in Table 2.1.

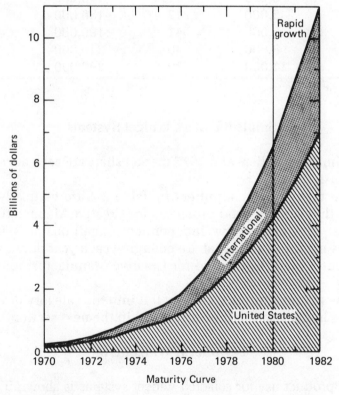

FIGURE 2.2. Worldwide widget system revenues for U.S. manufacturers, U.S. vs. international, 1970–1982

Worldwide OEM/End User Market Split

Since half of the top 20 widget systems suppliers are prospects for Creative Manufacturing's products, the OEM-end-user market split becomes important. Those widget systems sold on an OEM basis are potential users of widget products. The market split through 1982 is shown below:

Year	Revenue[a] ($M)	OEM (%)	Unit Shipments	OEM (%)
1977	2,700	40	88,000	65
1978	3,725	41	116,200	66
1979	5,000	42	150,000	66
1980	6,600	41	190,000	67
1981	8,600	40	240,000	67
1982	11,000	39	300,000	66

[a]worldwide

Small-Business Widget Systems

The primary suppliers and 1977 market shares of each are shown in Table 2.2.

Since many of the suppliers in Table 2.2 are vertically integrated, they are not good prospects for Creative Manufacturing's widgets. The many new, independent, small-business widget systems manufacturers that are emerging each year do, however, represent a market potential for Creative Manufacturing's products.

These manufacturers generally fall into the category of widget systems houses and will be discussed in the next section.

Peripheral Widget Use

Widget product use for selected widget systems is shown in Table 2.3. Widget system peripherals—widgees, widgums, and widguts—are significantly more popular with large widget systems than with traditional small ones. The average number used per

TABLE 2.1   Competitive Environment: 1977 Results

Supplier	Revenue ($M)	Percentage (%)	Unit Shipments	Percentage (%)
CED	1,100	40.7	37,500	42.6
PH	390	14.4	6,000	6.8
GD	279	10.3	11,000	13.2
SIH	130	4.8	1,600	1.8
ED	86	3.2	2,000	2.3
IAG	83	3.1	2,650	3.0
IT	80	3.0	5,000	5.7
ITC	70	2.7	1,3000	1.5
CCM	54	2.0	703	.8
IAC	52	1.9	5,228	5.9
CCP	50	1.9	626	.7
CM	38	1.5	996	1.1
C4	36	1.3	1,2000	1.4
CBC	36	1.3	330	.4
LES	35	1.3	165	.2
CCH	32	1.2	235	.3
MC	18	.6	1,250	1.4
SDR	12	.4	400	.5
CCT	11	.4	76	.09
CCL	10	.4	400	.5
Others	98	3.6	8,741	9.9
Total	$2,700	100 %	88,000	100 %

system is the same, regardless of size, except for widgets.

It is assumed that traditional small widget systems predominately use cartridge widgets, whereas the standard widget systems use standard widgets.

Widget termes are clearly more prevalent and used in greater numbers in the larger widget system.

For planning purposes, one can assume that other widget systems in the same size class will use the same ratio of widget products as the traditional small system.

What the Figures Mean to Creative Manufacturing, Inc.

The rapidly expanding widget systems market is creating an even greater demand for widget products.

The greatest demand for Creative Manufacturing's widgets will

TABLE 2.2 Primary Suppliers and Their 1977 Market Shares

Manufacturer	Model(s)	Systems	Share (%)	Millions ($)	Share (%)
ITC	32	14,810	31	630	33
CCW	3200	10,665	22	214	11
CED	Widgee Sys	5,037	10	205	11
CCB	80, 70, 80	3,550	7	206	11
CFB	35, 40, 50, 600, 700	2,350	5	111	6
CCW	2000	1,605	3	10	5
GDC	40	1,456	3	111	6
RCN	100, 200	1,115	2	73	4
NAQC	900, 1200, 1400	881	2	40	2
CCC	C-400, 900	865	2	26	1
QC	5500	750	2	22	1
Others		5,126	11	162	9
Total		48,250	100%	$1,900	100%

be in two application areas: automation and control systems.

Many of the vertically integrated widget systems and small-business widget systems suppliers will not be prospects for Creative Manufacturing's current widget products.

Creative Manufacturing's widget customers will be found mostly in the OEM widget systems house market.

A high percentage of widget systems and large widget systems use widgums and widgees, in multiple units per system.

The "bottom line" is that all the necessary ingredients for a profitable business opportunity exist in the OEM widget systems industry. Creative Manufacturing can look forward to entering an advantageous market situation poised for success.

REVIEW OF THE WIDGET SYSTEMS HOUSE MARKET

Creative Manufacturing's current and near-term customer base is the widget systems house marketplace. This section describes

TABLE 2.3   Widget Product Usage for Selected Widget Systems

Manufacturer	Model(s)	Percentage with Widgees (%)	Average Number	Percentage with Widgums (%)	Average Number	Percentage with Widgets (%)	Average Number	Percentage with Widgoons (%)	Average Number
				Traditional Widget Systems					
CED	8	38	1.7	32	1.9	26	1.2	61	2.4
	11	41	1.5	69	2.4	54	1.3	68	6.9
GD	1200	35	1.5	43	1.8	54	1.3	68	9.8
	2	30	1.3	46	1.8	53	1.2	45	2.5
	3	29	1.1	52	1.5	34	1.3	59	3.8
PH	200	59	1.4	48	1.8	39	1.2	56	8.8
	21.9	59	1.2	66	2.1	55	1.6	53	14
Subtotal		42	1.5	46	1.9	39	1.3	60	5.9
				Super Widget Systems					
CED	11 45	78	1.8	79	2.4	69	1.3	71	14.5
	11 70	86	1.4	79	2.3	75	1.6	76	12.8
GD	200	72	1.3	55	2.3	69	1.3	61	7.6
PH	3000	88	1.4	56	2.4	82	1.4	62	8.8
Subtotal		78	1.5	88	2.3	71	1.4	68	11.4

the four major types of companies in the OEM widget systems house marketplace, the number of companies in each, their widget use, and the reasons for Creative Manufacturing's interest.

Definitions

The term *widget systems house* describes a company that buys universal widget controllers (UWCs) and integrates independent widgets to create a total system for resale as the company's own product. The term *turnkey system* describes the typical ready-to-use systems house product.

Widget systems houses add value to their hardware purchases by means of application engineering and marketing ability. They contribute 48 percent of the value added to the widget systems house marketplace.

There are approximately 2500 widget systems houses in the United States, a figure that grows by 10 percent a year.

Traditional OEMs are established companies that make large-quantity purchases from widget systems and small-size widget suppliers, then add their own manufaturing value to produce their own product for resale. Traditional OEMs contribute 34 percent of the value added in the widget systems house marketplace.

There are approximately 800 traditional OEMs in the United States.

Internal widget systems houses are large companies that have consolidated their widget systems buying under one division or group to enable the entire company to take advantage of OEM discounting. Internal widget systems houses sell their systems by means of in-house transfer. Their value-added contribution is in the area of application engineering. Internal widget systems houses contribute 35 percent of the value added in the widget systems house marketplace.

The number of internal widget systems houses in the United States is not known.

Dealer/distributor is a term often used synonymously with widget systems house because it shares many of the same characteristics. The dealer/distributor generally buys a complete widget system from one or more manufacturers for resale as its own product.

The dealer/distributor has closer ties to the manufacturer than the widget systems house company. They share advertising and marketing support costs, are assigned exclusive territories, and enjoy a discount structure higher than the most-favored OEM.

Value is added in the form of application engineering and targeted marketing ability. The dealer/distributors contribute 21 percent of the value added in the Systems House marketplace.

The number of dealer/distributors in the United States is not known.

Peripheral Use

What follows is an analysis of the peripheral use in widget systems houses, traditional OEMs, and dealer/distributors. Peripherals use data for internal widget systems houses are not available.

Widget Systems House.   Based on DIC's* April 1979 data on 946 systems houses.

	Product	Number Buyers	Percentage of Database
1.	Widgoons	739	78
2.	Widgees	372	39
3.	Widgets	354	37
4.	Widgums	253	27
5.	Cartridge widgets	221	23

*DIC (a fictitious name) publishes an annual directory of known system houses in the United States. It includes their names, addresses, personnel contacts, products manufactured, and the types and quantities of widget and other peripherals they use on the annual basis.

Traditional OEMs. Based on DIC's April 1978 data on 654 traditional OEMs.

1.	Widgoons	474	72
2.	Widgums	251	38
3.	Widgees	230	35
4.	Widgets	216	33
5.	Cartridge widgets	151	23

Dealer/Distributors. Based on DICs April 1978 data on 383 dealer/distributors.

1.	Widgoons	297	78
2.	Widgums	175	46
3.	Widgets	164	43
4.	Widgees	143	39

Reasons for Creative Manufacturing's Interest

Widget systems houses will provide most of our near-term business. The reasons are several: Generally, widget systems houses are small and undercapitalized. Because they are smaller, they lack the time and staff to run extensive product evaluations. These limitations also mean that approval cycles are shorter.

Because widget systems houses are undercapitalized, they are dependent on timely deliveries from their suppliers. Unmet delivery schedules severely affect cash flow, and widget systems houses generally cannot afford an inventory.

They are also a high credit risk. As such they usually receive a low credit limit and a low delivery priority from their suppliers. The natural result is little supplier loyalty on the part of widget systems houses. They do, however, order from suppliers who extend credit and deliver in a timely manner.

Because of their shaky credit and their generally small orders, they pay a higher unit price, which provides a higher profit on each unit sold. The overall picture is one of higher-risk, lower-credibility customers who provide higher profits than more established customers.

The above reasons make widget systems houses the best market for Creative Manufacturing, Inc., at the outset. As we gain credibility and the manufacturing capability, we can compete for the volume OEM programs.

Traditional OEMs and widget systems manufacturers are long-term customer goals. With few exceptions, this market is generally unavailable to us at this time because of our start-up status and limited manufacturing capability. More of this market will become available as we gain credibility.

We will gain credibility by providing our products at a fair price, supporting the customer before and after delivery, delivering on time, and supporting the product after delivery—in sum, by being responsive to the market needs.

INDEPENDENT WIDGET PRODUCT MARKET

This section is included to define the relative sales revenues and projected growth rates of the nine major product areas. It provides an insight as to what revenue goal we can strive to achieve with our own products.

No attempt is made in this section to evaluate the profits of any product area, single product/multiple product companies, or any specific companies, for that matter. For the purposes of this section, it is sufficient to state that any company that turns a 5.8 percent net profit or more has enjoyed a good financial year in the independent widget product industry.

Definitions

An *independent* company is one that is solely engaged in the manufacture of widget products and one that manufactures and markets widget products separately from the widget systems portion of its business. A *product* is any machine used in conjunction with (or related to) a widget system but not necessarily attached to such unit. The term *manufacturer* includes true manufacturers and those who buy equipment on an OEM basis and do some engineering as their value-added contribution.

Widget Product Area

Widgoons: Operator-oriented products.
Widgets: Specific models, such as the Widget II.
Widbets: Add-in products.
Widgums: Shipping products.
Widgame: Communication products.
Widkings: Credit card products.
Widqueens: Graphic products.
Widjacks: Airline products.
Widdow: Optical products.
Widdim: Medical products.

WIDGET MARKET

The 1977 worldwide widget market was $3.1 billion dollars. This total includes the captive and independent market shares and is distributed across three widget classes: (1) rigid-fixed (2) rigid-removable (3) flexible-removable.

Rigid-fixed, representing the largest market segment, was $2.8 billion in 1977, shared by 38 worldwide manufacturers. This is the market segment which Creative Manufacturing, Inc., is interested in. Market growth is expected to be 14 percent through 1981 with revenues increasing to $4.75 billion. The share of U.S. manufactures was 91.5 percent in 1977, which will decrease to 87.3 percent in 1981. Industry growth results from demand for new widget models, including rigid-fixed of all sizes.

Of the 1977 total, $2.25 billion belongs to the captive market and the remaining $500 million is shared by the independent manufacturers. The $500 million independent market is roughly

Revenue Growth—Independent Widget Peripheral Manufacturers
1977–1982

	1977 Revenues ($M)	Percentage of Total (%)	5-Year Compound Rate of Growth (%)	Revenues ($M)	Percentage of Total
Widgoons	1,370	28	20	3,345	30
Widgets*	1,265	26	19	3,010	27
Widgums	510	11	19	1,225	11
Widgums	390	8	7	560	5
Widqueens	290	6	18	670	6
Widjacks	245	5	6	335	3
Widkings	220	5	6	730	7
Widgame	270	6	24	780	7
Widdow	165	3	15	330	3
Widdim	110	2	8	165	1
Total	$4,835	100%	19%	$11,150	100%

Product area in which Creative Manufacturing is a participant.
Total Revenue between 1977 and 1982 will increase by 131 percent.
Creative Manufacturing, Inc., is a participant in the second-highest revenue growth product area.

41

divided between the large-size widget systems market with $310 million and the standard-size widget market with $190 million.

The large size Widget Systems market generally uses rigid-removable widgets. It also uses rigid-fixed models like Creative Manufacturing's Widget II. The standard-size widget systems market generally uses low-capacity cartridge widgets. It can also be expected to use the emerging low-cost, rigid-fixed widgets.

Traditional rigid-fixed, a $50 million market in 1977 shared by 15 worldwide manufacturers, has been stagnated at this level since 1970. This market will erode as new rigid-fixed Widgets like the Creative Manufacturing Widget II gain greater market acceptability.

Flexible-removable was a $289 million market in 1977 shared by 15 worldwide manufacturers. This market will have no effect on Creative Manufacturing's current market plans.

Rigid-Fixed and Rigid-Removable Widget Market

Product Mix.   There are eight distinct categories within the rigid-fixed and removable widget family. These are:

Widget cartridge: less than 12M DUPS*

Widget cartridge: more than 12M DUPS

Widget pack: 29–58M DUPS

Widget module: 25–80M DUPS

Widget pack: more than 100M DUPS

Widget fixed: less than 30M DUPS

Widget fixed: 30–200M DUPS

Widget fixed: more than 200M DUPS

The market size for each widget category for years 1978 to 1981 are shown for OEM worldwide shipments in Table 2.4.

OEM Market.   71.7 percent of worldwide OEM revenues are expected to be derived from removable widget in 1981, with major

---

*A DUP is a fictitious figure of merit for a widget product.

TABLE 2.4 OEM Worldwide Shipments Product Category Review and Revenue Summary

Worldwide Revenues All Manufacturers	Shipments		1978		forecast 1979		1980		1981	
	$M	%	$M	%	$M	%	$M	%	$M	%
Widget cartridge										
Less than 12M DUPS	156.1	41.1	170.5	36.1	153.6	29.9	134.7	23.2	111.0	17.5
Widget cartridge drives										
More than 12M DUPS	2.7	.7	20.4	4.3	43.5	8.5	79.6	13.7	121.5	19.1
Widget pack										
29–58M DUPS	48.7	12.8	40.3	8.5	17.9	3.5	6.0	1.0	1.7	.3
Widget module										
25–80M DUPS	53.0	14.0	79.6	16.8	106.6	20.8	134.0	23.1	154.0	24.3
Widget pack										
More than 100M DUPS	110.6	29.1	121.3	25.7	97.9	19.1	81.0	14.0	61.1	9.6
Widget module (Old)	.9	.2	5.1	1.1	6.7	1.3	7.5	1.3	5.8	.9
Fixed Widget										
Less than 30M DUPS	6.6	1.8	27.0	5.7	34.0	6.6	43.0	7.4	54.5	8.6
Fixed Widget										
30–200M DUPS	1.1	.3	4.9	1.0	31.0	6.0	58.8	10.2	78.1	12.3
Fixed Widget										
More than 200M DUPS	—	—	3.6	.8	22.0	4.3	35.3	6.1	46.9	7.4
Total worldwide revenue	*379.7	100.0	472.8	100.0	513.4	100.0	579.9	100.0	634.6	100.0
% U.S. manufacturing	88.9%		90.3%		88.5%		84.4%		83.4%	
Annual growth rate	—		+24.5%		+8.5%		+13.0%		+9.4%	

contributions from widget modules, widget cartridges of all sizes, and widget packs over 100M DUPS.

Fixed widgets, like Creative Manufacturing's Widget II, will grow in revenue generation from 2.1 percent of the total in 1977 to 28.3 percent in 1981.

Creative Manufacturing's Market. Creative Manufacturing's Widget II product line allows us to effectively compete in the widget-fixed (30–200M DUPS) market.

Widget Fixed, Less Than 30M DUPS

Definition. The category under consideration is all widget fixed with a total capacity of less than 30M DUPS. The 30M DUP maximum limit includes fixed widgets designed to be sold at the lowest cost per unit, like the ASC 4000 series and the DCC 1000 series.* Most products in this category use some form of advanced technology.

Manufacturers. There are over 20 worldwide manufacturers who supply the captive and independent market areas, or both. Examples of the captive market manufacturers include CCD, DCC, EDC, ITC, and ETC, and examples of the independent (OEM) market manufacturers include CCA, DCC, MME, and MIC. Some captive manufacturers also compete in the independent market, namely, DCC, CMC, and ENC.

Market Status. OEM worldwide shipments in 1977 for this widget class totaled 3300 units. U.S. manufacturers shipped only a few hundred units with advanced technology. The balance was with baseline technology.

The 1978 product announcements of widgets with advanced technology include the AS 4000 and DCC 1000. These models are designed to provide highly reliable advanced performance at minimum cost by simplification of the basic design and through

---

*ASC and DCC and others are fictitious companies for purposes of this discussion.

use of inexpensive stepping rotor systems. Both products are designed for OEM prices of below $1500.

Fixed widgets with less than 30M DUPS are intended for use in small widget systems configured without the widgums normally used for backup protection. Loading and limited backup protection on such systems will be provided by flexible-removable widgets.

Now that IRC has made 8-inch widgees "respectable," a number of new suppliers have joined the ranks of CMI with advanced-technology widgets. Application for the 8-inch widget will be in small-business widget systems.

Marketing Trends.   Most widget shipments of the fixed (less than 30M DUPS) class will incorporate advanced technology by 1980. Widget shipments using older technology are expected to decline rapidly in shipments after 1979.

OEM widget shipments are expected to reach 36,000 units worldwide in 1981, with about 83 percent of this total from U.S. manufacturers, representing an annual growth rate of 94 percent.

Conclusion for Creative Manufacturing.   The widget fixed (less than 30M DUPS) market is essentially a high-volume, low-cost, low-priced one. Creative Manufacturing's product and manufacturing strengths do not fit this product/market profile. In particular, Widget II fixed products in a partially populated configuration do not fit the cost-price profile requirements of this market. Consequently, Creative Manufacturing's products should not be considered for this sales area.

Widget Fixed, 30–200 M DUPS

Definition.   This market category includes all widgets fixed with a total capacity of between 30 and 200M DUPS. The widgets in this category all use advanced technology.

Manufacturers..   There are over 15 manufacturers worldwide who supply either the captive or independent market areas, or both. Captive-market manufacturers include CCB, DCC, ITC, SSI and ENC, and independent-market (OEM) manufacturers include CCA, DCC and SSI. Some captive manufacturers also compete in the independent market and include DCC, SSI, and ENC.

Market Status.   Production in this group in 1977 was 700 units split almost evenly between captive and OEM markets and consisting entirely of previously announced units from CBC and CMC.

Market Trends.   Production will be boosted by the growing requirement for more capacity on small-business and other widget-based systems. OEM production will grow to 27,100 units worldwide by 1981. Of this total, 68 percent will be shipped by U.S. manufacturers.

Widget production will reach significant levels this year, after the normal delays for evaluation by system OEMs and start-up of system deliveries.

OEM shipments will be predominantly (almost 100 percent) in the 80M DUPS range during 1979 and 1980.

Backup continues to be a problem with widget fixed products. Systems using widgets above 80M DUPS will probably use a widgum on the system, which makes routine backup protection reasonably fast and economical. Between 30 and 80M DUPS is an awkward stage because the backup protection requirement is too much for widget flexible products and many of the systems are too small to justify the cost of a widgum in addition to a widget.

Until the backup protection problem is solved, most independent widget system designers are reluctant to settle for systems without backup. As a result, widget shipments in the 30 to 70M DUPS are slow and are expected to remain that way.

Shipment and Price Summary.   Shipments, revenues, and unit prices through 1981 are shown in Table 2.5.

Conclusion for Creative Manufacturing.   The Widget fixed (30–200M DUPS) market is a high-growth market. A high-growth period is consistent with widget II availability. Creative Manufac-

TABLE 2.5 Shipment and Price Summary for the Widget Fixed (30–200M DUPS) Market

| | 1977 Net Shipments | | Forecast | | | | | | | |
| | | | 1978 | | 1979 | | 1980 | | 1981 | |
	U.S.	Worldwide	U.S.	Worldwide	U.S.	Worldwide	U.S.	Worldwide	U.S.	Worldwide
Non-Captive Shipments										
OEM Units (000)	.3	.3	1.4	1.4	6.2	9.7	11.6	19.8	15.6	27.1
Average Unit Price										
To OEMs ($000)	3.5	3.5	3.5	3.5	3.3	3.4	3.1	3.2	3.0	3.1
Value of Shipments										
To OEMs ($M)	1.1	1.1	4.9	4.9	20.5	33.2	36.0	63.3	46.8	84.0

[a]Average of all widget capacities shipped in this category.

turing, Inc., is not a late entrant into the OEM market with widget II, and its strengths fit this product/market profile. A widget II cost reduction program will be required, however, to meet this area's cost/price profile.

Widget II provides Creative Manufacturing with the opportunity to become a volume OEM supplier with a technologically current product. Success in this area will add to our credibility in future product areas.

CREATIVE MANUFACTURING, INC., PRODUCT SPECIFICATION

What follows is a condensed specification for a widget product that will be designed, manufactured, and marketed by Creative Manufacturing, Inc.

Widget II

Widget Fixed: Characteristics

Capacity in M DUPS
    22.4 (1 widgee)
    67.2 (2 widgees)
    112 (3 widgees)
    156.8 (4 widgees)
Proven advanced technology
Sealed environment/closed air filtration system
    High reliability
Valve density
    500
DUP density
    6200 per inch
Widgee rotational speed
    3600 rpm

DUP transfer rate
 10,000/per second
Valve position time
 6MS single valve
 30MS average valve
 55MS full valve
Valve position error rate
 1 in 1 million
MTBF
 6000 hours
MTTR
 1 hour

3

REVENUE DISTRIBUTION

THE BEST APPROACH: BOTTOM UP OR TOP DOWN?

The question of the best approach to revenue distribution is important to the development of a business plan. Two approaches are available: "bottom up and top down." This chapter begins with the bottom-up approach because it appears to be the most logical place to start.

BOTTOM UP

Bottom-up merely means that the financial plan begins with departmental budgets. The individual departmental budgets are then combined to produce an initial company budget, which is used in turn to aid in the development of the income and cash flow statements.

The income statement is a business score card. It tells you how much money your company made or lost. It determines, in essence, if you have made a bank deposit or withdrawal. Some of the intermediate steps that comprise this approach will now be discussed.

Marketing Plan

Before your company budget can be developed, a marketing plan must first be completed. The marketing department makes an educated guesstimate about the number of units that will be sold during the next one, two, or three years, and possibly through the fifth year. The time span depends on the type of budget you are making. The word *guesstimate* is used because it accurately depicts the process. Budgets derive from estimates based on the available facts, salted, more frequently than not, by human frailty and misjudgment.

The facts usually include data on the market size, or, put another way, how many units the entire market will consume. Some determining factors are:

Market conditions.   Is it a buyer's or sellers' market?

Economic climate.   Is the country or world experiencing an economic expansion or recession?

Competitors.   Who are they, and what is the expected market share for each.

Product acceptability.   Will the market buy your product?

Sales force.   What type (i.e., OEM or end user), size, and skill requirements are required.

Selling prices demanded by the market.

Credibility of the guesstimators.

Department Approvals

After Marketing has completed its estimates, other managers must determine the feasibility of the resulting plan relative to their own departments.

As an example, if a new product design is required or if changes are needed to an existing one, the enginerring department must decide if it can meet the announced market-driven requirements. The manufacturing department must determine if it can obtain the raw materials, prepare the facilities, hire and train personnel, and, ultimately manufacture the product in the quantity and time specified by the marketing plan. The financial department must determine if the company can make a profit at the prices demanded by the market, given the estimated costs of all departments for the entire operation.

Any disputes must be negotiated by the department managers until an agreement is reached by all. When an agreement is reached, all parties should sign the plan to prevent future disputes.

Department Budget Development

Once the marketing plan is approved, departmental budgets are developed. They are based on the labor, material, overhead, and capital equipment required to meet the marketing forecast. Detailed budgets for a three year plan are usually estimated for monthly requirements during the first year, quarterly for the second year, and annually for the third and subsequent years.

Setting goals is an essential part of the process. You can do so by thinking through each step and making a list of all things that must be accomplished. Start and completion dates, which must be established for each budget item, can sometimes be usefully displayed in a bar chart.

Labor Costs. All aspects of labor costs must be estimated. Some factors to be considered are the total number of labor hours that will be required to begin a given program, to continue it, and— if it is in the plan—to bring it to an end. Skill levels and their corresponding labor rates must be estimated.

When considering a manufacturing company, "labor standards" must be set. Labor standards define, under ideal conditions, the total number of hours of each skill level required to produce the end product. Since "ideal" is not often achieved, a multiplier correction constant must be appended to this standard to more accurately define the actual labor hours required. Holidays, vacations, paid sick days, and fringe benefits are all part of the labor costs and must be included as a part of the total.

Indirect Labor Costs. Indirect labor is comprised of those functions not directly involved with the manufacture of a product. Examples include material planning, production planning, purchasing, and quality assurance. Even janitorial services could be included in this category.

The engineering department requires engineers, technicians, designers, draftspeople, print control, secretarial, and other support personnel to make it function.

Labor costs for the marketing department may include the national sales manager, regional and district sales managers, salespeople, product managers, service personnel, an advertising group, and administrative support personnel.

Sales managers, salespeople, and product managers often receive some form of commission, bonus, or a combination of both. These forms of compensation as well as basic salaries vary with the industry. Commissions and bonuses can, and usually do, amount to a significant percentage of the marketing department's labor costs.

The finance and administration department's labor costs will generally include the payroll clerks, accounts receivable and accounts payable clerks, posting and collections personnel, and supporting secretarial services for the department. It may even include the receptionist for the visitors' lobby.

Plant (Facilities) Costs. Since the plant facilities are shared by all departments, the related costs must be shared according to their use. Shared costs usually include the building rent or other site payments, utilities, garbage collection, and maintenance. Although shared-costs formulas vary with the company, they are often based on the square footage each department occupies. Costs unique to a department, such as the telephone and telex, are usually paid by the department that incurs them. Responsibility for maintaining the plant (facilities) in most manufacturing firms usually rests with the operations department.

Capital Equipment Costs. Capital equipment costs are different for each department. A manufacturing firm, such as Creative Manufacturing, will have different requirements than, say, service firms. But this discussion should give you a reasonable idea of the logic involved.

The first department to be discussed, *Operations,* may include the purchasing, production control, material control, manufacturing, test, inspection, stores, and shipping and receiving functions. Each function will have its own unique requirements according to the products being manufactured. There is, however, some common ground for all functions, regardless of the product. For instance, all functions need office furniture such as desks, chairs, file cabinets, tables, calculators, and so on.

The *manufacturing* department may need work benches, conveyors, specialized machinery, specialized tools—even hand tools. An example of specialized machinery is an industrial robot of the kind now becoming popular in the automotive industry. An *inspection* department may also require specialized equipment and hand tools, for instance, to inspect raw materials, goods in the process of being manufactured, and finished goods. Examples range from a simple gauge to a sophisticated computer, depending on the product and industry.

A *stores* department needs cabinets and storage racks as well as scales to measure small items such as nuts and bolts.

A *shipping and receiving* department may need hand trucks and fork-lift trucks to move goods and material. It also needs packaging materials (boxes, tape, staplers) as well as packaging equipment (shrink wrap machinery, labelers).

The *engineering* department, obviously, can't operate with office and drafting-room furniture alone. Engineering usually has responsibility for print control, which requires a blueprint duplicating machine and special flat filing cabinets to store odd-sized drawings. Other capital equipment requirements will vary with the industry, but may include oscilloscopes, signal generators, cameras (for photographing oscillographs), optical test equipment, clean rooms, work benches, computers, hand tools, calculators, and an array of related equipment.

The *marketing* department also needs office furniture, usually of a better grade than most other departments because the marketing area is often more accessible to customers. A marketing department may be located in a different building or perhaps even in a different city than the main plant. Additionally, the sales department may have regional and district offices located throughout the city, state, country, or world, each having its own facility costs to be included in the total budget. The marketing department's capital equipment allocation may also have to cover the cost of automobiles for managers and sales and field service personnel.

The field service department, which in many companies is part of the marketing organization, has its own capital equipment needs. Its personnel often employ the same specialized test equipment used by the engineering and manufacturing departments for final testing, except that it may be packaged for surface and air travel.

Finance and Administration has responsibility for supplying any capital equipment used by the company's chief executive officer, general manager, and chief financial officer. Their tastes may run to automobiles, air planes, and other big-ticket perks, Their furniture will probably be of better quality, and higher priced, than that of any other company executive. The remainder of this department's capital equipment requirements are generally limited to furniture, calculators, typewriters, and the like. In some companies this department may also be responsible for the copying equipment and supplies.

Once you have determined how many people will be working in your company, their job skills, and pay grades, and have provided them with a place to work and tools to work with, you can estimate your company's day-to-day operating expenses.

Day-to-Day Operating Costs. Day-to-day operating expenses include such items as telephone and telegraph (TWX or telex)— necessary for all departments if you are doing business on an interstate or international basis. A complete communication service is probably an absolute necessity for the marketing department. Travel and entertainment costs are inevitable and one of the largest marketing department line items. They can be also incurred by the engineering and manufacturing departments and are usually associated with delivery of a new product. New products have a habit of being delivered with "bugs" (defects) that can only be corrected by an engineer or a manufacturing specialist. Automobile and delivery truck operating expenses are also to be included in departmental travel budgets.

Other items contributing to day-to-day operating expenses are easily overlooked: writing paper, pencils, and erasers, and, perhaps most significant, photocopying costs. These will increase as your company grows. Remember that the firm must supply items of a most mundane character: toilet tissue, hand towels, soap, and other toiletries. Their absence, however, would create the greatest of problems.

The whole object of this discussion is to prod you to think through and itemize all of the cost elements for each department. Usually, a company will have a form that enables each department to do this in a uniform manner (see fig. 3.1). Costs can then be uniformly charged to the proper accounts. The procedure also prevents departmental managers from forgetting to include some cost items.

With your company's itemized departmental expenses completed, the plan is slowly getting closer to the "up" part of the bottoms-up approach. A proforma income and cash flow statement can be generated with the available cost data. These statements will inform you if, financially, your company is on target, marginal, or way off base.

The Income and Cash Flow Statements

An income statement begins with sales revenue. Sales revenue, obtained from the marketing forecast, is calculated by multiplying the number of units sold for each month by the average unit price. Cost of goods sold is the next line item on an income statement and is the sum of the material cost and the direct- and indirect-labor and manufacturing overhead costs. These can generally be obtained from the operations department budget. Sales revenue minus cost of goods sold provides you with the operating margin. The operating margin, if a positive number, pays for the remaining expenses, including the operating expenses for Engineering, Marketing, and Finance and Administration. Profits and taxes must also come from the operating margin. If the gross margin is a negative number, you are clearly losing money.

A similar exercise is performed for the cash flow statement, which tracks the cash coming into and going out of your company. Capital equipment is included here, not in the income

Expense by Sub-Account

Date _____ FY _____

Sub-Acc't	Description	Jan.	Feb.	Mar.	Apr.	May	June	July	Aug.	Sept.	Oct.	Nov.	Dec.	Total
01	Executive salaries													
02	Supervisory salaries													
03	Technical salaries													
04	Administrative salaries													
05	Production wages (dir. chg. indirect)													
06	Training													
07	Special assignments													
08														
09	Overtime premium													
10	3rd Shift differential													
11	Proposals													
12	Loaned labor													
13	Bonuses													
14	Marketing support													
15	Consultants													
16	Casual labor													
17	EDP services													
18	Other outside services													
19	Photography													
20	Dues & memberships													
21	Subscriptions													
22	Vehicle operations													
23	Travel													
24	Mileage allowance													
25	Entertainment													
26	Business conferences													

FIGURE 3.1. Department itemization form

Expense by Sub-Account

Date _____   FY _____

Sub-Acct	Description	Jan.	Feb.	Mar.	Apr.	May	June	July	Aug.	Sept.	Oct.	Nov.	Dec.	Total
27	Tooling													
28	Small tools													
29	Expendable equipment													
30	Equipment maintenance													
31	Equipment rental													
32	Production supplies													
33	Shipping supplies													
34	Non-productive supplies													
35	Re-sale material													
36	Office supplies													
37	Scrap (MRB)													
38	Reproduction supplies & service													
39	Peripheral support													
40	Printing forms & form design													
41	Recruiting													
42	Employee relocations													
43	Employee education program													
44	Manuals													
45	Freight in													
46	Allocated production expenses													
47	Allocated payroll expenses													
48	Allocated general expenses													
49	Sales literature													
50	Direct mail													
51	Advertising													
52	Exhibits & shows													

FIGURE 3.1. Continued

Date _____ Expense by Sub-Account Page _____ of _____

FY _____ Dept. No. _____

Sub-Acc't	Description	Jan.	Feb.	Mar.	Apr.	May	June	July	Aug.	Sept.	Oct.	Nov.	Dec.	Total
53	Demonstration and field service amortization													
54	Freight out													
55	Commissions													
56	Warranty expense													
57	Sales office expense													
58	Publicity & public relations													
59	Accounting & legal													
60	Contributions													
61	Franchise taxes													
62	Officers' life insurance													
63	Bad debt expense													
64	Miscellaneous expense													
65	Licenses & taxes													
66	Organization expense													
67	Acquisition expense													
68	New product line investment													
69	Depreciation & amortization													
70	Insurance													
71	Plant maintenance & repair													
72	Plant re-arrangement													
73	Janitorial supplies													
74	Building rent													
75														
76	Property tax													
77	Utilities													
78														

FIGURE 3.1. Continued

Expense by Sub-Account

Date _____ Page _____ of _____
FY _____ Dept No. _____

Sub-Acc't	Description	Jan.	Feb.	Mar.	Apr.	May	June	July	Aug.	Sept.	Oct.	Nov.	Dec.	Total
79	Sick leave													
80	Holiday													
81	Vacation													
82	Payroll taxes													
83	Group insurance													
84														
85	Workmen's compensation													
86	Other personnel fringes													
87	Other paid absences													
88	Telephone													
89	Postage													
90	Directors' expense													
91	Executives' supp. insur.													
92	Employee stock purch. plan													
93	Dealer franchise fees													
94	Training course fees													
95	Amortization of field service inventory													
96														
103	Total	$												

FIGURE 3.1. Continued

statement. The point to be made is not how to construct each statement, as that will be covered in a later chapter, but what is the bottom line for each.

The bottom line of an income statement measures profit before taxes and its percentage of total sales. The bottom line of a cash flow statement is significant according to whether it is positive or negative, and by how much. A positive flow essentially means that your company is making a bank deposit or adding to its cash reserves. A negative flow means the opposite.

What's good, bad, or marginal varies with the industry and the prevailing risk-free investments. U.S. government T bills are a good example of a risk-free investment. Your company's profit before taxes should be at least as much as is available from the highest interest-yielding bank account. Otherwise it would be better to avoid the problems of running a business altogether by investing in a secure and certain financial instrument.

An exception to this advice is a start-up (new) company, which is expected to lose money during its first years of operation.

Generally the bottom-up approach projects profits before taxes, and cash flow is substantially lower than expected prior to the summing together of departmental budgets. The reason is that departmental managers and others responsible for estimating the budget invariably overestimate or "pad" their share to ensure that they receive what they need (and more) to do their job. They are not deliberately being dishonest, just human. When all the extras are added together for each department, the result has a depressing effect on profits and cash flow.

The major benefits of bottom-up approach are that it involves the department managers, makes them think about what is required to get the job done, and prepares them for the top-down approach.

TOP DOWN

Top-down merely means that in the preparation of a budget a percentage of sales is allocated for each department. For instance, in an OEM manufacturing company, such as Creative Manufacturing, it is highly desirable to have a 40 percent gross margin. What this means is that 60 percent of the sales dollar is spent on direct labor, materials, and manufacturing overhead. How this 60 percent is divided varies with the product being manufactured. A labor-intensive product means that labor costs are higher than material costs. A material-intensive product means that material costs are higher than direct-labor costs, and so on.

In the present example, the 40 percent of the sales dollar that remains is known as the gross or operating margin. It is divided to pay for profit before taxes, Engineering, Marketing, and Finance and Administration (also known as general and administrative, or G&A).

Consider profits first. An arbitrary allocation of 16 percent to profit before taxes will leave 8 percent after taxes, assuming a 50 percent corporate tax rate (actually 48 percent).

The marketing department usually requires the next largest percentage of the sales dollar in this type of company. For purposes of this example, I will arbitrarily assign 9 percent to Marketing.

Engineering traditionally is the next largest user of funds, as it should be. A company can not grow unless it has a new-product development program. Engineering will thus be assigned 8 percent.

Because Finance and Administration should be the lowest user of funds in this type of company, 7 percent will be allocated for this function.

The next step in the top-down approach is to have department managers resubmit their budgets based on their assigned percentages or state their reasons why this cannot be done. Managers are expected to indicate what must be sacrificed to conform to these percentages. Often, the changes are minimal.

Now for the $64 question. Which of the two is the best approach? As it turns out, both have something to offer. The bottom-up approach makes department managers think about what is required to meet the overall objectives of the company. The top-down approach is more objective in that it establishes profits and costs at the outset. Both can be used to the advantage of management.

Start with bottom-up as a course adjustment and fine tune it with top-down. This might produce some grumbling from the budget planners, but the extra effort may be worth it.

4

ALLOCATING INCOME AND OUTGO FOR MAXIMUM PROFIT

In a free-enterprise system, the primary objective of most business organizations is to maximize profit and to return as much as possible to the owners and stockholders. To an extent, you can do this by allocating a percentage of revenue (sales) to meet your profit objectives (Chapter 3).

No chapter in this book attempts to show you how to maximize profits by taking advantage of the exemptions in the U.S. tax laws. This a matter for the tax experts. This chapter, rather, shows you how to allocate revenue to maximize pretax profits.

INCOME STATEMENT FUNDAMENTALS

First, a review of the fundamentals of an income statement is in order. This business score card has the following major components:

1. Sales or revenue.
2. Cost of goods sold.
   a. Material.
   b. Direct labor.
   c. Manufacturing overhead.

3. Operating margin.

4. Expenses.
   a. Engineering.
   b. Marketing.
   c. General and Administrative (G&A).

5. Pretax profit.

Revenue or *sales* is the total income received from products sold, which include prime equipment and spare parts. In its simplest form, revenue is the arithmetic product of units sold multiplied by the average unit price (AUP). This is the starting or 100 percent base point.

Cost of goods sold is the cost of providing a product for sale. In a manufacturing company such as Creative Manufacturing, it is the sum of material, direct labor, and manufacturing overhead.

Material includes all of the raw material or parts that are required to manufacture a unit. These are usually itemized on the "final" or "top" assembly drawing prepared by the engineering department. Some examples from Creative Manufacturing's widget include the electronic printed circuit boards, interconnecting cables, nuts bolts, screws, and shipping container, to name just a few of its many parts.

Material costs for the subassemblies manufactured by Creative, such as electronic printed circuit boards, cover only the raw materials such as the printed circuit board itself and components such as resistors, capacitors, diodes, and integrated circuits. Other costs such as those for direct labor are accounted for separately. If the same subassembly is purchased from an outside vendor, then the entire unit is counted as a material cost.

Material costs are usually a significant part of each revenue dollar in a manufacturing company with an advanced-technology product. The material cost of Creative's widgets is 40 percent of each sales dollar for new equipment and 15 percent for spare parts.

Direct labor is the labor cost associated with manufacturing a product. For example, the direct-labor component of Creative's widget products includes an assembler to insert components into printed circuit boards, a laborer to supervise passing the boards through a flow solder machine to secure the parts mechanically and electrically, assemblers to cut wires and to form them into wire harnesses and cables, mechanical assemblers to secure sub-assemblies to the widget's base plate with nuts and bolts, and finally, technicians to test the completed product.

For Creative Manufacturing's widget products, direct labor accounts for 7.2 cents of each revenue (sales) dollar for prime equipment and 1.4 cents for spare parts. Total direct labor, which is the sum of prime equipment and spare parts, therefore costs 8.6 cents of Creative's sales dollar.

Material and direct-labor costs are called variable costs because they vary directly with the quantity produced. The more produced, the greater the costs.

Factory overhead or manufacturing overhead consists of those costs that do not contribute directly to the manufacture of a product but without which it could not be built. Overhead might include the buyers, expeditors, and secretaries of the purchasing department and also, depending on the organizational structure, the firm's material planners, production control planners, receiving clerks, storekeepers and shipping clerks. In a quality assurance department, it will include all of the inspectors. In the manufacturing department, it includes supervisors, foremen, facility maintenance engineers, industrial engineers, facility, utility, and other costs.

Factory overhead is a fixed expense because it does not change appreciably over a minimum/maximum range of output. For example, a purchasing function is needed to buy parts for Creative's products whether 100 or 1000 widgets are manufactured a year. One person may be able to handle the job for up to 500 units annually, but two people may be required for 500 to 1000 units. Similarly, a 20,000 square foot building may be adequate for up to 500 units a year. But 40,000 square feet may be required when the annual rate reaches 500 and 1000 units. Costs are therefore fixed over some range of output.

Many manufacturing companies do not include their engineering costs as part of their cost of goods sold. They will generally, however, include them as an expense item.

EXPENSE ITEMS

Under expense items, Engineering may include basic and applied research, new product development, and sustaining engineering. Basic research is the art of exposing nature's secrets without planning how they might be used commercially for profit. Usually only the very large companies, an IBM or a General Electric, can afford this luxury. Applied research attempts to use nature's secrets for some useful purpose. Development is the use of a known technology in the creation of a product, commercial or otherwise. Sustaining engineering corrects design mistakes or improves on an existing design.

Many manufacturing companies, especially those with high-technology products, have some development and sustaining engineering efforts. In high technology, where a product's life is only three to five years, development of new products is an absolute must. Without it, a company would soon wither and die. Sustaining engineering does more than keep existing products marketable by correcting design mistakes or oversights; it also keeps them competitive through cost reduction designs or by adding capability to extend the product's life. Both engineering jobs are expensive but necessary.

Marketing/sales brings to mind the old adage that nothing happens until something is sold, which is indeed true. The cost of selling something is usually the highest of the three expense items (engineering, marketing, and G&A). Creative Manufacturing's formative first and second years were an exception to this rule because of expensive start-up engineering costs. Creative's marketing costs have been more expensive than engineering in later years, which is more typical.

The salespersons' salaries, commissions, and expenses are only the more visible components of marketing costs, there are many marketing support people and their expenses to consider. These may include the product managers who define and champion their products, administrative personnel who process and keep track of orders, advertising people who give the product exposure to the marketplace, service personnel who fix inevitable product failures, and finally, marketing and/or sales managers who orchestrate the whole operation. In a company such as Creative Manufacturing, these costs are higher than for many manufacturing firms because all except the administrators and advertising personnel are usually technicians.

Finance and administration or General and Administrative (G&A), as it is more widely known should be the smallest of the three expense items. It usually includes the chief executive officer, president or general manager, and staff. It can also include the financial staff, which is responsible for payroll, accounts payable, accounts receivable, and cost accounting, and ledger clerks, who keep track of all receipts and expenditures. G&A is frequently the home of the personnel function, or to call it by its new euphemism, the human resources department. Personnel is responsible for screening, hiring, and firing human resources, processing insurance claims, salary and job classification changes, and maintenance of personnel records.

MAXIMUM-PROFIT ANALYSIS

With the income statement's basic components explained, an analysis of how to allocate income and outgo for maximum profit is now possible. First, all major items of the income statement are listed with their corresponding dollar value and a percentage of sales. The procedure is illustrated for Creative Manufacturing's second-year sales, costs, and percentage of costs in Table 4.1.

To maintain profitability, sales (revenue) must be sufficient to pay for all costs with enough remaining to provide for the planned profit. Some business managers sometimes forget this basic principle, yet keeping income (sales) and outgo (expenses) in proper balance for maximum profit is the responsibility of all department managers.

As stated earlier, sales (revenue) represent the total income from all products sold. Extraordinary income or income from other than product sales, such as profits from stock dividends or real estate, is excluded from this discussion. In a manufacturing firm like Creative Manufacturing, revenue is the result of sales of prime equipment (widgets), widget parts, and service. Revenue from prime equipment and spare parts is the arithmetic product of the number of units sold times the unit price. Total revenue from service is simply the sum of all income from each job.

Market Analysis

Marketing's objective is to keep the price of each product (widgets and widget parts) and service as high as possible while remaining competitive. This is where the value of a good market analysis begins to pay off. The analysis must be sufficiently ac-

TABLE 4.1   Creative Manufacturing, Inc.,
Second-Year Sales, Costs and Percentages

Item	Amount ($000)	Percentage (%)
Revenue (sales)		
	4888	100
Prime equipment	4444	90
Spare parts	444	10
Material	1902	38.4
Prime equipment	1835	37.5
Spare parts	67	1.4
Labor	419	8.6
Prime equipment	352	7.2
Spare parts	67	1.4
Overhead	662	13.5
Cost of goods (COG)	2893	61.0
Gross margin = sales − COG	1905	39.0
Expenses		
Engineering	450	9.2
Marketing	361	7.4
G&A	342	7.0
Total expenses	1153	23.6
Pretax profit		
(Gross margin − expenses)	752	15.4

curate to determine what the market is willing to pay for your product and service and what the competition is charging for something comparable.

If your market analysis reveals low market demand and competitive prices generally lower than yours, you may be pricing your products too high and inviting a decline in sales. If you ignore your market analysis, the reason for declining sales may become apparent only months later. After the problem is recognized and corrected, it may take the sales department additional months to turn the situation around and increase sales.

If, on the other hand, your market analysis indicates high market demand and prices that are high relative to yours, then you may be pricing your product too low and unnecessarily sacrificing profits or, to put it another way, "leaving money on the table."

Another danger of ignoring your market analysis and undercharging is that it may be counterproductive. A sales strategy to price slightly below the competition in hopes of capturing a larger market share might actually price significantly below the competition and thus set off a "price war."

Price Wars

In a price war, your competitors may reduce their prices below market value in hopes of recapturing market share. Their reasoning in this situation is that if they reduce their selling price and therefore their profit, the later will eventually be regained with increased sales volume. In many instances, this just does not happen. Competitors may continue with round after round of price reductions until no profit is left for anyone.

Price wars can eventually condition customers to pay a lower than fair-value price. If this happens, the manufacturer is obliged to sell at cost just to "keep the doors open." The effects of below-market pricing can last for years and from one product cycle to the next. If a market is conditioned to pay a below fair-value price for a product with an established price-to-performance ratio, a new product must have an equal or better ratio even though its manufacturing costs may be higher.

The cartridge widget market experienced a price war that went on for years, with effects lasting form one product generation to the next. Fortunately for Creative Manufacturing, it decided not to participate. The OEM market for this product emerged in the late sixties after a major manufacturer announced a cartridge widget that would be used in its own systems. Several new OEM widget manufacturing companies were founded to compete against the major manufacturer. They were generally managed by technicians—capable as engineers and scientists, but inexperienced as business managers. The result was that many good widget products, all with similar or identical characteristics, were offered to the market.

The market value for each Widget was underestimated, and they were consequently underpriced. Across the industry, immature management tried to increase market share through price-cutting tactics. The resulting price reductions extended well into the late seventies, near the end of the product's life.

As prices plummeted, gross margins and profits followed. Gross margins were reduced from an OEM manufacturer's ideal goal of 50 percent, which provides a good profit, to 30 percent, which is a near break-even point. Many of the cartridge widget manufacturers were forced out of business or were acquired by other companies—or wish they had been acquired.

By 1978 management matured, market conditions improved, and though prices rose more in line with costs, they did not reach a comfortably profitable level. As a consequence, prices for new products required an even better price-to-performance ratio than for earlier products. This situation puts an even greater burden on manufacturers to provide a better and more efficiently designed and built product so that a reasonable profit can be realized.

The moral of this example is: Don't underestimate the value of an accurate market analysis, and put it to use!

Spare-Parts Products

One line of products whose value is often underestimated is spare parts, also known as the after market. It is sometimes difficult to motivate sales people to sell spare parts because of their "unglamourous" nature. Nevertheless, spare parts are, and should be, the most profitable product sold by a manufacturer. They commonly provide a 70 percent gross margin and can oftentimes represent 10 to 13 percent of total sales revenue.

A 70 percent gross margin means that the cost of goods is only 30 cents of each sales dollar. Creative Manufacturing's prime equipment (widgets) provide only a 40 percent gross margin, which means that the cost of goods represents 60 cents of each sales dollar. Therefore, one obvious way to improve profits is to keep the ratio of spare parts to prime equipment as high as possible.

Volume spare-parts sales for OEM products can be expected after the second year a product has been on the market. An OEM customer needs about one year to plan to support a product and prepare for its inevitable failures.

There are methods of keeping spare-parts sales high. Discount incentives can be offered if purchased with prime equipment. When discounts are offered they are generally structured so that the lowest selling price will net the manufacturer a minimum gross margin of 70 percent. The price of some individual items may be priced to provide a 95 percent gross margin. Or put another way, cost of goods can be as low as five cents of each sales dollar. The spare-parts after market is indeed profitable!

Material Cost Savings

As Creative Manufacturing's income statement shows, to calculate cost of goods sold, one begins with the material required to produce the products. Material includes all parts, components, and subassemblies necessary to build, test, and ship a product. Although this cost is fixed on a per unit basis, it can be adjusted for maximum profit through proper planning.

For Creative Manufacturing's widgets, material represents 38.9 cents of each sales dollar, divided between prime equipment ($.375) and spare parts ($.014). This share is not uncommon, but it can and should be kept as low as possible.

The engineering department can contribute to low material costs with a value engineering program. Simply stated, value engineering is designing or redesigning a product for the lowest cost without compromising its performance. A value engineering program is usually initiated after the first design is released to Manufacturing. It starts with the examination of each part or subassembly to determine if the same function can be accomplished at a lower cost by using a different material, component, manufacturing process, and in the case of purchased subassemblies, a different vendor.

For example, an extruded plastic part may be less expensive than a machined metal part. If tooling is required to produce the substitute part, it should be included and amortized over the entire program cost. Components with a 5 percent tolerance might be replaced by ones having a 10 percent tolerance, providing a worst-case design analysis finds the substitition acceptable.

Design changes can often result in the use of less-expensive components. A process change such as cleaning a part before or after a machining or an assembly step might result in lower costs. Buying an identical subassembly to the same form, fit, and function specification from a different vendor may provide significant cost reductions.

When a product is released to manufacturing, production engineers should examine their assembly procedures to reduce waste. Doing things in a different way can reduce spoilage for considerable savings of material.

Purchasing raw materials is an area where significant savings can be realized through careful planning and buying. Success depends heavily on the marketing forecast because a purchasing department buys material according to its estimated requirements. If the marketing forecast is too optimistic, then too much material is purchased, which increases inventory unnecessarily. Interest, inventory taxes, handling and storage charges must then be paid on the unneeded material, which increases their effective cost. If the marketing forecast is too low and too little material is purchased, the result can be late product deliveries, customer dissatisfaction and possibly lost sales. Once again, the effective material cost increases.

Adjusting inventory to actual needs is a never-ending balancing act. One technique often used to minimize inventory balance problems while obtaining the lowest possible price is volume purchase agreements with suppliers. A purchasing department contracts with suppliers to buy the maximum number of parts expected to be used over a fixed time, usually one and sometimes two years. The buyer then releases a monthly purchase order with minimum and maximum quantity limits as stipulated by the purchase agreement. This allows a buyer to adjust inventory needs within limits and to known requirements. The procedure only works, of course, if the marketing forecast is reasonably accurate.

Suppliers also benefit from this type of arrangement because it allows them optimally to adjust their inventory and manpower. Suppliers can pass some of their savings on to their buyers as discounts.

Discounts can be based on the number of units purchased or the total dollar value of the purchase agreement. Checks and balances are included in this instrument to protect both the buyer and seller. The buyer is assured of a continuous material flow at the lowest possible price and is allowed to adjust the flow within limits.

Part of the checks and balances is a bill-back clause, which protects the supplier if a buyer does not order the minimum specified quantity over an agreed-upon time period. The supplier can bill back the buyer according to a defined discount schedule and the actual quantity purchased. If a buyer wants to accelerate purchases more than the maximum limits, the seller may impose a price premium or an extra discount, depending on the terms of the agreement. This instrument provides a win/win situation for both buyer and seller.

Material costs can also be minimized by shopping around with different suppliers for the same material. A supplier who is working to capacity is less inclined to provide the best possible discount. He may even impose a premium coupled with an increased delivery charge to discourage a customer from ordering.

On the other hand, a supplier who is eager for business is likely to offer discounts and improved delivery terms. Perhaps a local supplier is working to capacity while an out-of-town supplier is looking for business. There are additional costs of doing business with an out-of-town supplier that must be fully considered. They include the expense, as well as the inconvenience of communications and shipping outside the local area.

Suppliers, on occasion, suggest different methods, processes, materials, or manufacturing tolerances that can save you money. Although their suggestions are often valid, to be safe, consult the engineering department before making any serious changes. A change in one area often affects performance in another.

Savings can frequently be realized on material costs simply by paying your bills on time. If commercial credit is established with suppliers on a 30 day account, make sure that they are paid in 30 days, not 45 or 60. Suppliers are not in business to finance their customers' businesses. If your company earns a reputation as a slow payer, prices on subsequent orders will probably increase to cover the cost of money being extended to you through credit and to pay for the added inconvenience of doing business with you. If this happens, you may exchange your most-favored-customer position for a new one at the end of the queue and as a result suffer late material delivery. This can cause you to deliver your product late and thereby lose sales.

An additional means of saving on material costs often overlooked is the discount offered by many suppliers for paying an invoice within a specified time period. This is a painless way to save a couple of percentage points on your material cost, providing, of course, you have the cash available.

Direct-Labor Cost Savings

Direct-labor cost for Creative Manufacturing's widget products is only 8.6 cents of each sales dollar. Of this figure, prime equipment requires 7.2 cents and spare parts 1.4 cents. However low this is for this type of product, good management practices will keep it even lower. One way to do so is to keep personnel turnover down.

Low personnel turnover means that your training costs are reduced. Additionally, trained personnel can accomplish the same job in less time with fewer errors which pays off in reduced manufacturing and inspection time, fewer service calls, and improved customer satisfaction. Keeping employees happy and turnover low, though difficult, is worth the effort.

For a company like Creative Manufacturing located in a manufacturing center of the country, labor is a cherished commodity, especially during a period of economic expansion. It is far better to keep turnover low by keeping employees happy than to try to keep them through fear tactics. Fear tactics are sometimes used by short-sighted companies during periods of recession or by others located in remote locations where employees are required to endure the conditions or suffer the consequences. But a short-sighted employer eventually becomes one that is short changed. Unhappy employees produce expensive products.

If a product is labor intensive and if labor costs are prohibitively expensive, there are alternative methods to keep costs down. One method adopted by technology companies in the San Francisco Bay area is to locate their manufacturing facilities in a less-expensive part of the country, such as the Pacific Northwestern states. Another method is to subcontract assembly work to companies located in geographic areas with lower labor costs.

Certain products with a high labor content are suitable for manufacture in countries where labor costs are low such as Mexico, Puerto Rico, Korea, and Hong Kong. A manufacturer is cautioned to ensure that a product is well designed and all processes and procedures well defined before undertaking an off-shore operation. Failure to do so can result in higher costs, owing in part to mistakes caused by communication problems. The real key to keeping labor costs low is imagination—imaginative management, and imaginative programs.

Manufacturing Overhead Cost Savings

Manufacturing overhead, the last factor in the cost-of-goods equation, is an area where a little more management control can keep costs down. For Creative Manufacturing, overhead accounts for 13.5 cents of each sales dollar. It is often stated in management circles that a 10 percent reduction in the overhead budget will not significantly affect manufacturing efficiency.

Whatever the truth of this observation, if a program is properly planned and executed at the outset, costs can be kept in check without any budget cutting.

Overhead costs are generally divided into three major categories:

1. Facilities, communications, and data processing.
2. Indirect labor.
3. Operating expenses.

Facilities. Facilities should be selected for immediate space requirements with expansion options that will support planned growth. Choose an affordable area with the lowest utilities cost and an abundance of inexpensive but highly skilled labor. Sounds like a ridiculous wish list, doesn't it? In reality, however, these parameters must be considered and a cost/benefit trade-off made when selecting a facility.

Communications Costs. Communications costs include telephone, telex, and postage, in that order. Telephone and telex costs are mostly incurred by the purchasing department. They can be minimized by using telephone company WATTS (Wide-Area Telephone and Telegraph Service) lines if many of your suppliers are located in distant cities. A common-sense approach to the length of telephone and telex messages also helps to reduce cost: the shorter, the better. Telephone extensions with outside lines and long-distance connections should be kept to a bare minimum throughout all departments. Pay telephones should be located in appropriate locations throughout the manufacturing facility for employee use.

Data Processing Costs. Data processing costs are primarily affected by the work of the material planning department. Material requirements are often planned and purchased with the help of MRP (material requirements planning) computer programs. These services are often purchased on an hourly basis from tima-sharing data processing service companies. These costs can be kept down by analyzing actual data processing needs and using the service only when necessary.

Given today's low-cost computer systems, it may be less expensive in the long run to purchase one of these electronic marvels. The recent advent of low-cost but powerful personal computers supported by increasing amounts of flexible software packages now make this possible.

Indirect-Labor Costs.   Indirect-labor costs for all of the operations departments, as the second-largest expense, is an area where a great deal of control can and should be exercised. In a start-up company, "cheap labor" may be the most expensive. In many instances it may be less expensive to employ trained personnel (when possible and when available) who can be immediately productive. Training lower-skilled personnel is a luxury only established companies can afford.

Avoid the temptation for "empire building" by department managers. Insure that all people hired are really needed to avoid future employee layoffs. A company that gains a reputation for its indiscriminate hiring and firing policies soon finds it difficult to attract the people they want when it really counts. Encouraging interdepartmental communications, mutual trust, and camaraderie helps to ensure efficiency and lower labor costs.

Operating Expenses.   Operating expenses are the least-expensive category. They generally include development material and scrap, office and shipping materials, employee travel, and freight costs. The key to keeping them down is to avoid waste. Informing employees through periodic educational programs about costs, their meaning, and how they affect profits and jobs will help to reduce costs in this area. If management has done its job in keeping employees happy, the employees will reciprocate by reducing costs. Satisfied employees do care about the company they keep!

Cost of Goods Sold

Cost of goods sold is the sum total of the three cost items: material, labor, and overhead. For Creative Manufacturing, this item amounts to 61 percent of each revenue (sales) dollar. Each percentage point saved here is added directly to pretax profit—the bottom line.

Gross Margin

Gross margin is the difference between sales and cost of goods sold. An OEM manufacturer like Creative Manufacturing has a target goal of 50 percent gross margin. It is not often achieved in today's market, however. A 25 to 30 percent gross margin is usually a survival or break-even point. This depends somewhat on a company's engineering, marketing, and G&A expenses. What remains is pretax profit. The three components of cost—engineering, marketing, and G&A—are often evenly divided, within a few percentage points. Each percentage point saved on any one adds directly to pretax profit.

Engineering Expenses

During Creative Manufacturing's first and second years, Engineering was the most expensive of the three cost centers. In year two, it accounted for 9.2 cents of each sales dollar, owing to the many changes that were required to make the company's widget products salable in the OEM market. Engineering expenses should take second place behind marketing, in the third and subsequent years.

Engineering expenses are really an investment, today and in the future. Products must be kept current for today's market, and new products are required for tomorrow's. All the same, this expense can be minimized through thoughtful planning and skillful management. At the outset of each fiscal year, a listing should be made of all projects necessary to meet the marketing objectives for the year(s) under consideration, annotated with a description and a completion schedule for each. Once the projects are listed, described, and scheduled, they can be estimated in terms of time, material, and ultimate cost.

To describe a project basically means to define it as a "statement of work." Such a statement helps the engineering manager to divide each project into its basic components of skill and time requirements. In Creative Manufacturing's engineering department, skill requirements are specified in terms of certain positions: a manager of advanced development, an electronic engineer, mechanical engineer, mechanical designer, component engineer, electronic technician, draftsman, secretary, and document control clerk. A job description for each skill is given in a later section of this book.

A majority of these skills are required for each project, though in differing proportions. Adding the number of hours for each skill determines how many people are required to complete a project and also determines its schedule. Adding more people can often improve a schedule, but not always. Multiplying the number of hours for each skill by its basic hourly rate (plus fringe benefits) provides a labor cost for each project.

Supplies and material must also be included in total project costs. These costs usually include special tooling, material for prototypes and preproduction models, and expendable supplies. When the costs and schedules are established for each project, they should be reviewed by the rest of management to determine if the benefits justify the costs and if the schedule fulfills the requirements of the program.

When other management members are faced with the realities of a project's cost, they often modify their original requirements to bring costs in line with benefits. They may change a product's specification, schedule, or pricing, or they may modify a combination of these and other variables. The important point is that a manager cannot begin to reduce costs until they are quantified. Objective and accurate estimates of engineering costs contribute significantly to cost reduction. This skill only develops through experience and with good common sense.

Marketing Expenses

As stated earlier, nothing happens until something is sold. Unfortunately, the costs of marketing and selling are generally the highest of the three expenses. They can range from a low of 7 cents of each sales dollar to over 50 cents, depending on the type of business and the markets served. Creative Manufacturing's marketing expenses were 7.4 cents of each sales dollar during the second year of operation. This increased to 9 cents in subsequent years, which is more typical for an OEM manufacturing firm.

Keeping marketing and sales costs down is a management skill—an art and a continuous struggle. These costs include the salaries and commissions of salespeople and the commissions for manufacturer's representatives. They also include the salaries for product managers and service and administrative personnel and the costs of advertising, travel, communications, and supplies. Creative and imaginative management can help to keep some if not all of these costs down.

Salespersons' compensation packages, which are the sum of their salaries, commissions, and other perquisites, should be reviewed on an annual basis to ensure that both they and the company are both receiving maximum value for the money and effort expended. Income is a great motivating force, and proper remuneration can often increase sales. On the other hand, if territory sales quotas are too low, salespeople, like everyone else, have a tendency to get lazy. Your job is to keep the goals difficult but achievable and profitable to both sides when achieved.

If manufacturer representatives (who generally work strictly on commission) are used to supplement the sales force, it is important to select one whose other products are complementary (and not competitive). Check that they have a successful sales history, and set their commissions at a competitive and nonpenalizing level to ensure maximum productivity. Some OEM manufacturers have a commission plan that in effect penalizes representatives for increasing sales by reducing their commissions. This is frequently counterproductive.

Product managers can enjoy a share in profits through a commission or bonus plan. The arrangement provides them with an incentive to keep sales up and costs down. Service departments should be managed for maximum on-site working time and minimum travel between calls. Administrative needs should be evaluated periodically to ensure that only those positions that are actually required are filled. This simple practice avoids empire building and extra and unneeded costs.

Ensure that value is being received from your advertising programs by keeping a tally of qualified leads received from each advertisement. If the tally is low, change the advertisement or the media or the manager—or a combination of all three.

Travel and communications costs are significant expenditures in a marketing budget. Air travel expense can be reduced by planning trips to take advantage of the special commuter and discount rates offered by many airlines. Additionally, make each trip serve a multiple purpose by grouping calls in the same city during the same trip.

Telephone and telex costs can be kept down by keeping messages short. If many calls are made to distant time zones—for instance, calls from a West Coast firm to East Coast customers—it may be advantageous to change employee working hours to benefit from the lower telephone rates for calls made before 8:00 A.M. These are but a few of the more-obvious, common-sense ways to keep costs down. Creative Management should provide more of the less-obvious savings devices.

General and Administrative

General and Administrative (G&A) costs are the last and should be the least of the three expense items. For Creative Manufacturing, G&A expenses claim seven cents of each sales dollar. This is par for an OEM manufacturing firm of this type. Anything more usually signifies an inefficiently run operation. G&A items generally include the chief executive officer and his staff, Finance and Accounting, and Personnel.

The primary expenses in this area are salaries. Competitive salary structures should be monitored on a regular basis to ensure that full value is received from each dollar spent. If salaries are too low, people will leave, which will increase your training costs. Low salaries also promote inefficiency. The results of maintaining salaries that are too high are obvious.

The seven percent rule should be tested frequently to determine if the G&A function is on target or needs revision.

Total Expenses

Total expenses for Creative Manufacturing account for 23.6 cents of each sales dollar. The remainder is pretax profit, which is 15.4 cents. Assuming a 50 percent tax bracket, Creative Manufacturing would net a 7.7 percent after-tax profit, which is better than average for U.S. corporations. Average after-tax profit for all manufacturing firms is approximately 5 percent.

SUMMARY

This section was designed to show how to distribute your sales dollar and how to keep costs down to maximize pretax profits. The sample income statement that was presented was described and analyzed part by part in terms of costs. Some common-sense approaches to minimizing costs were also presented. Central to the discussion was how each component's percentage of cost contributed to the sum total. This notion illustrates how each component can be adjusted to maximize profits. Of course, the total cannot be greater than the sum of its parts.

5

COMPETITIVE DATA SOURCES AND HOW TO EVALUATE YOUR INFORMATION

One of the best ways to obtain valuable and informative data on how to and, equally important, how not to manage an organization is the study of successes and failures of competitors. This part of our study investigates where to obtain and how to evaluate competitive information.

The first and most logical place to start is with a listing of your company's competitors. If you don't know who they are, then visit a major public library, where you should be able to locate the pertinent information. For those who do not know how to use a business library, a book on this subject may help: *How to Use the Business Library, with Sources of Business Information*, by H. Webster Johnson and S. W. McFarland (fourth edition, 1957, paperback, Southwestern Publishing Company, 5101 Madison Road, Cincinnati, Ohio 45227). The major part of this book covers specific publications (handbooks, periodicals, business services, government publications), but there are also brief sections on the mechanics of locating information in libraries, writing reports, and using audio visual aids, as well as on data processing.

DIRECTORIES

Business directories are usually available through library services that provide information on products, manufacturers, potential buyers, and trade associations. A good place to start is the reference book *Guide to American Directories* (ninth edition, 1975, B. Klein Publications, Inc., 11 Third Street, Rye, N.Y. 10580). Its information on directories, classified by industry, profession, and function, is useful for identifying specific directories to locating sources of supply (competitors) and new markets.

Library services can also provide manufacturers' directories, often by state and industry. One of these comes in three volumes, the *United States Industrial Directory*, published by the Cahners Publishing Company, 89 Franklyn Street, Boston, Massachusetts 02110. It lists manufacturers alphabetically and gives a description of the firm's product lines, the number of its employees, the address, and telephone numbers. A classified section includes products with names and addresses of manufacturers (competitors). The directory also offers special sections with chemical and mechanical data and trademark and trade name identifications.

Another good directory is the *Thomas Register of American Manufacturers*. This 11 volume set is published annually by the Thomas Publishing Company, One Penn Plaza, New York, N.Y. 10001. It is a purchasing guide, listing names of manufacturers (competitors), producers, and similar sources of supply in all lines.

Financial directories are an invaluable source of information. The *Dunn & Bradstreet Reference Book*, published six times a year, contains the names and ratings of nearly three million businesses of all types located throughout the United States and Canada.

An excellent financial reference source for the electronics industry is the *Electronic News Financial Fact Book and Directory* published annually by the Book Division of Fairchild Publications, 7 E. 12th Street, New York, N.Y. 10003. An alphabetical listing of most publicly held electronics corporations, it includes company addresses, corporate officers, directors, areas of work, divisions, subsidiaries, and a five year financial history covering sales and earnings, revenues by line of business, common stock, common stock equity, income account, assets, liabilities, and a statistical summary.

Another useful directory for studying competitive successes and failures is the *World's Who's Who in Finance and Industry*, published by Who's Who, Inc., 200 East Ohio Street, Chicago, Ill. 60611. It provides biographical information of men and women prominent in finance, industry, and trade.

To illustrate the above, I have included as Figures 5.1 through 5.6, a single-page excerpt from "How to Use the Business Library, *Guide to American Directories, Thomas Register of American Manufacturers, The Dunn & Bradstreet Reference Book (Million Dollar Directory), Electronic News Financial Fact Book and Directory,* and *World's Who's Who in Finance and Industry.*

SEC REPORTS AND OTHER PUBLIC SOURCES

A listing of your competitors and data on each can be compiled by researching privately published directories and other sources. If your competitor is a public corporation, the job is simplified. Extensive company data are found in the registration statements, prospectus, proxy statements, and other reports resulting from SEC, ICC, FPC, FCC, CAB, and NYSE full-disclosure requirements.*

A registration statement is the basic disclosure document for a public distribution of securities registered under the Securities Act. It is made up of two parts. The first section, the prospectus, is the only part that is generally distributed to the public. It contains a wealth of information on company history, investment risk factors, use of stock proceeds, and capitalization; a financial statement of operations (usually covering several years); and a description of the business. It will include a general description

---

*Securities and Exchange Commission (SEC), Interstate Commerce Commission (ICC), Federal Power Commission (FPC), Federal Communications Commission (FCC), Civil Aeronautics Board (CAB), and the New York Stock Exchange (NYSE).

Standard and Poor's Corporation Services. *Standard Corporation Records* is published currently in loose-leaf form and lists corporations and other organizations offering investment opportunities. Information, alphabetically arranged, covers capitalization, corporate background, financial statements, properties with their locations, officers, stock data, stockholders, price range of securities, dividends, and other information pertinent to the firm. Bond quality ratings for the investor give the expert opinions of qualified men in the firm of Standard and Poor's. Use of this extensive service facilitates buying securities for both the individual and institutional investor.

The Bond Outlook is a publication giving up-to-the-minute information on various bond issues, governmental and corporate. Included is a section on Canadian and foreign bonds.

Called Bond Record gives bonds and stocks called for redemption together with the numbers of the securities that are called. These are cumulated weekly and quarterly. Another section covers bonds in default.

Daily Dividend Record gives information on dividends declared and presents precise facts on each. This is accumulated weekly, and an annual cumulative record is also issued.

Facts and Forecasts Service gives daily sheets covering recommended stock market policy, advice on separate issues, analysis of the better issues, stock price indexes, market action, and trading activity, including both United States and Canadian issues.

Industry Surveys is a current series dealing with various segments of industry that present detailed facts and figures enabling the investor to analyze merits of various investment opportunities.

Convertible Bond Reports gives current information and ratings on bonds in various corporations. Much statistical and comparative data are included in these reports.

American Exchange Stock Reports gives reports on individual companies — corporate analysis, company forecast, balance sheet and income account data, ratios, dividends, and earnings.

FIGURE 5.1.   How to use the Business Library. (Standard and Poor's Corporation Services)

of the products and their market, the percentage of sales for each, and how the products are marketed. Competition, product development, manufacturing facilities, number of employees, officers, remuneration of officers, stock option plans, principal and selling shareholders, balance sheet—all these are also discussed. The prospectus, in other words, offers everything you always wanted to know about your competitor but were afraid to ask.

Part 2 of the registration statement contains information of a more technical nature dealing with such matters as marketing

NAMES AND NUMBERS — JOURNALIST'S GUIDE TO THE MOST NEEDED INFORMATION SOURCES AND CONTACTS
Covers magazine, radio and television, public relations and advertising fields. Lists names, telephone numbers, addresses and general information to which a journalist might wish access. Entries include public information officers and press contacts for federal, state and local governments; colleges, important U.S. businesses, police agencies, educational scientific and technological, sports, weather, labor and trade organizations. 560 pp. John Wiley & Sons, 605 Third Ave., New York, NY. 10158. (212) 850-6000. $24.95.

SOURCE NO 1 — COMMUNICATIONS
A guide to 1,000 print and media groups, books, films, periodicals useful as communications resources for initiating social change. 120 pp. The Swallow Press, Inc., 811 W. Junior Terrace, Chicago, IL. 60613. (312) 871-2760.

SOURCE NO 2 — COMMUNITIES
A bibliography of reference material on tenant housing problems, active groups, community programs etc. 256 pp. The Swallow Press Inc., 811 W. Junior Place, Chicago, IL. 60613. (312) 871-2760.

SPEECH COMMUNICATION DIRECTORY
This directory lists over 7,000 members' names, 2,000 colleges and 200 books that are related to speech communications. Alpha-geographically arranged. 350 pp. Annual. Speech Communication Association, 5105 Backlick Road, Annandale, VA. 22003. (703) 379-1888. $9.00.

U.S. PUBLICITY DIRECTORY — COMMUNICATION SERVICES
Features news bureaus in the United States including personnel, wire services, syndicates, columns, columnists, circulation. Also covers picture service companies. Alphabetical and subject category index. 400 pp. Every six months. John Wiley & Sons, 605 Third Ave., New York, NY. 10158. (212) 867-9800. $65.00. Four other volumes of "U.S. Publicity Directory" covering: Newspapers, Magazines, Business & Finance and Radio & Television available. Complete 5 volume set: $185.00.

WOMEN IN COMMUNICATIONS MEMBERSHIP DIRECTORY
Roster of members of the organization by chapters. Includes professionals in communications and journalism and students in the field. More than 6,900 entries. 160 pp. Every other year. Women in Communications, Inc., PO Box 9561, Austin, TX. 78766. (512) 345-8922. $6.00.

WORLD COMMUNICATIONS: A 200 COUNTRY SURVEY OF PRESS, RADIO, TELEVISION, FILM
This one-of-a-kind global communications survey describes the situation of the four principal media (press, radio, television, film) in over 200 countries. Each country entry indicates, with statistical support, the general structure, facilities, output, distribution and coverage in local and national contexts. This compact reference source is based on information regularly supplied to UNESCO (United Nations Educational, Scientific and Cultural Organization). 500 pp. Published by Unipub/UNESCO and available from Bowker, 1180 Avenue of the Americas, New York, NY. 10036. (212) 764-5100. $23.25.

COMPUTERS AND DATA PROCESSING

ANNOTATED BIBLIOGRAPHY OF ELECTRONIC DATA PROCESSING
An alphabetical by author listing of books, and articles in professional journals on electronic data processing. 50 pp. University of Florida Press, University of Florida, Gainesville, FL 32601. (904) 392-1686.

AUERBACH ON ALPHANUMERIC DISPLAYS
A text on new products designs and technology in the field. Also provides a directory of manufacturers. 297 pp. Auerbach Publishers Inc., 121 N. Broad St., Philadelphia, PA. 19107. (215) 564-8200.

BIBLIOGRAPHY OF COMPUTER-ORIENTED BOOKS
An alphabetical list of about 1,200 books which are useful in teaching business applications of the computer. 22 pp. Annual. Computing Newsletter, University of Colorado, Box 7345, Colorado Springs, CO. 80933. (303) 593-3318. $4.00.

BUSINESS AUTOMATION REFERENCE SERVICE — COMPUTER EQUIPMENT AND SOFTWARE
Contains information for 250 product categories including word processing, microfilm devices and copiers. Over 700 pp. Alltech Publishing Company, 212 Cooper Center, North Park Drive & Browning Road, Pennsauken, NJ. 08109.

COMPJOB
Contains listings nationwide of 125 major companies in the Data Processing Industry with information about their hiring needs. 75 pp. Every three years. Employment Information Services, PO Box 3265, Chico, CA. 95927. $6.95.

COMPUTER DISPLAY REVIEW
A comprehensive reference on alphanumeric terminals and graphic display systems manufactured in the United States and abroad. Contains in three volumes, information on cost, availability and application of all types of Display terminal equipment. 1,400 pp. Loose leaf bound and updated every four months. GML Corp., 594 Marrett Rd., Lexington, MA. 02173. (617) 861-0515. $650.00 per year.

COMPUTER AND INFORMATION SYSTEMS
Devoted to complete and comprehensive coverage of the world literature in this field. Cambridge Scientific Abstracts Inc., 6611 Kenilworth Ave., Suite 437, Riverdale, MD. 20840. (301) 864-5753.

FIGURE 5.2. Guide to American Directories

BAGS: PLASTIC (Contd)

WA: SEATTLE
Davidson Products Co. 402-T Baker Blvd. Andover Industrial Park .... 1M+
Fisher Bag Co. 1560-T 1st Ave. S. .... 1M+
WA: TUKWILA
Cello Bag Co. Inc. P.O. Box 88883 .... 1M+
WA: YAKIMA
Shields Bag & Printing Co. 1009-T Rock Ave. (Printed) .... NR
WV: KENOVA
Zims Bagging Co. P.O. Box 455 (Polyethylene & Cellophane) .... NR
WV: PINEVILLE
Hargis Mine Supply, Inc. P.O. Box 130 .... NR
WI: APPLETON
Duralam Inc. 2621-T W. Everett St. P.O. Box 862 ...NR
Presto Products, Inc. P.O. Box 2399 .... 25M+
WI: COLFAX
Dairyland Plastics Co. P.O. Box 328 .... NR
WI: DE PERE
Valley Packaging Supply Co. 300-T James St. .. 1/4M-
WI: DELAVAN
FOF Products 1450-T Racine St., P.O. Box 80 ....NR
WI: GREEN LAKE
Fabriko, Inc. 745 South St. ((Imprinted Vinyl Tote, Advertising)) .... 1M+
WI: JANESVILLE
Badger Transparent Bag Co. 1412-T S. Jackson (& Cellophane) 1/4M-
WI: MILWAUKEE
Associated Bag Co. 160 S. 2nd St. (Polyethylene) .... 5M+
Crest Convectors Inc. 7330-T N. Teutonia Ave. ......NR
Fredman Bag Co. 5801 W. Bender Ct. (Polyethylene) .... 1M+
Hamilton Box & Specialty Co. 5110 N. 35th ... 1/4M+
Sealcraft Packaging Corp. 7074-T W. Parkland Court .... 1M+
WI: OCONTO
Wisconsin Film & Bag, Inc. P.O. Box 259 (Polyethylene) .... 1/4M+
WI: SOUTH MILWAUKEE
Luetzow Industries 1105 Davis Ave. (Polyethylene) .... NR
WI: TOMAH
Union Camp Corp., Bag Div. 503 Williams St. ...10M+

★ BAGS: PLIOFILM
(see Bags: Plastic)
CA: LOS ANGELES
POLY PAK AMERICA INC. 2939 E. Washington Blvd. T (ZIP 90023) (213—264-2400) .... NR
CA: SONOMA
SULLIVAN INDUSTRIES 103 Fremont Dr. (ZIP 95476) (Synthetic) (707—938-3355) .... 1M+
CA: TORRANCE
ARMIN PLASTICS CALIFORNIA, INC. 414-A Alaska Ave. (ZIP 90503) (213—320-7373) .... NR
NJ: ELIZABETH
ARMIN POLYETHYLENE FILM 100-A Dowd Ave. (ZIP 07206) (201—353-3850) .... NR
NJ: JERSEY CITY
ARMIN POLYETHYLENE BAG 301-A West Side Ave. (ZIP 07305) (201—432-7260) .... NR
NY: JERSEY CITY
ARMIN ROTOLITH, LTD. 49-A Fisk St. (ZIP 07305) (201—451-7600) .... NR
NY: NEW HYDE PARK
UNITED PACKAGING CORP. 1327 2nd Ave. (ZIP 11040) (516—352-8000) .... NR
NY: ROCKVILLE CENTRE
CENTURY POLY FLEX, INC. 100-T North Village Ave., P.O. Box 466 (ZIP 11571) (516—764-6111) .... NR
OK: TULSA
ARMIN PLASTICS OKLAHOMA, INC. 10001-A 54th St. (ZIP 74146) (918—628-0200) .... NR
PA: PHILADELPHIA
PLASTIC MANUFACTURERS INC. 4041-T Ridge Ave., Bldg. 31 (ZIP 19129) (215—438-1082) .... 1/2M+ (Extruded & converted; plain & printed; of mylar, acetate, polyethylene, polypropylene, vinyl-stitched/sealed; stock & custom)
★ See our catalog in THOMCAT vols. 13-18
SC: GREENVILLE
ARMIN PLASTICS SOUTH CAROLINA, INC. 609-A Worley Rd. (ZIP 29609) (803—235-3863) .... NR

★ BAGS: POLYESTER
(see Bags: Plastic)
CA: LOS ANGELES
POLY PAK AMERICA INC. 2939 E. Washington Blvd. T (ZIP 90023) (213—264-2400) .... NR
GA: MACON
BONAR INDUSTRIES INC. P.O. Box 10196 (ZIP 31297) (Woven Polypropylene Bulk Containers) (Out Of State Call Toll Free: 800-841-4982) .... 1M+
NJ: ASBURY PARK
UNIVERSAL FILTERS, INC. 1225-T Main St. (ZIP 07712) (A08, Media, Screens Stock Or Custom) (201—774-6655) .... 1/4M+
NJ: ELIZABETH
ARMIN POLYETHYLENE FILM 100-A Dowd Ave. (ZIP 07206) (201—353-3850) .... NR
NY: BROOKLYN
GIBRALTAR INDUSTRIES, INC. 254 36th St., Bldg. 2 (ZIP 11232) (212—965-5666) .... 50M+
NY: ROCKVILLE CENTRE
CENTURY POLY FLEX, INC. 100-T North Village Ave., P.O. Box 466 (ZIP 11571) (516—764-6111) .... NR
OH: DAYTON
DAYTON BAG AND BURLAP CO., THE Drawer 8-T (ZIP 45401) (513—258-8000) .... 1/2M+
(See Our Full Page Ad At Burlap)
PA: PHILADELPHIA
PLASTIC MANUFACTURERS INC. 4041-T Ridge Ave., Bldg. 31 (ZIP 19129) (215—438-1082) .... 1/2M+ (Extruded & converted; plain & printed; of mylar, acetate, polyethylene, polypropylene, vinyl-stitched/sealed; stock & custom)
★ See our catalog in THOMCAT vols. 13-18
TX: DALLAS
B.A.G. CORP. 11510 Data Drive (ZIP 75218) (PVC/Polyester, Semi-Bulk Bags) (214—340-7060) .... 1M+

★ BAGS: POLYETHYLENE
(see Bags: Plastic)
CA: LOS ANGELES
POLY PAK AMERICA INC. 2939 E. Washington Blvd. T (ZIP 90023) (213—264-2400) .... NR
CA: MONTEBELLO
LANDSBERG, KENT H., CO. 1640-T S. Greenwood Ave. (ZIP 90640) (213—726-7776) .... 50M+

CA: SAN FRANCISCO
PACKAGING AIDS CORP. P.O. Drawer 77203, 496 Bryant, M/S 28 (ZIP 94107) (Heat, Impulse & Vacuum Plastic Bag Sealers; Packaging Equipment;

(Complete Company Information, see Volumes 11 & 12)

Military Packaging; Bag Making Machinery; Lay-Flat Polyethylene Tubing) (415—362-9202) .... 1/2M+
★ See our catalog in THOMCAT vols. 13-18
CA: TORRANCE
ARMIN PLASTICS CALIFORNIA, INC. 414-A Alaska Ave. (ZIP 90503) (213—320-7373) .... NR
CO: COLORADO SPRINGS
HARLOFF MFG., CO., INC. 752 Garden of the Gods Rd. (ZIP 80907) (303—598-5081) .... 1/4M+
CT: DANBURY
SEALED AIR CORP. Old Sherman Tpke. (ZIP 06810) (203—792-2360) .... 50M+
UNION CARBIDE CORP. HOME & AUTOMOTIVE PRODUCTS DIV. Old Ridgebury Road (ZIP 06817) (203—794-5300) .... 50M+
CT: NEW LONDON
AMERICAN ENGINEERING & DESIGN CORP. Box 729 (ZIP 06320) (Complete Single-Operator & Unattended Bagging Systems. Compact & Economical Fully & Semi-Automatic Bag Opening, Filling & Heat Sealing Machines Which May Be Combined With Conveyors, Automatic Weighing & Counting Devices) (Out Of State Call Toll Free 800-243-8160) .... 1M+
GA: MACON
BONAR INDUSTRIES INC. P.O. Box 10196 (ZIP 31297) (Woven Bulk Containers) (Out Of State Toll Free: 800-841-4982) .... 1M+
IL: CHICAGO
AR-BEE TRANSPARENT PRODUCTS 4882 W. Cortland St. (ZIP 60639) (312—622-0400) .... 1/4M+
★ See our catalog in THOMCAT vols. 13-18

BURCOTT MILLS 304 N. Loomis St. (ZIP 60607) (Out Of State Call Toll Free: 800-621-3463) .... 1M+
CHICAGO TRANSPARENT PRODUCTS 2702 N. Paulina St. (ZIP 60614) (Extruders Of Packaging & Shrink Polyethylene) (312—281-3040) .... 1M+
CONTINENTAL GLASS & PLASTIC, INC. 817 W. Cermak Rd. (ZIP 60608) (Film & Custom Manufacturers - All Sizes) (312—666-2050) .... 5M+
LABELMASTER, DIV. OF MODULAR PRODUCTS CORP. 6724 N. Pulaski, Dept. TR2 (ZIP 60646) (Contour Liners For Fibre Or Steel Drums) (Out Of State Call Toll Free: 800-621-5808; In Illinois Call (312) 478-0900) .... 5M+
(See Our Company Profile in Volume 11)
LOWENTHAL MANUFACTURING CO. 2076-T N. Elston Ave. (ZIP 60614) (312—235-4416) .... 1M+

IL: HARVARD
LANNING BAG & SPECIALTY CO. P.O. Box 126-W (ZIP 60033) (815—943-4466) .... 5M+
IL: LAKE VILLA
VONCO PRODUCTS INC. 201 Park Ave., Plant B (ZIP 60046) (312—356-2323) .... 1/2M+
IN: SHELBYVILLE
KCL CORPORATION 1500 Prospect Ave. (ZIP 46176) (Out Of State Call Toll Free 1-800-428-5431. In Indiana Call 317-392-2521) .... 1M+
(See Our Company Profile in Volume 11)
KY: LOUISVILLE
WALKER BAG COMPANY P.O. Box 1188A (ZIP 40201) (Out Of State Call Toll Free 800-626-5315) .... 1M+
★ See our catalog in THOMCAT vols. 13-18
MA: BEDFORD
COHEN, ARNOLD DAVID CO. 261-T Old Billerica Rd. (ZIP 01730) (Clean Room Packaging, Sterile, Etc. Anti-Static) (617—275-2646) .... NR
MA: HYANNIS
SENTINEL FOAM PRODUCTS DIV. PACKAGING INDUSTRIES GROUP, INC. 130-T North St. (ZIP 02601) (Pouches, Standard & Anti-Stat) (617—775-5220) .... 1M+
MA: SCITUATE
CDF CHEMICAL CORP. P.O. Box 212T (ZIP 02066) (617—545-1378) .... 1M+
MI: KALAMAZOO
TOTAL PLASTICS INC. 5273 Wynn Rd. (ZIP 49001) (Plastic Sheet, Rod, Tubing, Film, Tapes, Shapes & Fabricated Parts) (Out Of State Call Toll Free: 800-231-0013) .... 1/2M+
(See Our Full Page Color Ad At: Plastic Material Manufacturers)
MI: SPARTA
PAK-SAK INDUSTRIES, INC. 120 S. Aspen Dr. (ZIP 49345) (Plastic Bags, Over 60 Million In Stock, & Other Flexible Packaging Materials) (616—887-8837) .... 1/2M+
(See adv. page 630)
MI: STERLING HEIGHTS
CADILLAC PRODUCTS, INC. 7004 E. 15 Mile Rd. (ZIP 48077) (Polyethylene Bags, Plain & Printed; Perforated On Rolls; Shrink & Stretch Bundling Film & Pallet Covers; Trash Can Liners On Perforated Rolls For Industrial, Consumer & Institutional Use) (313—264-2525) .... 1M+
MN: LAKEVILLE
STAR-TEX CORPORATION 8233 220th St. (ZIP 55044) (Out Of State Call Toll Free: 800-328-4080) .... 5M+
★ See our catalog in THOMCAT vols. 13-18
MN: MINNEAPOLIS
AMERICAN MARKETING OF PLASTICS, INC. Hwy. 55 W., 1840 Berkshire Lane (ZIP 55441) (Polyethylene Plastic Bags, Tubing, Sheeting, Etc.) (Out Of State Call Toll Free: 800-328-3348) .... 1/2M+
(See Our Full Page Ad Under Bags: Plastic.)
★ See our catalog in THOMCAT vols. 13-18
(See adv. page 630)

629/BAG

FIGURE 5.3. Thomas Register of American Manufacturers

Dun's Million Dollar Directory® Series... the most frequently used source of business data.

Dun's *Million Dollar Directory* can help you build your business and increase profits. The number and variety of uses you find for it are limited only by your imagination.

• **Target** your sales efforts and develop prospect leads by matching your customer profile to similar businesses listed in the *Million Dollar Directory.*

• **Personalize** your sales approach by locating the offices and addresses of key corporate executives. Impress each sales contact by having his or her correct name and title and knowing the bottom-line facts about their business. Feel confident when you make that initial sales call, knowing that Dun's information is accurate and timely.

• **Confirm** data you already have, or avoid expensive errors caused by misinformation.

• **Reduce selling costs** by using the directory to cluster sales calls geographically. Identify your prime sales areas, then assign your key sales personnel to those locations or direct them into territories with hidden potential.

• **Know your market** by studying your clients that are listed in the *Million Dollar Directory.* You may learn some valuable new information about them.

• **Research** minor details that can affect major decisions—and expenditures. Librarians and business researchers tell us that the *Million Dollar Directory* frequently helps

them put their fingers on specific, hard-to-find data items that are needed by sales and marketing executives.

• **Identify** new (or back-up) sources of supply for critical materials or services.

• **Pinpoint** sales programs and direct mail campaigns by location, type and size of business.

• **Possess** the richest, most productive marketplace in the world...right at your fingertips!

Call Dun's Marketing Services toll-free at **(800) 526-0651** and learn how to make this trio of volumes a working partner in *your* business.

Dun's Marketing Services

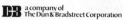

a company of
The Dun & Bradstreet Corporation

MD983

FIGURE 5.4. The Dunn & Bradstreet Reference Book

90

ITI Electronics, Inc.

Income Account*

Year ended Jan. 31	1979	1978
Net sales	$ 1,100,0816	$ 834,291
Cost of sales	653,833	543,110
Expenses	208,365	164,237
Interest expense	21,757	20,228
Bad debts	965	350
Other charges (income)	(653)	1,347
Income before taxes	$ 215,814	$ 105,019
Income taxes	79,500	40,000
Net Income	$ 136,314	$ 65,019
Extraord. credit	–	31,000
Net Income & extraord. credit	$ 136,314	$ 96,019

* Included in Costs and Expenses, Depreciation: $10,359 in 1979 and $10,987 in 1978.

Assets

As of Jan. 31	1979	1978
Cash	$ 146,432	$ 86,916
Short-term invest.	50,902	50,570
Accts. receiv., net	111,015	64,936
*Inventories	302,399	251,132
Other assets	2,737	2,213
Current Assets	$ 613,485	$ 455,767
# Fixed assets	169,228	157,352
Other assets	17,547	17,530
Total Assets	$ 800,260	$ 630,649

Liabilities

	1979	1978
Long-term debt curr.	10,082	9,202
Notes payable	40,000	56,200
Accts. payable & accruals	33,823	31,080
Accrued payroll	17,023	12,638
State taxes	12,932	7,841
Other taxes	3,312	2,634
Federal taxes on income	62,000	–
Curr. Liabilities	$ 179,172	$ 119,595
Long-term debt	118,110	139,390
+ Preferred stock	130	130
+ + Common stock	50,951	50,951
Add. paid-in capital	727,286	727,286
Deficit	(270,389)	(406,703)
Total Liabilities & Shareholders' Equity	$ 800,260	$ 630,649

* At lower of cost (FIFO) or market.
# Less accumulated depreciation.
+ $0.05 par value, Series A, cumulative convertible.
+ + $0.05 par value.

Statistical Summary

%Income bef. Taxes to Sales	19.62	19.34
%Net Income to Sales	12.39	11.97
%Net Income to Equity	27.10	17.49
Sales to Inventories	3.64	2.16
Working Capital	$ 434,313	$ 336,172
Current Ratio	3.42	3.81
Shareholders' Equity	$ 502,978	$ 371,664

Jaco Electronics, Inc.

145 Oser Avenue
Hauppauge, New York 11787
(516) 273-5500

Officers: Charles B. Girsky, president; Michael Gentile, Denis A. Haggerty, v.p.'s; Joel H. Girsky, secretary-treasurer; Stanley M. Zimmerman, corp. controller & asst. secretary.

Directors: Charles B. Girsky, Joel H. Girsky, Martin B. Bloch, Stephen A. Cohen.

Areas of Work: Distributes electronic components manufactured by others to various electronics enterprises. The company specializes in the distribution of capacitors, semiconductors, integrated circuits and resistors used in electronic consumer products, and electronic equipment for commercial, space and defense industries.

Subsidiaries:

Jaco Overseas Inc.
Components Supply Company, Inc.

Transfer Agent(s):

Manufacturers Hanover Trust Company
New York, New York

Stock Exchange(s): Over-the-Counter

Ticker Symbol: JACO (NASDAQ)

Number of Employees:

1978	320	1977	260

Plant Footage:

1978	72,100 sq. ft.	1977	62,600

Sales and Earnings

	Net Sales	Net Income
1977	$ 35,588,269	$ (664,867)
1976	31,625,695	(12,152)
1975	31,755,700	697,187
1974	29,513,738	1,968,943
1973	20,644,480	789,963

	No. of Com. Shares #	Earn. per Share #
1977	751,125	$ –
1976	751,125	–
1975	751,038	0.93
1974	750,206	2.62
1973	763,499	1.03

(Loss)
Based on weighted average number of shares outstanding.

Common Stock Equity

	Total Equity	Equity Per Share #
1977	$ 5,692,406	$7.58
1976	6,357,273	8.46
1975	6,369,425	8.48
1974	5,671,338	7.56

Based on weighted average number of shares outstanding.

Income Account *

Year ended June 30	1977	1976
Net sales	$ 35,588,269	$ 31,625,695
Cost of sales	28,146,329	24,048,434
Expenses	8,268,541	7,143,394
Interest expense	522,267	549,819
Loss before taxes	$ (1,348,868)	$ (115,952)
Tax credit	(684,001)	(103,800)
Net Loss	$ (664,867)	$ (12,152)

* Included in Costs and Expenses, Depreciation and Amortization: $223,101 in 1977 and $221,809 in 1976.

Assets

As of June 30	1977	1976
Cash	$ 174,846	$ 623,786
Accts. receiv., net	3,947,468	4,782,405
Refundable taxes	685,873	372,137
*Inventories	8,588,723	9,544,627
Prepaid expenses	284,529	67,778

	1979	1978
Current Assets	$ 13,681,439	$ 15,390,733
# Fixed assets	1,966,609	2,087,412
Other assets	34,686	124,576
Total Assets	$ 15,682,734	$ 17,602,721

Liabilities

Long-term debt, curr.	$ 63,093	$ 788,541
Bank loans	4,283,812	–
Accts. payable	4,161,641	4,526,495
Accruals	383,384	481,363
Income taxes	11,560	51,101
Curr. Liabilities	$ 8,903,490	$ 5,847,500
Long-term debt	1,086,838	5,359,748
Deferred inc. taxes	–	38,200
+ Common stock	75,113	75,113
Add. paid-in capital	1,111,127	1,111,127
Retained earnings	4,506,166	5,171,033
Total Liabilities & Shareholders' Equity	$ 15,682,734	$ 17,602,721

* At lower of cost (FIFO) or market.
# Less accumulated depreciation and amortization.
+ $0.10 par value.

Statistical Summary

Sales to Inventories	4.14	3.31
Working Capital	$ 4,777,949	$ 9,543,233
Current Ratio	1.54	2.63
Shareholders' Equity	$ 5,692,406	$ 6,357,273

Jamesbury Corp.

640 Lincoln Street
Worcester, Massachusetts 01605
(617) 852-0200

Officers: Howard G. Freeman, chairman & president; Daniel L. DeSantis, v.p.-industrial relations; William W. Rawstron, v.p.-engineering & planning; Maxwell H. Reck, v.p.-marketing & sales; Clyde S. Reynolds, v.p.-mfg.; Joaquim S.S. Ribeiro, v.p.-finance, international; Robert S. Bowditch, secretary-clerk; James B. Reynolds, treasurer.

Directors: Robert S. Bowditch, Howard G. Freeman, Arthur E. Gilman, John A. Lunn, Arthur F.F. Snyder, Paul F. Hartz, C. Vincent Vappi, Paul S. Morgan, John H. Freeman, S. Warner Pach.

Areas of Work: Manufactures and sells ball valves, butterfly valves, valve actuators, and on-off throttling control valves and subsystems, used by the chemical processing pulp and paper, petroleum, steel and power industries; also manufactures and sells punched-tape readers and accessories for the graphic arts, machine tools, computer peripherals and paper tape controlled equipment industries.

Division(s):

Decitek Division
129 Flanders Road
Westboro, Massachusetts 01581
(617) 798-8731
 Manufactures punched tape-readers used in computer peripheral equipment and by machine tool control producers.

Subsidiaries:

Jamesbury Canada Ltd.
1282 Algoma Road
Mobile Route 1
Ottawa 15, Ontario, Canada
(613) 746-2211

Jamesbury Nippon Ltd.
18-7 Shibuya, 3-chome
Tokyo, Japan

Jamesbury Singapore (Pte.) Ltd.
Units 1-2, Block 1
1200 Depot Road
Singapore 4

FIGURE 5.5. Electronic News Financial Fact Book and Directory

91

WHO'S WHO IN FINANCE AND INDUSTRY

CRAWFORD, OLIVER RAY, investment exec.; b. Amarillo, Tex., July 19, 1925; s. George Gordon and Bell Elizabeth (Allston) C.; student Wash. State Coll., 1943-44, S. Tex. Sch. Law, 1953-55; m. Nancy Rose Hudson, Sept. 22, 1979; children by previous marriage—Lynda Ann, Carolyn Rae, Alan Richard. Div. mgr. Phillips Petroleum Co., Midland, Tex., 1947-62; mgr. tax and tile dept. Houston Oil Co. Tex., 1952-56; asst. to gen. mgr. Southwestern Settlement and Devel. Co., Jasper, Tex., 1956-59; gen. mgr. Southwestern Timber Co., 1959-73; v.p. Eastex, Inc., 1956-73; asst. to chmn. bd. and pres. Temple Industries, Inc. div. Time Inc., 1973-74; cons. investments, real estate, govt. and pub. relations, 1974-75; pres. Austin Unltd. Inc., 1974-75; chmn. Lincoln Securities Corp.; pres. Lincoln Realty Co., Lincoln Land Mgmt. Co., Lincoln Devel. Co., 1974-75; pres., chmn. bd. Tecom Inc., 1975—, Chaparral Land and Devel., Inc., 1979—; dir. First State Bank, Jasper. Pres. So. Forest Research Inst., 1963-74; past mem. Tex. Alcoholic Beverage Commn.; dir. Tex. forest industries com. Am. Forest Products Industries. Pres. Jasper Youth Baseball Assn., 1958-74. Bd. dirs. A.R.C., Operation Orphans, Inc., Tex. Law Enforcement Found.; mem. century council, trustee research council Tex. A. & M. U.; mem. regents' devel. council Lamar U.; trustee S.W. Research Inst. Served as fighter pilot USAAF 1943-45. Named Man of Month, East Tex. C. of C., 1961; recipient hon. Lone Star Farmer degree Tex. Assn. Future Farmers; Forest Mgmt. award Nat. Lumber Mfrs. Assn.; Mr. East Texas award, operating dirs. of Tyler County Dogwood Festival, 1967; decorated Comdrs. Cross Order of Merit (Germany). Hon. life mem. Jasper Youth Baseball, Nat. Congress P.T.A., Future Farmers Am.; mem. Tex. Forestry Assn. (dir. pres. 1970-74), Sportsman's Clubs Tex. (pres. 1975-76), Jasper C. of C. (pres. 1964). Presbyn. Home: 7507 Stepdown Cove Austin TX 78731 Office: 3636 Executive Center Dr Suite 201 Austin TX 78731

CRAWFORD, STEPHEN EVERETT, fisheries biologist; b. Pawtucket, R.I., Oct. 29, 1947; s. Earl Smith and Ruth C.; B.S., U. R.I., 1970; M.S. in Zoology, U. Okla., 1979; m. Judith Ann Collins, Jan. 3, 1975. Fisheries biologist R.I. Dept. Fisheries, 1970; Peace Corps vol., Rajasthan, India, 1971-73, fisheries trainer in Nepal, Africa and India, 1973-74; mgr. Sooner Fish Farm, Washington, Okla., 1974-75; pres., mgr. Crawford's Catfish Acres, Inc., Shawnee, Okla., 1977—; fisheries cons. Am. Peace Corps. Mem. Am. Fisheries Soc. Republican. Congregationalist. Home and Office: Route 1 Box 435 Shawnee OK 74801

CRAWFORD, WILLIAM F., corp. exec., cons.; b. Chgo., Apr. 11, 1911; s. William Wilberforce and Mona (Richards) C.; student Northwestern Mil. and Naval Acad., 1925-29, U. Chgo., 1929-31; m. Ruth M. Fellinger, May 4, 1935; children—Judith Crawford Smith, Susan (dec.), Constance Crawford Dry, Barbara Crawford Boger, William Edwin. Sec., Edward Valves, Inc. (formerly Edward Valve & Mfg. Co., Inc.), East Chicago, Ind., 1931-37, v.p., 1937-41, pres., dir., 1941-63; pres., dir. Republic Flow Meters Co., Chgo., 1957-61, Valve Products, Inc., Knox, Ind., 1950-63, W.E. Bowler Co., Phila., 1954-63; v.p., dir. Rockwell Mfg. Co., Pitts., 1945-73, chmn. fin. com., 1963-73; adv. dir. Rockwell Internat., Pitts., 1973-79; v.p., dir. Chgo. Fittings Corp.; dir. U.S. Flexible Metallic Tubing Co., San Francisco, Atlantic India Rubber Works, Inc., Flex-Weld, Inc., Keflex, Inc., Tec-Line Products, Inc. (all Chgo.), Mogul Rubber Corp., Goshen, Ind., Rubbernek Fittings Ltd., Birmingham, Eng.; chmn. W.F. Crawford & Assos., Chgo.; mem. valve industry adv. com. WPB, 1941-45, 50-52. Trustee Ill. Inst. Tech., IIT Research Inst., The Crawford Found., Chgo. Mem. Valve Mfrs. Assn. (pres. 1959-61, 64-65), ASME, Art Inst. Chgo., Field Mus. Natural History, Shedd Aquarium Soc., Delta Upsilon. Republican. Congregationalist. Clubs: Union League, Tavern, Adventurers, Econ. (Chgo.); Duquesne (Pitts.). Home: 4950 Chicago Beach Dr Chicago IL 60615 also PO Box 1800 Sun Valley ID 53353 Office: 185 N Wabash Ave Chicago IL 60601

CRAWFORD, WILLIAM WAIT, securities dealer; b. Louisville, July 10, 1928; s. Malcolm Henry and Mary Louise (Webb) C.; A.B., Centre Coll. of Ky., 1950; m. Shelia Mason, Jan. 28, 1977; children—William Wait, Louise Wallis, Elizabeth Stuart, Barbara Webb. Mem. sales staff Pepsi Cola Louisville Bottlers, 1955-56, Bunte Bros. Chase Candy Co., 1957-60; partner W.L. Lyons & Co., Louisville, 1960-65; dir. J.J.B. Hilliard, W.L. Lyons Inc., Louisville, 1965—, dir. sales and mktg., 1979—, mem. exec. com., 1979—. Served with USNR, 1950-55. Bd. dirs. Ky. Ind. Coll. Found., 1979—. Mem. Nat. Assn. Securities Dealers (dist. com. chmn. 1971-73), Centre Coll. Alumni Assn. (pres. 1970, dir. 1965-71). Republican. Episcopalian. Clubs: Louisville Country, Pendennis, Jefferson, Bond (pres. 1966) (Louisville). Home: 503 Ridgewood Rd Louisville KY 40207 Office: J J B Hilliard W L Lyons Inc 535 S 3d St Louisville KY 40202

CRAWLEY, JAMES BENJAMIN, oil co. exec.; b. Simsboro, La., Aug. 5, 1926; s. John Earl and Lottie (Robison) C.; B.S., Tex. A&M U., 1947; M.B.A., Harvard U., 1956; m. Mary Colby Williamson, June 5, 1956; children—Sara Beth, Linda Sue, Martha Jane. Petroleum engr. Stanolind (now Amoco) Midland, Tex., 1947-51; asst. prodn. supt. Blackwood & Nichols, Midland, 1951-55; v.p. Consol. Prodn. Corp., Oklahoma City, 1957-71, pres., 1971-72; pres. Crawley Petroleum Corp., Oklahoma City, 1972—. Served with AC, U.S. Army, 1945. Registered profl. engr., Okla. Mem. Ind. Producers Assn. Am., Soc. Petroleum Engrs., AIME. Democrat. Presbyterian. Club: Petroleum. Home: 525 Merkle Dr Norman OK 73069 Office: 740 Hightower Bldg Oklahoma City OK 73102

CRAYS, THOMAS COLLISON, banker; b. Danville, Ill., Apr. 26, 1934; s. John Asbury and Lillian Claire (Battershell) C.; B.S., U. Ill., 1958; m. Barbara Ann Huffman, Dec. 9, 1967; children—Anne Elizabeth, Jennifer Courtney, John Forrest. Spl. rep. Fed. Reserve Bank of Chgo., 1958-62; corr. bank rep. Harris Trust & Savs. Bank, Chgo., 1962; exec. v.p. First Nat. Bank of Rossville (Ill.), 1962-66; with Palmer American Nat. Bank, Danville, Ill., 1966—, now pres., chmn. bd. dirs. Chmn., Danville United Way Campaign, 1978, bd. dirs., 1979—; bd. dirs. Center for Children's Service, 1972-79; bd. dirs. Lake View Med. Center, Danville Indsl. Park. Served with U.S. Army, 1954-56. Mem. Ill. State C. of C. (dir.), Ill. Bankers Assn., Am. Bankers Assn. Republican. Clubs: Danville Country, Elks Country, Danville Rotary. Office: 2 W Main St Danville IL 61832

CREAGER, CHARLES EDWIN, lawyer, economist, educator; b. Hagerstown, Md., Oct. 20, 1925; s. Charles Edwin and Mary Edith (Bloyer) C.; B.S., U. Balt., 1950, J.D., 1973; M.B.A., Am. U., Washington, 1959, postgrad., 1966-68; m. Alice Eleanor Hollenbach, Oct. 9, 1948 (div. Jan. 1970); children—Charles Edwin, Karen Elaine and Roger Thomas (twins); m. Dolores C. Yanuk, Nov. 1970. Traffic rep. Charlton Bros. Transp. Co., Inc., Balt., 1946-49; transp. cons., 1950—; gen. freight agt. Novick Transfer Co., Inc., Balt. 1949-58, So. div. sales mgr., Winchester, Va., 1958-59, gen. traffic mgr., 1960-62, v.p. traffic, 1962-64; dir. sales Halls Motor Transport, Sunbury, 1959-60; v.p. traffic Nat. Transport Co., Inc., Bridgeport, Conn., 1964-65, cons., 1965—; partner Germelman, Alt & Creager, 1966-68; owner Charles E. Creager & Assos., Silver Spring, Md., 1968-73; individual practice law, Hagerstown, 1974-76; pres., treas. Law Offices Creager & Newhouse, P.A., 1976—; asst. prof., dir. transp. insts. Am. U., 1965-68, practitioner ICC, 1955—; admitted to Md., D.C., U.S. Ct. of Appeals, U.S. Supreme Ct. bars; asst. prof. mktg. Lord Fairfax Community Coll. Served with USAAF, 1943-46. Bd. dirs. Middle Atlantic Conf., Washington, 1963-68. Mem. Am., Md., D.C. bar assns., Eastern Shipper-Motor Carrier Council (pres. 1964-65; chmn. exec. com. 1965-66), traffic clubs Hagerstown, Shenandoah (past pres.), Nat. Shipper Motor Carrier Conf. (chmn. exec. com. 1964-66), Assn. ICC Practitioners, Motor Carrier Lawyers Assn., Internat. Platform Assn., Phi Alpha Delta. Episcopalian. Elk. Clubs: Fountain Head Country, Rotary. Home: 133 Overhill Dr Hagerstown MD 21740 Office: Creager & Newhouse PA 1329 Pennsylvania Ave PO Box 1417 Hagerstown MD 21740

CREAN, JEREMIAH PAUL, constrn. engring. co. exec.; b. Waterbury, Conn., June 29, 1911; s. Richard Martin and Anna Catherine (Denehy) C.; B.A., Fordham U., 1933, LL.B., 1938; m. Oct. 22, 1938; children—Paula Marie, Christine Angela, Maryanne. Teller, trust dept. Guaranty Trust Co. of N.Y., 1934-42; admitted to N.Y. State bar, 1940; with M.W. Kellogg Co., N.Y.C., 1942-66, mgr. sales adminstrn., 1966; mgr. proposals and contracts, mgr. sales adminstrn. Stone & Webster Engring. Corp., N.Y.C., 1966—. Pres., Burdsall Manor Assn., N.Y.C., 1955-57, West Norwalk (Conn.) Assn., 1974-76. Mem. Bar Assn. State N.Y. Office: Stone & Webster Engring Corp One Penn Plaza 250 W 35th St New York NY 10019

CREECH, SALLY WOOD, real estate broker; educator; b. Raleigh, N.C., Apr. 10, 1939; d. Larry Faison and Harriet Alpha (Dickinson) Wood; A.B. cum laude, Salem Coll., 1961; M.A., U. N.C., 1965; postgrad. U. Oslo (Norway), N.C. State U., Duke U.; m. William Ayden Creech, Jan. 13, 1968; children—Lawrence Wood, Ezekiel Hollingsworth, Charles Alderman. Instr. dept. social scis. U. N.C., Wilmington, 1965-68, Raleigh, N.C., 1975—; Pres. Wake County Democratic Women, 1937-75; mem. Raleigh Hist. Sites Commn. Mem. LWV, Raleigh Fine Arts Soc., Raleigh Bd. Realtors, Salem Coll. Alumni Assn. (dir. 1973-74), Phi Alpha Theta. Methodist. Clubs: Jr. League of Raleigh, Twentieth Century Book. Home: 1208 College Pl Raleigh NC 27605

CREEDON, JOHN J., ins. co. exec.; b. N.Y.C., Aug. 1, 1924; s. Bartholomew and Emma (Glynn) C.; B.S. magna cum laude, N.Y. U., 1952, LL.B. cum laude, 1955, LL.M., 1962; m. Vivian Elser, Aug. 17, 1947; children—Juliette, Michele, John, David. With Met. Life Ins. Co., N.Y.C., 1942—, v.p., asso. gen. counsel, 1970-73, sr. v.p., gen. counsel, 1973-76, exec. v.p., 1976-80, pres. and dir., 1980—, chmn. bd. Met. Property & Liability Ins. Co., 1979-80; admitted to N.Y. State bar, 1955; adj. prof. law N.Y. U. Law Sch., 1962-73; bd. dirs., pres. Am. Bar Found.; chmn. bd. Met. Life Found.; trustee N.Y. U., N.Y. U. Law Center Found., Am. Coll., Practising Law Inst.; mem. legal adv. com. N.Y. Stock Exchange. Served with USNR, 1943-46. Mem. Am. (assembly del. 1972-75, chmn. sect. corp. banking and bus. law 1975-76), N.Y. State bar assns., Assn. Bar City N.Y., Assn. Life Ins. Counsel (pres. 1977-78), Life Ins. Council N.Y. (chmn.), Am. Law Inst., N.Y. State C. of C. and Industry. Editor The Bus. Lawyer, 1973-74: contbr. articles to profl. jours. Office: 1 Madison Ave New York NY 10010

CREEGER, ALLAN DAVID, equipment rental co. exec.; b. Boston, Dec. 9, 1921; s. Herbert S. and Jane S. (Nelson) C.; B.A., Columbia U., 1942; I.A. with distinction, Grad. Sch. Bus., Harvard U., 1943; m. Louise V. Rosenthal, Feb. 12, 1944; children—Lawrence A., Carol J. Pres., Creeg-Rose Corp., Richmond, Va., 1947-56, Karol Distbg. Co., Richmond, 1952-54, Handy Distbrs. Inc., Richmond, 1954—. Served to lt lt. U.S. Army, 1943-46. Mem. Am. Rental Assn. (dir. 1959-62, pres. 1972-73, chmn. 1973-75, Disting. Service award 1979), Retail Mchts. Assn. Greater Richmond (2d vice chmn.), Va. Equipment Rental Assn. (pres.). Club: Richmond Kiwanis (dir.). Contbr. articles to trade jours. Home: 43 Old Mill Rd Richmond VA 23226 Office: 2367 Staples Mill Rd Richmond VA 23230

CREEK, JOHN DENNIS, mfg. co. exec.; b. Roswell, N.Mex., Apr. 5, 1951; s. Webster Bennett and Edna Ore (Lott) C.; B.A., Tex. Tech U., 1974, postgrad., 1974-75; m. Billie Lou Kingsbery, June 19, 1976; 1 dau., Courtney A. Field technician Tait-Andritz Co., Lubbock, Tex., 1976, sales staff, 1977-78, sales mgr., 1978, dir. mktg., 1978—, v.p., 1980—, gen. mgr., 1981—; cons. U. Wis., Madison, 1978-79. Mem. TAPPI, AIME, Am. Mgmt. Assn. Republican. Baptist. Clubs: Rotary, Lubbock Country. Contbr. articles to profl. jours. Home: 4811 Tamanaco Ct Arlington TX 76017 Office: 1010 Commonwealth Blvd S Arlington TX 76063

CREEL, JAMES PEARLIE, advt. exec.; b. Conway, S.C., Mar. 6, 1939; s. John P. and Hazel M. Creel; B.S. in Indsl. Mgmt., Clemson (S.C.) U., 1961; m. Carolyn Willism, Aug. 8, 1959; children—James Pearlie, Carolyn Alicia. Mgmt. trainee Shell Oil Co., 1961; from sales dir. to v.p. Tyson & Co. Advt., Myrtle Beach, S.C., 1963-78; pres. Creel Outdoor Advt., Inc., Myrtle Beach, 1978—, Cabana I Devel. Co., Inc., Myrtle Beach, 1979—; partner T.W.C. Properties, 1969—, Bayview Acres, 1973—; sec. Fairway Corp., 1971—; dir. Standard Savs. & Loan Assn., Myrtle Beach. Co-chmn. Horry County Indsl. Council, 1967; bd. dirs. Horry County Dept. Public Welfare, 1966-71, S.C. Hall of Fame, 1973—, Jr. Achievement Horry County, 1975; chmn. dist. adv. com. Pee Dee Area council Boy Scouts Am., 1968-71; mem. Horry County Planning Commn., 1977-79; chmn. coliseum com. Myrtle Beach Auditorium, 1973; sec. Horry-Georgetown Tech. Edn. Commn., 1972; gen. chmn. United Way Horry County, 1973, bd. dirs., 1973—, v.p. agy. ops., 1975; chmn. Gov. S.C. Com. Hwy. Safety, 1980. Served to 1st lt. USAR, 1961-63. Decorated Army Commendation medal. Mem. Outdoor Advt. Assn. Am. (dir. 1978—), Inst. Outdoor Advt. (gov., exec. com. 1979—), S.C. Outdoor Advt. Assn. (pres. 1970-73), Carolina's Electric Sign Assn., Myrtle Beach C. of C. (chmn. coms.), Dunes Property Owners Assn. (v.p., dir. 1977-80), Med. Exec. Assn. (past pres.). Methodist. Clubs: Kiwanis (pres. 1967-68), Rotary (pres. 1980) (Myrtle Beach). Home: 411 Wildwood Trail Dunes Myrtle Beach SC 29577 Office: PO Box 157 Hwy 317 at 501 Myrtle Beach CA 29577

CREIGHTON, JOHN EVERETT, spl. events planner; b. Bakersfield, Calif., Oct. 23, 1931; s. John Lyon and Grayce (Mills) C.; B.S. in Animal Sci., U. Calif., Davis, 1958; m. Janice Rakestraw, Mar. 17, 1951; children—John K., Larry B., Kathrine A., Linda M. Mgr., Nev. State Fair, Reno, 1969-71, Navajo Nation Fair, Window Rock, Ariz., 1971-73; coordinator Ariz. State Fair., Phoenix, 1973-74; mgr. Ariz. Nat. Livestock Show, Phoenix, 1974-76; owner The Connection, Phoenix, 1976—. Served with U.S. Army, 1952-54. Mem. Ariz. Fairs Assn., Western Fairs Assn. Club: Ariz. Showman's. Office: PO Box 39452 Phoenix AZ 85069

CREMONA, VINCENT ANTHONY, banking adminstr.; b. Valetta, Malta, Nov. 5, 1925; s. Henry and Jane Mary (Cachia) C.; came to U.S., 1959, naturalized, 1965; B.S., Stella Maris Coll., Malta, 1945; M.S. in Finance, London Sch. Accountancy, 1950. Ships purveyor Peninsular and Oriental Steam Nav. Co., Valetta, 1945-50; asst. supr. Gen. Motors, Oshawa, Ont., Can., 1950-55; accounting supr. Ind. Groceries Assn., Toronto, Ont., Can., 1955-59; accounting mgr. Air India, N.Y.C., 1960-65; dir. adminstrn. and finance Commonwealth Services, Dhahran Internat. Airport, Saudi Arabia, 1965-66; mgr. internal audits Litton Industries, Carlstadt, N.J., 1966-67; v.p. Fashioncade, N.Y.C., 1967-68; tng. dir. FRS, Washington, 1969—. Certified internal auditor. Mem. Am. Mgmt. Assn., Inst. Internal Auditors, Assn. Govt. Accountants, Order St. John of Jerusalem. Home: Columbia Plaza Envoy 2450 Virginia Ave NW Washington DC 20037 Office: Fed Reserve System Washington DC 20551

CREQUÉ, MARCELYN ELLEN, telephone co. ofcl.; b. Cleve., Mar. 15, 1931; d. Spearman D. and P. Edwinetta (Reed) Lark; student Keller Grad. Sch. Mgmt., 1975-77; m. Carl Crequé, May 14, 1972. Long distance operator AT&T Co., Chgo., 1950-54, clerk, various depts., 1954-63, service rep., 1963-66, sales supr., 1966-73, staff supr., 1973-74, service mgr., 1974-76, ops. mgr. telegraph and radio, 1976-78, dist. engr. customer services, 1978—. Del., bd. dirs. Chgo. Conf. on Race and Religion, 1975—; mem. support com. Urban Bishops Coalition, 1977. Mem. Stony Island Assn., Dorchester Civic Assn., Chgo. Fiber Guild. Episcopalian. Home: 8732 S Dorchester Ave Chicago IL 60619 Office: 10 S Canal St 25th Floor Chicago IL 60606

CRESON, WILLIAM T., corp. exec.; b. 1929; B.S., Purdue U., 1948; M.A., U. Pa., 1950; married. With Packaging Corp. of Am. prior to 1968; sr. v.p., gen. mgr. Brown Co., 1968-75; with Crown Zellerbach Corp., San Francisco, 1976—, exec. v.p., mem. exec. com., now pres., dir. Office: Crown Zellerbach Corp 1 Bush St Box 7809 San Francisco CA 94119*

CRESWELL, DONALD CRESTON, mgmt. cons.; b. Balt., Mar. 28, 1932; s. Carroll Creston and Verna Moore (Taylor) C.; student Johns Hopkins U., 1951-52; M.B.A., U. Dayton, 1966; postgrad. bus. Stanford U., 1975; m. Terri Sue Tidwell, Dec. 27, 1958; 1 son, Creston Lee. Cons. engr. A.D. Ring & Assos., Washington, 1956-58; sales and mktg. mgr. Ampex Corp., Redwood City, Calif., 1959-68; dir. mktg., magnetic products div. RCA Corp., N.Y.C., 1968-71; staff v.p. sales and advt. Pan Am. World Airways, N.Y.C., 1971-74; mktg. v.p. Rocor Internat., Palo Alto, Calif., 1975; v.p., chief operating officer, gen. mgr., Am. AmBuCar Services, Inc., San Francisco, 1976; prin. strategic mgmt. cons. Stanford Research Inst., Menlo Park, Calif., 1977—; lectr. planning and mktg. mgmt. Am. Mgmt. Assn., 1968-69; program chmn. Grad. Bus. Assn., 1965; rep. to Electronics Industries Assn., 1968-71, to Internat. Air Transport Assn., 1971-74; spl. cons. Devtronix Organs, Inc., 1978-79. Mem. Am. Theatre Organ Soc. (dir. 1978-79). Republican. Home: 3328 Brittan Ave San Carlos CA 94070

CRETSOS, JAMES MIMIS, sci. info. co. exec., chemist; b. Athens, Greece, Oct. 23, 1929; s. Basil D. and Chrissa B. (Thomaidou) Kretsos; came to U.S., 1946, naturalized, 1955; B.S. in Chemistry, Am. U., 1960, postgrad., 1960-62; m. Barbara Ann Deitz, Mar. 10, 1952; children—Maurice William, Christopher James. Research chemist Melpar, Inc., Falls Church, Va., 1961-63, info. scientist, 1963-64, head tech. info. center, 1964-65, mgr. info. services lab., 1965-67, dir. instructional materials center, Tng. Corp. of Am., Falls Church, 1966-67; dir. info. systems lab. Litton Industries, Bethesda, Md., 1967-69; head sci. info. systems dept. Merrell-Nat. Labs., Cin., 1969—; dir. Infoflow, Inc.; cons OEO, Ohio, Ky.-Ind. Regional Library and Info. Council; lectr. U. Cin., 1973-74, U. Ky., 1976-77. Mem. Creative Edn. Found., Buffalo, 1967—. Served with M.C., AUS, 1954-56. Mem. Am. Chem. Soc., Am. Mgmt. Assn., Am. Soc. Info. Sci. (chmn. So. Ohio chpt. 1973-74, chmn. SIG/BC 1973-74, chmn. profl. enhancement com. 1974-75, chmn. 5th mid-year meeting 1976, Watson Davis award 1976, chmn. membership com. 1977, exec. com. 1979, nominations com. 1980, pres. 1979), Assn. Computing Machinery, Drug Info. Assn., IEEE Computer Soc., Am. Fedn. Info. Processing Socs. (dir. 1981—), Spl. Libraries Assn. (pres. Cin. chpt. 1974-75, consultation officer 1976-77), Pharm. Mfrs. Assn., Nat. Micrographics Assn. Club: Indoor Tennis. Editor: Health Aspects of Pesticides Abstract Bull., 1967-69; adv. bd. Chem. Abstracts Service, 1981—. Home: 10701 Adventure Ln Cincinnati OH 45242 Office: 2110 E Galbraith Rd Cincinnati OH 45215

CREW, CHARLES ANTHONY, mfg. corp. exec.; b. Balt., Mar. 23, 1943; s. Charles Albert and Nellie Elizabeth (Zurgable) C.; B.S. in Accounting and Fin., U. Balt., 1966; m. Linda Carol Bilson, Sept. 7, 1963; children—Alisa, Carol, Charles. Cost accountant Green Spring Dairy, Inc., Balt., 1963-66, cost, budget supr., 1966; sr. div. accountant Am. Trading & Production Co., Balt., 1966-69; accounting mgr. Sealtest Foods, Kraft Corp., Balt., 1969-70; plant controller Eastern Products Corp., Roper Corp., Balt., 1970-72; controller Unitote div. Gen. Instrument Co., Balt., 1972-73, fin. exec. data systems & services group, 1973-79; v.p. fin. Dur-O-Wal, Inc., Balt., 1979-80; dir. fin. Dutch Boy, Inc., Balt., 1980—. C.P.A., Md. Mem. Candlewicke Community Assn. (treas. 1976-77), Md. Assn. C.P.A.'s, Nat. Assn. Accountants, Am. Mgmt. Assn. Home: 101 Talloway Ct Sykesville MD 21784 Office: 2325 Hollins Ferry Rd Baltimore MD 21230

CRICHTON, BRUCE NELSON, coal co. exec.; b. Rahway, N.J., Sept. 17, 1936; s. Harry Alan and Imelda R. Crichton; B.S. in Bus., Lehigh U., Bethlehem, Pa., 1958; s. Baily Haines, Nov. 24, 1959; children—Lissa, Douglas, Garrett. With Irving Trust Co., N.Y.C., 1959-61; pres. Crichton Co. Inc., N.Y.C., 1961-75; pres., dir. John K. Irish Co. Inc., Red Bank, N.J., 1975—; dir. Jersey Shore Bank, Long Branch, N.J. Served with USAR, 1958-64. Mem. Coal Exporters Am. (dir.), Nat. Coal Assn. Republican. Presbyterian. Clubs: Navesink Country, Saucon Valley Country, Seabright Beach, Madison Sq. Garden. Home: 6 Azalea Ln Rumson NJ 07760 Office: 176 Riverside Ave Red Bank NJ 07701

CRICHTON, JOHN HAYES, investment banker; b. Minden, La., July 21, 1920; s. Thomas and Bernard Moore (Hayes) C.; B.S., Davidson Coll., 1942; J.D., La. State U., 1949; Exec. Program, Stanford, 1970; m. 2d, Dale Cowgill, July 3, 1967; children by previous marriage—Kate, Bunnie, Lili, John Hayes. Admitted to La. bar, 1949; mem. firm Smitherman, Smitherman & Purcell, 1949-51; mng. dir. Better Hotels of La., Shreveport, 1951-61; exec. v.p., asst. to pres. Allied Properties, San Francisco, 1961-62; pres., dir. Guaranteed Reservations Inc., Palm Beach, Fla., 1962—; pres., dir. Computer Controls Corp., 1967-70; chmn., dir. Commonwealth Group Inc., 1975—; dir. Three Two Corp., Southeastern Surg. Supply Co., Inverness Corp., Nat. Assn. Merger and Acquisition Cons. Served to maj., inf. AUS, 1942-46. Decorated Bronze star with oak leaf cluster. Mem. Am., La. bar assns., Bankers Club San Francisco, Phi Delta Phi. Republican. Mem. Anglican Ch. of N.Am. Club: Bath and Tennis (Palm Beach). Home: 2411 Pacific Ave San Francisco CA Office: 601 California St San Francisco CA 94108

CRICHTON, JOHN PETER, hand tool mfg. co. exec.; b. Greenwich, Conn., Dec. 9, 1934; s. William Edward and Elizabeth (Bowen) C.; B.A., St. Michaels Coll., 1952-56; postgrad. exec. summer program Harvard U., 1970; m. Mary Ellen Horsfall, Sept. 7, 1957; children—Susan, John, Kathleen, Melissa, Matthew. Dist. sales mgr. Power Tool div. Rockwell Internat., Pitts., 1960-63, merchandising specialist, 1963-64, Can. sales mgr., 1964-66, Can. dir. mktg., 1966-69, U.S. nat. sales mgr., 1969-71, dir. mktg., 1971-73, v.p. mktg., 1973-76, dir. internat. mktg., 1976-78; pres. New Britain Tool div. Litton Industries (Conn.), 1978—; instr. Grad. Sch. Indsl. Mktg., Carnegie-Mellon U., 1979. Served with CIC, U.S. Army, 1957-60. Recipient award of merit Nat. Retail Hardware Assn., 1976. Mem. Hardware Mktg. Council. Patentee pocket socket hand tool. Home:

FIGURE 5.6. World's Who's Who in Finance and Industry

arrangements, the expenses of distribution, relationships between the registrant and certain experts, sales of securities to special parties, recent sales of unregistered securities, a list of subsidiaries, and the treatment of proceeds being registered.

The Exchange Act has four types of disclosure requirements relating to registration, periodic reporting, proxy solicitation, and insider trading. Listed (New York and American Exchanges) and OTC (over the counter) registered companies are required to file certain periodic reports. The most important of these reports are Forms 8K, 10K, and 10Q, of which 10K is the most useful for obtaining competitive information.

Form 10K is an annual report due 90 days after the end of the fiscal year. It contains certified financial statements, including a balance sheet, a profit and loss statement for each fiscal year covered by the report, an analysis of surplus, and supporting schedules. It includes a breakdown of both sales and earnings for each major line of business, although a company with sales greater than $50 million does not have to carry an individual breakdown unless a product line contributes 10 percent or more to total volume or pretax profits. For smaller companies, the disclosure point is 15 percent. Although companies must break out such product line data on their annual 10K reports to the SEC, they need not disclose the information in the annual report to their shareholders.

The 10K report must reveal the amount spent on R & D in the preceding year, the size of order backlogs, the availability of essential raw materials, competitive conditions in the industry, and the financial statements of unconsolidated majority-owned subsidiaries. The 10K report must also disclose any leasing and rental commitments and their dollar impact on both present and future earnings. The 10K report is therefore an information bonanza for evaluating a competitor's business.

Since not all of the information in a 10K report finds its way into the company's annual report to the shareholders, competitive research should be done with the 10K supplementing the annual report.

Large public libraries, larger financial houses and leading business school libraries, have microfilm copies of 10K reports and up to 10 other reporting documents that are required by law. A company's 10K report can usually be obtained by requesting a copy in writing from the financial officer.

If a competitor is a private corporation, then the data, though more difficult to obtain, are not out of reach for an aware and observant analyst. Data are often published in the newspapers, trade journals, and information bulletins reporting on new contract awards and their value (companies love to announce these), contract losers, personnel movements, litigation (who is suing whom and for how much), new product announcements and prices, user-reported product problems and manufacturers' responsiveness in correcting them, and other pertinent data.

INDUSTRY SOURCES

Trade shows also offer a wealth of information. Visit your competitors' product booths and examine their products for the latest features, strengths, and weaknesses. Listen to their salesmen's stories, especially what they are telling other prospects. Many trade shows have seminars where competitors often present papers on their products and/or developments. This can be a rich source of information.

Another less-glamorous technique include interviewing your competitors' personnel for positions in your own company. Much can be learned through intelligent questioning about their operations without compromising an employee's position.

If a competitor is local, a periodic inspection of its parking lot during working hours will reveal if its employee count is up or down, which has a direct relationship to its business activity.

Keep a current file on your competitors' product brochures and specifications. Often, changes in these indicate trends in a company or in the industry itself. Competitive information is available, if only you have the imagination, alertness, and determination to uncover it.

Evaluating the collected data to determine why a competitor is a success or a failure is the more difficult side of information gathering. With a public corporation, first examine the profit (bottom line) on their income statements for several years to determine if they are a success or a failure. Since one good year doesn't make a success and one bad year doesn't make a failure, look for trends. A consistent growth in net profit in actual dollars and percentages of sales over a period of years certainly indicates a successful operation. Conversely, a consistent decline would seem to indicate failure. If a business is sensitive to national economic expansion and recession, then national conditions figure into your calculation.

A further examination of a business's income statement will reveal how it has allocated its sales dollar among labor, material, overhead, engineering, marketing, and G&A. If its allocation has been a success, try to duplicate it. If not, compare the expenditures against those of a successful company and try to determine the cause of failure. Knowing why a company has failed is as valuable as knowing why it succeeded. Keep digging!

If labor costs are too high or low, question why. If labor costs are too high, perhaps the firm has priced itself out of the market. If too low, it may have caused high labor turnover and thus incurred increased training costs and inefficiencies. This liability may show up in other cost areas, such as increased overhead and scrap. If labor turnover is high, question why. Is it because of low wages, poor working conditions, poor management, or even a high turnover in management itself?

If material costs are out of line, is it because a company cannot buy in the same quantity as a successful competitor? Or perhaps the cause is an inexperienced purchasing staff.

If overhead costs are too high, perhaps your competitor has a staff larger than is required to do the job. Or perhaps building rent and operating costs are more than they should be. If overhead costs are too low, it could mean there is inadequate supervision to maximize labor's efforts. The same logic holds true for engineering, marketing and G & A. Not spending enough is just as bad and sometimes is worse, than spending too much. Striking the right balance is the key.

If it is possible, and it often times is, visit and tour your competitor's facility. Be observant. Are their offices and manufacturing areas neat, clean, and well organized for a smooth logical flow of raw materials to completed and shipped products? Or are they unkempt and helter-skelter? It is often stated that the cleanliness and physical organization of a company is a direct reflection of its management's thinking and a yardstick for measuring a product's quality. The author, in visits to hundreds of manufacturing firms, has found this correlation holds true. Neatness and organization usually reflect efficiency, whereas the opposite reflects inefficiency and waste.

The behavior of a firm's personnel is very revealing. If they are neat about themselves, it usually means that they generally take pride in their work. This point should not be taken lightly because it is people, not things, that make a company succeed or fail.

Observe the offices and how they are decorated. And the type of factory equipment employed. If a facility's furniture, floor and wall trappings, and manufacturing equipment are more expensive than required, it is also a reflection of management's thinking. Its priorities indicate whether the company will succeed or fail.

If financial statements are not available and facility tours are not possible, much can still be learned about a competitor's success or failure by examining its product—in detail! Buy one and have a manufacturing, purchasing, and engineering team dissect and examine it objectively.

A manufacturing expert can determine how it was put together and how much it cost to do so. The engineers can evaluate its performance, and estimate its design and manufacturing cost. The industrial engineers and purchasing department buyers can estimate piece parts and subassembly costs. Put all the pieces together, and the development and manufacturing costs will be known.

The marketing people will know its selling price, competitor's discount policies, facility size, manufacturing capability, sales force, and customer base. The marketing data provides the remaining puzzle pieces. Product costs, gross margins, expenses and profits (or losses) can then be estimated.

Knowing your competition's customer base even reveals the likelihood of their (your competition) being paid on time and discloses something about their financial condition. Added finance charges must either be absorbed (subtracted from profits) or passed on to the customer (higher prices).

Executive and first-level management stability is also an indicator of a successful or failing company. If the financial reports are available for several years, examine the names filling the executive management posts. If the same names appear year after year, it indicates stability. If not, it may mean that the company is still trying to find the right combination to make it work.

The same holds true for the first-level managers. Trade journals regularly report their comings and goings. Management changes are expensive. They cause morale problems, which foster inefficiency. This in turn is reflected in lower productivity, lower quality, higher costs and the bottom line: lower profits.

There are many ways to be an effective industrial management detective and to evaluate competitive reasons for success or failure. It just requires imagination and common sense.

SUMMARY

In summary, valuable lessons can be learned about how to and, equally important, how not to manage your organization by studying competitors' successes and failures. The first step is to determine who they are, using the resources of local public library.

If your competition is a public corporation, a library that carries its 10K report can provide much of the financial data needed to evaluate its profit and loss situation and how it spends its revenue. Compare the same type expenses for a successful and a not-so-successful competitor to determine what was done right and what was wrong.

If your competitor is a private corporation, the business section of newspapers, trade journals, and trade shows are valuable sources for competitive information. They can often provide insights into what the other guy is doing, right or wrong.

Facility tours will reveal clues as to how management thinks and spends money, which has a direct bearing on success and failure. Product dissection and examination also tell a story about a product's performance and costs, which will be reflected in your competitors' profit and loss statements.

Finally, an examination of your competitions management stability will provide additional clues to its success or failure. Being successful in evaluating competitors requires only imagination and common sense.

6

EXAMPLES OF
COMPETITIVE SUCCESSES
AND FAILURES

The study of competitive successes and failures yields valuable information on how to, and how not to, manage an organization. This chapter puts this general principle into operation by reviewing the income statements of three companies: Print Corporation, a very successful, privately held manufacturer of printers for the OEM minicomputer and systems house market; MME Corporation, a division of a publically held corporation that failed as a manufacturer of cartridge disk drives for the OEM minicomputer and systems house market; and Diskco Corporation, which is a division of a publically held corporation and a not very successful, but recovering, manufacturer of cartridge disk drives for the OEM minicomputer and systems house market.

The respective income statements for these three companies (Tables 6.1, 6.2, and 6.3) will be examined to determine what Print Corporation did right and what MME and Diskco did wrong.

These three companies were selected as a case study because of their product and market similarities so that an "apples to apples" and not an "apples to oranges" comparison could be made. The three are manufacturers of sophisticated computer peripheral equipment. All are located in California's electronic manufacturing centers, and each serves the OEM minicomputer and systems house market. The single major difference is that Print is a privately held corporation. MME and Diskco are divisions of

TABLE 6.1 Print Corporation Income Statement Years 1, 2, 3, 4, and 5

| | Year 1 | | Year 2 | | Year 3 | |
	($000)	%Sales	($000)	%Sales	($000)	%Sales
Net sales	11	100	1,872	100	9,957	100
Cost of sales	24	218	2,201	117	6,732	67.6
Gross margin	(13)	(118)	(329)	(17.5)	3,226	32.4
Expenses						
Engineering	524	4,764	461	24.6	628	6.3
Marketing	62	564	332	17.7	738	7.4
G&A	181	1,645	433	23	988	9.9
Total expenses	767	6,973	1,226	65.3	2,354	23.6
Pretax profit	(780)	(7,091)	(1,555)	(83.1)	872	8.8

| | Year 4 | | Year 5 | |
	($000)	%Sales	($000)	%Sales
Net sales	21,591	100	69,101	100
Cost of sales	13,369	61.9	37,159	61.8
Gross margin	8,222	38.1	22,942	38.2
Expenses				
Engineering	1,384	6.4	2,889	4.8
Marketing	1,241	5.8	2,816	4.7
G&A	2,040	9.4	4,649	7.7
Total expenses	4,665	21.6	10,345	17.2
Pretax profit	3,557	16.5	12,588	21.0

publically held corporations. A biographical sketch of each company is presented, followed by an analysis of their respective income statements.

PRINT CORPORATION

Print Corporation was founded during the early 1970s (in a recession). It is located in the greater San Francisco Bay area,

TABLE 6.2 MME Corporation Income Statement Years 9 and 10

	Year 9		Year 10 Proforma	
	($000)	%Sales	($000)	%Sales
Sales drives	4,606	73.4	11,287	87.3
Sales spares	1,473	23.5	1,640	12.7
Subtotal	6,079	96.9	—	—
Service and other	197	3.1	—	—
Total revenue	6,276	100.0	12,927	100.0
Direct cost of sales				
Direct labor	764	12.2	1,036	8
Material	2,853	45.5	6,570	50.8
Shipping	148	2.4	112	0.9
Expense material	78	1.2	—	—
Warranty, scrap	236	3.8	281	2.2
subtotal	4,079	65.1	—	—
Intercompany	7	0.1	—	—
Subtotal	4,086	65.2	—	—
Cost of service	210	3.5	244	1.9
Total direct costs	4,296	68.7	8,243	63.8
Indirect costs				
Manufacturing	956	15.2	1,289	10.0
Engineering	440	7.0	726	5.6
Total, indirect	1,396	22.2	2,015	15.6
Cost of sales	5,692	91.0	10,258	79.4
Gross margin	584	9.0	2,669	20.6
Operating expenses				
Selling/marketing	369	5.9	853	6.6
G&A	400	6.4	422	3.3
Total operating expenses	769	12.3	1.275	9.9
Other expenses	32	—	130	1.0
Pretax profit	(217)	(3.3)	1.264	9.7

TABLE 6.3   Diskco Corporation Income Statement Year 6

	Year 6	
	($000)	%Sales
Net sales	11,238	100
Cost of sales		
Direct labor	990	8.8
Material	4,558	40.6
Overhead	2,989	26.6
Total cost of sales	8,537	76.0
Gross margin	2,701	24.0
Expenses		
Engineering	Not available	
Marketing	Not available	
G&A	Not available	

which is also known as the electronics capital of the world.

Labor rates in the San Francisco Bay area are generally higher than in the rest of the United States. During periods of national economic expansion, there is usually a labor shortage, which creates severe competitive pressures for the available labor pool.

The absence of unions in the electronics industry contributes to the mobility of the labor force. As a rule, employers show little loyalty to their employees and as a result, employees show little loyalty to their employers. The labor force is therefore one large, transient mass of skilled individuals, looking for the highest wages, shortest hours, and best working conditions. A company must do "something extra" under these conditions to keep its labor force from turning over and to keep costs down.

Though this was difficult for a new company such as Print Corporation, as a start-up it was able to prosper under these difficult circumstances. The evidence is in its income statement, Table 6.1. In only two years, it was able to develop an advanced-technology product and establish a market, while only spending $2.3 million. By the end of its third year, Print was able to earn a pretax profit of 8.8 percent, which is only 1.2 percent below the average for all U.S. manufacturers. Years four and five provided profits substantially above the average for U.S. manufacturers, the computer peripheral industry, and the computer industry itself.

Print Corporation's income statement gives several clues about what it did right to achieve success. It first established a market by finding a need (better printers) in a growing industry (minicomputers) and effectively, and profitably, filling that need. The proof is in its growth from $11,000 to $60 million in sales in a five year period in a market that grew from $413 million to $510 million during the same time. Print grew because it made the necessary engineering and marketing expenditures to design a good product and bring it to market at the outset of the program.

The path it chose was expensive but necessary. The absolute dollars spent and the expenses, on a percentage-of-sales basis during years one and two, tell the story. Expenses were quickly reduced as a percentage of sales during the following years. Engineering and sales expenses in year five were at least 3 percentage points below the industry average for similar products. These are two important clues for the serious investigator to follow up. Why could this company spend less than 5 percent of its sales on engineering and the same percentage for marketing while the rest of the industry spends approximately 7 percent on engineering and 8 to 10 percent on marketing?

Lower engineering costs are attributable to higher-caliber engineers who designed a better product requiring fewer engineering changes and allowing the staff to concentrate on new developments in subsequent years.

Lower marketing costs are attributable to the use of a then-novel marketing approach for peripherals: using distributors to sell products rather than employing a large, direct sales force and manufacturers' representatives.

Distributors are customers who buy products at a discount, stock an inventory, and resell to low-volume accounts for a profit. Salespeople who service distributor accounts, which may require a minimum of time and effort, usually do so on a reduced-commission basis. A salesforce can then concentrate on higher-volume OEM accounts. Manufacturers' representatives, who are usually employed to sell this type of product (and who operate on a commission-only basis) are eliminated altogether.

Print Corporation's achievement in these two areas in its fifth year added 7 percentage points to its pre-tax profit. Cost of sales (labor, material, and overhead) during the fourth and fifth years was maintained at 62 percent of sales, which provided a 38 percent gross margin and which is 8 to 10 percentage points above the break-even point of most companies in the OEM peripherals industry.

The only anomaly in Print Corporation's income statement is its General and Administrative costs, which should not exceed 7 percent. The actual figure was explained by a note in the company's income statement to the effect that a special disbursement was made to the officers of the corporation. There is certainly nothing wrong with this practice when the recipients are the owners of a profitable and private corporation. Print Corporation has continued to outpace its competitors and is growing and profitable today.

MME CORPORATION

MME Corporation is on the opposite side of the performance spectrum. One of the first independent manufacturers of cartridge disk drives, MME was founded at the end of the sixties. It is also located in the competitive labor market of the San Francisco Bay area.

At one point in its rocky history, MME captured 27 percent of the OEM cartridge disk drive market, yet failed to stay profitable. The company was plagued at the outset by severe management problems. It was also known for its flamboyant and expensive spending. These problems were compounded by poor product design and manufacturing-quality problems.

As a result of poor management, financial losses, and product failures, the company reduced its staff from 600 to 40 employees during the mid-seventies. The object was to begin anew, solve the product-related problems, accept a smaller market share, and achieve profitability.

The firm solved its design-related product problems. Market

share, which had dropped to 2 percent, increased to 4 percent through the new efforts, and employment eventually grew from 40 to 150 persons over a three year period. "Creative bookkeeping" practices made MME appear to be marginally profitable.

Because MME continued to be plagued by top-management problems at the division and corporate levels, lower management and the technical and production ranks suffered from high employee turnover. In one 11 month period, employee turnover was 110 percent. The company developed a very poor reputation in the competitive San Francisco Bay area labor pool and was not able to attract quality personnel. As a result, product quality declined and customers were lost. The high employee turnover also made it impossible for the company to reduce product costs. It was always in a training mode of operation. Corporate management tried to sell the division, but because of its history and reputation there were no buyers. Corporate management decided to close operations at the end of 1979.

This is a classic case of how not to run a business!

Table 6.2 is MME's income statement for its 9th year of operation and includes its 10th year proforma statement. MME's objectives for year 10 were not realized, owing in part to the later decision to cease operations and phase out the division.

An analysis of MME's income statement for the 9th year shows that cost of goods (labor, material, and manufacturing overhead) amounted to 83.9 percent of each sales dollar, leaving only 16.1 percent available for engineering, marketing, G&A, and profit. This is clearly out of line by at least 20 percentage points. Engineering expenses of 7 percent (noted as indirect cost in MME's method of reporting), marketing at 5.9 percent, and G&A at 6.4 percent were within the range of industry practice. The real villain was material costs.

When the shipping material (2.4 percent), expense material (1.2 percent), and warranty and scrap (3.8 percent) costs are added to prime material cost of 45.5 percent, the total is 52.9 percent. These costs could not be reduced because of high personnel turnover in the purchasing department, which caused a loss of buying continuity and poor buying habits. Slow payment to suppliers also contributed to greater material costs because suppliers increased their prices to compensate for the added costs of doing business with MME.

The 10th year proforma income statement attempted to correct the mistakes made in the 9th year and to improve the profit picture. But the improvements were made in the wrong places. Total material costs increased by 1 percentage point. Management apparently did not recognize its real enemy. The company reduced direct labor (8 percent) by 4.2 percent and manufacturing overhead (10 percent) by 5.2 percent with the same products in a year that was to see an inflation rate of 13 percent. At the time the proforma income statement was written (January 1979), the inflation rate was 8 percent. Engineering (5.6 percent) and sales/marketing (6.6 percent) were within acceptable limits but G&A (3.3 percent) was reduced dangerously low.

This was a plan that was doomed to fail, and it did.

DISKCO CORPORATION

Diskco Corporation was six years old in 1979. MME's direct competitor, it was located in southern California's electronic manufacturing center. Labor rates and overhead costs were a few percentage points lower than in northern California at that time. Competition for the available labor pool in southern California was just as fierce as it was in northern California.

Diskco Corporation was a private corporation for the first five years of its history, after which it was sold to a large business computer conglomerate at a substantial profit to its owners.

Diskco had achieved a good deal of its cartridge disk drive sales success because of aggressive pricing practices. It undercut all of its competitors to achieve large-volume OEM orders. Profit was not a motive at the time. Though the acquiring company corrected this pricing policy on new business shortly after taking control, they were obligated to honor existing contractual commitments.

Table 6.3 is Diskco's income statement for its sixth year of operation. Although Diskco had other peripheral equipment product lines with the same profit profile, only figures for the cartridge disk drive income statement are shown. Because engineering, marketing, and G&A functions were shared by other product lines and other corporate divisions, they are not shown on the income statement.

Diskco's cartridge disk drive sales were almost three times as large as MME's for the same calendar period (year 9), owing in part to its aggressive pricing policies. Diskco's material costs (40.6 percent) were 12.3 percent below MME's, and direct labor (8.8 percent) was 4.2 percent lower. The firm's real mistake was in not keeping down its overhead expenses (26.6 percent), which caused total cost of sales to increase to 76 percent. This increase left a gross margin of only 24 percent, which was a break-even situation at best when distributed over engineering, marketing and G&A. The acquiring company corrected the overhead problems, installing a new general manager shortly after taking control. Diskco is still in business and is well on its way to becoming a profitable company.

In summary, valuable lessons can be learned on how to, and how not to manage a company through the study of competitive successes and failures. An income statement, if available, is a good place to start. It shows how a company has spent its income and whether it did so wisely and in the right proportions.

The income distribution of the three companies discussed is right, or wrong, only for the OEM minicomputer peripheral manufacturing industry and only for the time period discussed. Time has a habit of changing things.

Studies of company successes and failures should concern your industry of interest to determine what income distribution is right or wrong for it. This is a valuable management tool and should be used to its fullest extent.

7

DEPARTMENT PLANS

This chapter is a study of department plans and what they should include. An appendix of department plans for Creative Manufacturing shows how departmental data are prepared for inclusion into a business plan. The objective of a department plan is to determine the department's needs and the operating costs required to complete its responsibilities in a given time period be it one, three, or five years.

A department plan should begin with a charter to define its purpose and responsibility within the company structure. Charters are generally assigned by the chief executive officer, president or general manager. They should specify a department's goals and responsibilities so that they do not overlap those of other departments. If overlap occurs, it can be a source of interdepartmental friction which can result in inefficiency. Though not usually a problem in a small firm like Creative Manufacturing, it is often an issue in large corporations.

Department plans should include projects that are to be accomplished within the time frame established by the plan, perhaps in the form of a simple listing of all projects, each annotated with a descriptive paragraph or two. It is important that the listing be comprehensive so that nothing will be omitted from your cost and schedule estimates. Once a budget has been approved, it is usually difficult and sometimes impossible to include a forgotten project after the fact.

After all projects are accounted for, time schedules can be estimated. A chart listing the projects on the abscissa and time on the ordinate provides a helpful graphical display of a schedule.

Personnel requirements follow logically from the project listing and time schedule. It is now possible to determine the types of skills required and when they will be needed to meet your schedules. Job descriptions should be included that clearly define the responsibilities and pay level of each skilled position. An industry's professional organizations, such as the American Electronics Association for the electronics industry, or your state employment service may be able to provide information about pay levels for specific jobs and geographic areas.

The plan's discussion of capital equipment requirements should include a list of the equipment itself, when it's needed, and how much it costs. This information is necessary to determine your company's cash requirements and to prepare its cash flow statement.

Capital expenditures are generally defined as investments that provide future benefits. For Creative Manufacturing and other small firms, the investment is usually a piece of necessary equipment costing more than $100. Depreciation, for tax purposes, occurs over several years. Examples are an oscilloscope for an engineering department, a flow solder machine for a manufacturing department, an automobile for the marketing department, and a calculator for the accounting department. Most departmental furniture is included in the capital equipment category.

Other costs peculiar to each department must be included in their budgets, such as development material for the engineering department or facility costs for the manufacturing department. Other day-to-day operating costs, such as for photocopying and communications supplies, must also be included. When these costs are listed and defined, they can be summarized to provide an overall picture of the needs of a department for a given time. These data are used to construct your company's income and cash flow statements.

Creative Manufacturing's business plan evolved from the departmental plans and budgets included at the end of this chapter, including those for Engineering, Manufacturing, Marketing and Sales, and Finance and Administration (G&A). The departmental documents are based on a sales plan of 112 units of the widget product sold during the first year and 966 units in the second.

These sales provided a revenue base of $460,000 and $4,888,000, respectively. Because of the company's high start-up costs, a loss of slightly over $1 million was planned for the first year. A pretax profit of $752,000 was planned for the second year.

For each department plan, the information discussed in this chapter is included to illustrate how it is prepared for a business plan. The presentation is not intended for detailed study but is meant to be skimmed for essential content only.

Creative Manufacturing's plans were the result of a tops-down budget approach by which a percentage of sales was allocated for each department. The bottoms-up approach tried first resulted in expenses that far exceeded the income necessary for their support. The income statement of Print Corporation, discussed in the preceding chapter, was used as a guide for developing these department budgets. Percentages for cost of sales (labor, material, and overhead, engineering, marketing, and G&A) similar to what were spent by Print Corporation were allocated to Creative Manufacturing's departments for their second through fifth years. The approach produced trim but workable (and profitable) department plans and budgets.

In summary, a department's plan begins with a charter that define its goals and responsibilities. It lists projects and project schedules. It specifies what personnel are required and schedules when they should be hired. The plan contains descriptions of jobs, pay levels, capital equipment needs, and, finally, day-to-day operating costs. The totals establish your department needs and are then used to help prepare your income and cash flow statements. Department plans for Creative Manufacturing are appended to this chapter.

APPENDIX

DEPARTMENT PLANS AND BUDGETS

ENGINEERING DEPARTMENT PLAN AND BUDGET

Charter

The charter of the engineering department is to provide technical expertise to the company to support the following functions:

Specification and design of new widget products.

Technical support of products in production for Manufacturing, Marketing and Sales.

Design services for product enhancements and cost reductions.

Maintenance of mature products in production.

Technical assistance to customers and potential customers when required.

Recommendations to Marketing for new and innovative products and product improvements that can enhance the product line.

The engineering department consists of electronic and mechanical engineers and technicians supported by drafting and clerical personnel. The engineering area includes office space, a drafting office, and a development laboratory.

Additional engineering department details of job descriptions, comparative engineering department expenses, widget II tasks, equipment requirements, and so on are also included in this section.

Engineering Department Start-up Tasks

1. Set up department operating procedures.
2. Obtain engineering supplies: vellums, pencils, drawing tables, storage shelves, drawing files, etc.
3. Reconfigure Diversified Manufacturing Corp.'s drawings, as required.
4. Design and specify engineering test equipment.
5. Build, procure, checkout engineering test equipment.
6. Procure furniture.
7. Layout engineering drafting lab and office areas.
8. Perform cost studies of products.
9. Build proto widget II to revised engineering paper design.
10. Hire personnel.
11. Issue tech info and preliminary manuals and schematics.

Budget

The engineering budget, presented herein, is based on the following development plan:

Finish the checkout of the Widget II and issue all engineering and support documentation. In addition, certain additional features will be added to increase its ability to outperform competing devices. The design and checkout effort is scheduled to be completed by month 12.

Specify, design, checkout, and release the production design of Widget III.

Although the final specifications have not been drawn, Widget III will offer at least 3 to 4 times the performance of a comparable Widget II model. The Widget III design will be completed at the end of year 2.

The engineering budget is based on a close-knit, aggressive engineering group that will expend a maximum effort on behalf of the company. Initial expenditures are large, owing to the need to provide the new department with people, supplies, and equipment. Every effort will be made to reduce equipment expenditures by buying used equipment, renting equipment for short duration requirements, etc.

Engineering schedules will be detailed and will be reviewed with respect to project accomplishments on a regular basis. Engineering budgets will be reviewed in a likewise manner. Adherence to project budgets and schedules will be a primary goal of the engineering department management.

Engineering Budget as a Percentage of Revenue
($ Million)

	Year 1	Year 2
Revenue	$.46	$4.88
Engineering	$.393	$ .45
Percentage of revenue	85.4%	9.2%

Widget II Product Tasks

Assumptions:

1. The present design status of Widget II consists of engineering prototypes being tested, but still a lot of proof testing must be done.
2. Start date is 30 days following corporate founding.
3. The main design of the Widget II is finished. Only device compatibility must be assured.

Tasks:

1. *Dual-Port Option.* May have a major impact, owing to requirements for repackaging (i.e., no room for bigger power supply or additional PCBS). Marketing must supply the device spec for dual port.

2. *Electronic Masking.* The unit must have a option to allow it to appear as 5 valves and 820 pistons (not 14 & 560).

3. *Power Sequencing.* This option would allow the widget to be sequenced on/off by the use of two reserved interface lines.

4. *Connector Options.* The signal interface connector must provide the following options:
Widget or controller compatibility
   Flat wire or twister pair
Dual or single port
Sequencing or no sequencing

5. *Intelligent Interface.* This project involves a major redesign of the interface. This will be a microprocessor-controlled interface with error correction and internal mapping capabilities.

6. *Additional Widgee.* This task involves adding a valve to access an additional widgee.

Widget II Summary Production Table

Task/Activity	Material Cost ($000)	Man Months	Discipline[a]		
Complete Basic Engineering Design					
Checkout prototypes		5	DAD,	T	
Redesign		2	DAD,	EE	
Finish drawing package		3	DAD,	De,	Dr
Create manuals		2	De,	DAD,	Dr
Material	8	———			
		12			
Dual-Port Configuration					
Specifications prep		.1	DAD		
Preliminary Design		.5	DAD,	EE	

Task/Activity	Material Cost ($000)	Man Months	Discipline[a]		
Prototype (PCB, P.S. sheetmetal)		1.5	T,	MM,	EE
Test (power, perf. cooling)		1.0	T,	MM,	EE
Review design		.1	DAD,	EE	
Final drawings		1.0	De,	Dr	
ECN		.1	De		
Material	4.5	———			
		4.3			
Electronic Masking (SMD Cylinder, Identical)					
Specifications prep		.2	DAD		
Logic design		.5	EE,	DAD	
Prototype		.5	T		
Test		.7	T,	EE	
PCB layout		.8	De		
PCBA checkout		.5	T,	DAD	
Redesign		.2	EE,	DAD	
Checkout		.7	T,	DAD,	EE
ECN		.2	DAD,	De	
Material	4.0	———			
		4.3			
Power Sequencing					
Specifications prep		.2	DAD,	EE	
Logic design		.3	EE		
Prototype		.4	T		
Test		.4	T,	EE	
PCB layout		.5	De		
PCBA checkout		.2	T,	EE	
Redesign		.2	EE		
Checkout		.1	T,	EE	
ECN		.1	De,	EE	
Material	3.0	———			
		2.4			

Task/Activity	Material Cost ($000)	Man Months	Discipline[a]		
SMD Connectors					
Specifications prep		.1	DAD,	ME	
Competitive research		.2	ME		
Quality components connectors		.2	ME		
Layout		.2	ME,	Dr	
Prototype		.2	MM		
Final design		.2	ME,	De	
Prototype		.2	MM		
Review		.1	ME,	DAD	
ECN		.1	De		
Material	2	——			
		1.5			
STC Intelligent Interface					
Specifications prep		.5	DAD,	ME,	EE
Competitive research		.8	DAD		
Architectural design		1.0	EE		
Design review		.2	DAD,	EE	
Prototype		3.0	DAD,	EE,	T, ME
Final design		3.0	DAD,	EE,	Dr
Checkout		3.0	T,	PE,	EE
Review		.5	DAD,	EE	
Document		2.0	DAD,	EE,	De
Support		2.0	DAD,	EE	
Material	25	——			
		16.0			

[a]DAD—Director of advanced development
De—Designer
Dr—Draftsman
EE—Electronic engineer
MM—Model maker
PE—Project engineer
T—Technician

Widget III Design Summary Table

Task/Activity	Development Cost ($000)	Man Months	Discipline[a]		
Preliminary Design					
Prepare engineering specifications		1.0	DAD,	ME,	EE
Prepare cost estimates		1.0	DAD,	ME,	EE
Preliminary electronic design		4.0	EE		
Preliminary mechanical layout		——	ME,	De	
Prototype concept	10	13.0			
Mechanical Design					
Layout		1.0	ME,	De	
Detail drawings		5.0	De,	Dr	
Specs		2.0	ME,	Dr	
Review		1.0	ME		
Build Protos		4.0	MM,	ME	
Test		4.0	MM,	ME	
Review		0.5	ME		
Redesign		1.5	ME,	De	
Complete drawings		7.0	De,	Dr	
Complete manuals		1.0	ME,	De	
Complete specs (test)		1.0	ME,	De	
Manufacturing support		6.0	ME,	MM	
Material	20	——			
		34.0			
Electrical Design					
Preliminary logic designs		6.0	DAD,	EE	
Breadboard		3.0	EE,	T	
Test		4.0	EE,	T	
PCB layout		3.0	De		
PCBA checkout		2.0	T,	EE	

Task/Activity	Material Cost ($000)	Man Months	Discipline[a]		
Review		1.0	DAD,	EE	
Redesign		4.0	DAD,	EE	
Checkout		8.0	DAD,	EE,	T
Complete drawings		3.5	EE,	De,	Dr
Complete Specs		1.0	EE		
Complete manuals		2.0	EE		
Manufacturing support		6.0	DAD,	EE	
Material	10	——			
		43.5			

[a]DAD—Director of advanced development
De—Designer
Dr—Draftsman
EE—Electronic engineer
MM—Model maker
PE—Project engineer
T—Technician

Widget Schedule Summary Table

Activity	Man Months
Widget II	
Complete basic design	12
Dual-port option	4.3
Electronic masking	4.3
Power sequencing	2.4
Connectors	1.5
Intelligent interface	16.0
Widget III	
Preliminary design	10
Mechanical design	29
Electronic design	34.5

Engineering Development Schedule

Task	Months after startup 1	2	3	4	5	6	7	8	9	10	11	12	1st Yr Total	Quarters 1	2	3	4	2nd Yr Total
Startup tasks																		
Widget II																		
Finish checkout																		
Complete drawings																		
Dual port option																		
Pistons																		
Power sequencing																		
Connectors																		
Intelligent intf.																		
Support pilot prod'n																		
Widget III																		
Prelim. design																		
Electronic design																		
Mechanical design																		
Protos available																		

Page _____ of _____
Date _____

FIGURE 7.1. Engineering development schedule

Manpower Requirements

Job Description	Number of People on Board, FY																			
	Year 1				Year 2				Year 3				Year 4				Year 5			
	1	2	3	4	1	2	3	4	1	2	3	4	1	2	3	4	1	2	3	4
VP engineering	1	1	1	1	1	1	1	1												
Director of advanced development	1	1	1	1	1	1	1	1												
Mechanical engineer	–	–	1	1	1	1	1	1												
Mechanical designer	1	1	1	1	1	1	1	1												
Draftsman	–	1	1	1	1	1	1	1												
Electrical technician	1	1	2	2	2	2	2	2												
Electrical engineer	1	1	1	2	2	2	2	2												
Component engineer	–	–	–	–	–	–	–	–												
Document clerk	–	–	1	1	1	1	1	1												
Secretary	–	–	–	–	–	–	–	–												
Model maker	1	1	1	1	1	1	1	1												
	6	7	10	11	11	11	11	11												

Engineering Manpower Requirements

	Months after startup												Quarters			
	1	2	3	4	5	6	7	8	9	10	11	12	1	2	3	4
VP engineering	1	1	1	1	1	1	1	1	1	1	1	1	1	1	1	1
Director advanced development	1	1	1	1	1	1	1	1	1	1	1	1	1	1	1	1
Mechanical engineer			1	1	1	1	1	1	1	1	1	1	1	1	1	1
Electrical engineer			1	1	1	1	1	1	1	1	1	2	2	2	2	2
Mechanical designer		1	1	1	1	1	1	1	1	1	1	1	1	1	1	1
Draftsman		1	1	1	1	1	1	1	1	1	1	1	1	1	1	1
Electrical technician	1	1	1	1	1	1	1	2	2	2	2	2	2	2	2	2
Model maker		1	1	1	1	1	1	1	1	1	1	1	1	1	1	1
Document clerk								1	1	1	1	1	1	1	1	1
Total	3	5	6	7	7	7	8	10	10	10	10	11	11	11	11	11

FIGURE 7.2. Engineering manpower requirements

ENGINEERING DEPARTMENT JOB DESCRIPTIONS

Director of Advanced Development

The director of advanced development is responsible for the specification and overall technical leadership for product developments. He (or she) will also contribute directly to the design effort in his own specialty areas.

Electrical Engineer/Mechanical Engineer

Summary.

This classification covers those employees who are engaged in developmental engineering at the project level of company products.

Duties.

Make decisions independently for engineering problems and methods and coordinate activities with other departments to solve technical problems. Utilize advanced techniques and modifications and extensions of theories, precepts, and practices of the engineering field and related sciences and disciplines.

Carry out assignments requiring the development of new or approved techniques and procedures. Work is expected to result in the development of new or refined equipment, materials, processes, or products. Develop and evaluate plans or criteria for assigned projects and the activities of technical personnel assigned to the project.

Assess the feasibility and soundness of engineering tests, products, or equipment when necessary data are insufficient or confirmation by test is advisable. Coordinate and review the work of associate engineers and technicians.

Requirements:

Education: B.S. or M.S. degree.

Background: Minimum of five years directly related

experience.

Department: Engineering.

Mechanical Designer

Summary:

This classification covers those employees who, with a wide latitude for exercising initiative, inventiveness, and independent judgment, are responsible for the planning, coordination, and successful production of complete product design and development projects.

Duties:

Consult and collaborate with members of the technical staff to obtain the historical and operating data necessary to develop designs for the assigned design project. Responsible for translating and projecting this information into preliminary design data and sketches for initial engineering and/or customer approval. Decide on the number and types of drawings required, estimate completion dates, and prepare schedules for the various phases of the project. Break down a specific design into workable units for assignment to draftsmen or designers. Incorporate authorized documentation changes when necessary.

Responsible for all calculations necessary to determine proper fit and function of all allied parts, components, and materials, considering such design objectives as packaging, structural stability, manufacturability, etc. The designer will also make layout drawings to support initial product designs. Provide technical guidance and training to draftsmen and designers, checking their work for technical accuracy and conformance to accepted drafting and design standards.

May serve in a technical liaison capacity between Purchasing and vendors in cases involving specialized mechanical component purchases. Confer and maintain necessary liaison contacts with Engineering, Manufacturing, and vendors in matters pertaining to the design project. Perform other related assignments as required.

Requirements:

Education and background: A combination of directly applicable training and experience totaling at least 10 years, preferably including 4 years of applicable college-level study.
Department: Engineering.

Component Engineer

Summary:

This classification covers those employees who are responsible for the generation, manufacturing release, and change control of all specifications for electrical or mechanical components and associated hardware employed in the company's equipment.

Duties:

Establish specifications for all component parts employed in the company's products. Responsible for the manufacturing release and change control of these specifications. Modify existing specifications as necessary to reflect new requirements or changes in the "state of the art."

Procure and evaluate all types of technical data to determine the particular electronic or mechanical characteristics of the various component parts. Properly apply these parts for maximum effectiveness, considering performance, environmental conditions, reliability, contract requirements costs. Provide assistance to designers regarding component application. Prepare application notes and component use guidelines. Generate and submit value engineering proposals to reduce the cost of end products by lowering material or methods costs without impairing the functionality of products.

Maintain vendor liaison to keep abreast of current component types and performance improvements as well as pricing fluctuations. Collaborate with Purchasing, Manufacturing, and Quality Assurance to resolve problem areas related to component engineering. Conduct research into improved test methods and equipment to optimize the quality, performance, and cost factors of components. Perform other related assignments as directed.

Requirements:

Education: B.S. in engineering or equivalent.

Background: Minimum of four years' experience in component engineering.

Department: Engineering.

Electronic Technician

Summary:

This classification covers those employees who construct and check out experimental models of company products.

Duties:

Under the direction of a member of the technical staff, constructs, tests, and records data on experimental models related to a limited segment of a development project. Sets tasks or experiments requiring the selection, adaptation, or modification of test equipment or test procedures. Compiles, computes, and reports test results. May guide the efforts of lower-level technicians.

Requirements:

Education: High School graduation, or equivalent two years of technical schooling, or the military equivalent thereof.

Background: Three to five years in the field.

Department: Engineering.

Draftsman

Summary:

This classification covers those employees who prepare detailed drawings from sketches provided by engineers and designers.

Duties:

Prepare detailed and assembly drawings and/or schematics wiring, and logic diagrams from marked-up prints, layouts, and sketches. Detail all necessary parts and views. Prepare minor layouts under the direction of designers or engineers, making any mathematical calculations necessary for these layouts. Write engineering orders to incorporate authorized drawing changes.

Requirements:

Education: High School graduation or trade school courses in drafting and mathematics.

Background: Zero to two years in drafting field.

Department: Engineering.

Secretary

Summary::

This classification covers those employees who serve as secretary to a manager, relieving him of all possible clerical and administrative details of the organization.

Duties:

Take and transcribe dictation, set up and maintain all necessary files and records, review and sort incoming mail, screen telephone calls, schedule appointments, prepare special reports, graphs, and charts. Disseminate information to employees within the organization and to other authorized personnel, and perform other typical secretarial duties at a level requiring considerable independent judgment and discretion and demanding highest-quality performance. May guide the work of other clerical employees in the organization and assist in their training.

Requirements:

Education: High School graduate. 60 words per minute typing capability. 50 words per minute dictation.

Clerk, Document Control

Summary:

This classification covers those employees who maintain records of company documents and who perform clerical document control functions in an assigned area of the company.

Duties:

Prepare, maintain, and verify the status and history of all documents within an assigned area. Process all revisions and changes to appropriate documents, verifying the completeness of information and checking for required approvals. Assign drawing, vellum, and change numbers as necessary. Prepare work orders for supplementary distribution and reproduction requests. May be required to perform typing, filing, and other related clerical duties.

Requirements:

Education: High School graduation or equivalent.

Background: One or more years experience in related field.

Department: Engineering.

Enginnering Salary Analysis

	Monthly Salary				1st Yr Total	Quarters				2nd Yr Total
	Yr 1	Yr 2	Yr 3			1	2	3	4	
VP engineering	3333	3600	3883							
Director advanced development	3750	4050	4374							
Mechanical engineer	2500	2700	2916							
Electrical engineer	2500	2700	2916							
Mechanical designer	1667	1800	1944							
Draftsman	1550	1674	1808							
Electrical technician	1124	1214	1311							
Model maker	1640	1771	1913							
Comp engineer	1800	1944	2099							
Secretary	1050	1134	1225							
Document clerk	813	878	940							

FIGURE 7.3. Engineering salary analysis

Engineering Development Material Costs ($000)

	Months after startup												1st Yr Total	Quarters				2nd Yr Total
	1	2	3	4	5	6	7	8	9	10	11	12		1	2	3	4	
Widget II																		
Finish checkout		1.0	0.5	0.5	2.0	2.0	2.0						8.0					
Complete drawing		1.0	1.5										2.5					
Dual port				0.5		2.0							2.5					
Pistons				1.0		1.0	1.0	2.0					5.0					
Power sequencing							1.0	1.0	1.0				3.0					
Connections							0.5	0.5	1.0				2.0					
Intelligent interface						12.0	2.0	3.0	3.0	4.0	4.0	4.0	32.0	2.0	2.0	2.0	2.0	8.0
Buy (4) units	20.0												20.0					
II Subtotal	20.0	2.0	2.0	2.0	2.0	17.0	6.5	6.5	5.0	4.0	4.0	4.0	75.0	2.0	2.0	2.0	2.0	8.0
Widget III																		
Preliminary design								2.0	3.0	5.0	2.0		12.0					
Mechanical design												3.0	3.0	12.0	10.0	28.0	10.0	60.0
Electrical design											3.0		3.0	6.0	7.0	10.0	7.0	30.0
Widget III Subtotal								2.0	3.0	5.0	8.0	5.0	18.0	18.0	17.0	38.0	17.0	90.0
Total	20.0	2.0	2.0	2.0	2.0	17.0	6.5	8.5	8.0	9.0	12.0	5.0	94.0	20.0	19.0	40.0	19.0	98.0

FIGURE 7.4. Engineering development material costs

Required Engineering Test Equipment

Description	Quantity	Manufac-turer	Amount ($000)	Total ($000)
Oscilloscope	2	Tek	4	8
Plug-ins	4	Tek	1	4
Carts	2	Tek	.5	1
Camera	1	Tek	.5	.5
Probes	8	Tek	.05	.4
Strobe tach		GR	.6	.6
DVM's	2		.7	1.4
Signal generator	2	Wavetek	1	2
Counter	1	HP	3	3
Power supplies	2	—	.5	1
Computer test system	1	Bruning	12	12
Benches	4	—	.3	1
Power cables	lot	—	.35	.35
Variac	1	GR	.3	.3
Air flow & pressure measure	lot	Dwyer	1	1
Print repro machine			Rent	150/month
Model shop				
Lathe	1		5	5
Mill	1		5	5
Brake	1		2	2
Shear	1		2	2
Drill press	1		.5	.5
Saw	1		1	1
Granite block	1		1	1
Miscellaneous tools	lot		5	5
Benches	lot		2	2

Engineering Capital Equipment Plan (Units Required)

| | $ | \multicolumn{12}{c}{Months after startup} | 1st Yr Total | \multicolumn{4}{c}{Quarters} | 2nd Yr Total |
		1	2	3	4	5	6	7	8	9	10	11	12		1	2	3	4	
Oscilloscope	7000	1	1			.5	1								1				
Camera	500	1																	
Digital volt meter	500	1			1														
Signal generator	1500	1														1			
Counter	1000	1					1												
Power supply	200	3								1									
Test system	12000	1					1								1				
Variac	200	1																	
Cables	200	1																	
Flow measurement	500	1													'				
Strobe tach	500		1																
Sub-total		24000	7500		500	3500	8200			200									
Lathe	5000	1	1																
Mill	5000	1	1																
Brake	2000			1															
Shear	1500			1															
Drill press	400	1																	
Saw	1000		1																
Granite block	1000	1																	
Drills, etc.	5000	1																	
Benches	200	1	1	1															
Total cost ($)		35600	13700	3700	500	3500	8200			200				65400	19000	1500			20500

FIGURE 7.5. Engineering capital equipment plan (units required)

Furniture Prices

	Buy ($ ea)
Desk	350
Chair	65
Bookcase	80
Table	50
Lamp	40
Dwg. table	600
Stool	80
Cabinet	120
Bench (Lab)	200
Bench (Clean)	2000
Chair (for table)	40

Engineering Furniture Plan (Units Purchased)

	Cost Each	Months after startup												1st Yr Total	Quarters			
		1	2	3	4	5	6	7	8	9	10	11	12		1	2	3	4
Desk	$ 350	2		1			1	2							1		1	
Chair	65	2		1			1	2							1		1	
Bookcase	80	2	1	1				2			1				2		1	
Table	50	2	3	1	1		1	2							1		1	
Lamp	40	1	1		1		1								2		1	2
Drawing table	600	1	1		1												1	
Stool	80	1	1		1												1	
Cabinet	120	2	1	1					1								1	2
Lab bench	200	2	1						1									1
Clean bench	2000							1										
Small chair	40	2	1	1	1			2								1	1	
File cabinet	100	1	2			2	1	1										1
Drawing cabinet	400		1				1											
Typewriter	600								1						1			
Total $		2630	1910	625	850	200	1005	2200	720		80				1505	40	1385	620

FIGURE 7.6. Engineering furniture plan (units purchased)

Engineering Dept. Expenses($)

Personnel	Months after startup 1	2	3	4	5	6	7	8	9	10	11	12	1st Yr Total	Q1	Q2	Q3	Q4	2nd Yr Total
Regular salaries	8207	11514	14014	15564	15564	15564	18064	20001	20001	20001	20001	22501	200996	64800	64800	64800	64800	259200
Overtime	–	–	–	–	–	155	181	200	200	200	200	225	1361	750	800	800	900	3250
Benefits & taxes	1641	2302	2802	3112	3112	3112	3612	4000	4000	4000	4000	4500	40193	12960	12960	12960	12960	51840
Miscellaneous expenses	–	–	400	–	–	400	–	–	400	–	–	400	1600	1200	1200	1200	1500	5400
Total personnel costs	9848	13816	17210	18676	18676	19231	21857	24201	24601	24201	24201	27626	244150	79710	79760	80060	80160	319690
Headcount	3	5	6	7	7	7	8	10	10	10	10	11	–	11	11	11	11	–
Development material	20000	2000	2000	2000	2000	17000	6500	8500	8000	9000	12000	5000	94000	20000	19000	40000	19000	98000
Tel & Tel	150	75	75	100	100	100	100	125	125	125	125	125	1325	400	400	450	450	1700
Furniture	2630	1910	625	850	200	1005	2200	720	0	80	0	0	10140	250	300	250	300	1100
Small tools	3000	2400	1800	1300	800	500	300	300	300	300	300	300	11600	1000	1000	1000	1000	4000
Maintenance & repairs	50	50	70	70	70	70	70	100	70	500	100	100	1320	300	400	500	500	1700
Freight costs	50	50	50	100	100	100	100	100	100	100	100	100	1050	200	400	400	200	1200
Stationery & printing	500	500	300	300	350	600	400	300	600	300	300	300	4750	1000	1000	1000	1000	4000
Memberships & dues	10	10	10	10	10	10	10	10	10	10	10	20	120	50	50	50	50	200
Technical journals	100	50	20	20	10	10	20	20	20	20	20	20	330	100	100	100	100	400
Equipment rental	50	100	200	200	200	400	200	200	300	300	300	300	2750	600	800	1000	1000	3400
Temporary help	1000	250	–	–	–	1000	1000	–	1000	–	–	1500	5750	2000	–	2000	–	4000
Recruiting	1500	–	–	–	–	–	1500	–	–	–	–	3500	6500	–	–	–	–	–
Consultants	–	–	–	2000	2000	–	–	2000	2000	–	–	–	8000	3000	3000	3000	–	9000
Prepro machine rental	120	120	120	130	130	130	150	150	130	130	130	150	1570	500	500	500	500	2000
Misc subtotal	9160	5515	3270	5080	3970	3925	6050	4025	4655	1865	1385	6405	55225	9400	7950	10250	5100	32700
Total	19008	21331	22486	25756	24646	40156	34407	36726	37256	35066	37506	39031	393375	109110	106710	110310	104260	450390
Quarter total	–	–	82825	–	–	90558	–	–	108389	–	–	111683	–	–	–	–	–	–
Cumulative quarter	–	–	82825	–	–	173383	–	–	281772	–	–	393455	–	109110	205820	346130	450390	–

FIGURE 7.7. Engineering dept. expenses ($)

Engineering Dept Expenses ($)

Personnel	Months after startup												1st Yr Total	Quarters			
	1	2	3	4	5	6	7	8	9	10	11	12		1	2	3	4
Capital equipment	35600	13700	3700	500	3500	8200	0	0	200	0	0	0	65400	19000	1500	2000	2500

FIGURE 7.7. Engineering dept. expenses ($) (cont'd).

MANUFACTURING DEPARTMENT PLAN AND BUDGET

Charter

The charter of the manufacturing department is to produce the company's products:

To schedule.

At, or below, target costs.

With acceptable quality levels.

Overview

The above charter will be implemented by establishing a facility, hiring the necessary personnel, and assembling and testing the finished products. There are no plans to fabricate any of the required parts; all parts will be purchased from external sources.

Major Tasks

Most of the activities falling under the manufacturing department's responsibility will be standard functions that will be carried out in a straightforward manner. There are, however, a number of areas that are critical to the operation and that will consequently receive particular attention.

Sealed DUP Module. The requirements of this subassembly dictate that it be assembled in a contamination-free environment. In addition, the assembly and test process are complex and the material being assembled represents approximately two-thirds of the total material cost.

Material Costs. Material is approximately 39 percent of the total cost of sales.

Printed Wiring Board Test. Stringent testing of printed circuit board assemblies prior to their assembly into the final unit is mandatory for smooth product flow.

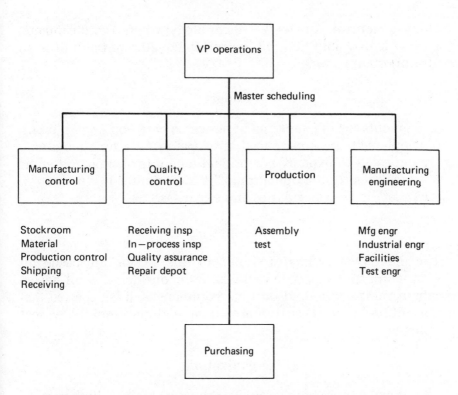

FIGURE 7.8. Creative Manufacturing, Inc., Organization chart: Reports
to president

Manufacturing Budget as a Percentage of Revenue
($M)

	Year 1	Year 2
Revenue	.46	4.88
Manufacturing (cost of sales/goods)	.690	2.98
Percentage of revenue	150%	61%

Quality Control. In widget technology, where the customers' DUP is irrevocably tied to the unit, the quality of the unit is an all-important factor.

Budget

The manufacturing department budget is based on a small group of people who are experienced in widget manufacturing and who are expected to expend exceptional amounts of time and effort to the success of the operation. The 1979 figures in this section are based on current salaries and expenses.

Manpower

The manpower estimates shown in this section are based on planned output schedule and take into consideration all necessary learning curves and start-up requirements. It is expected that most of the indirect personnel will be recruited from the widget industry.

Organization

The organization shown hereafter represents the initial start-up organization of the manufacturing department.

JOB DESCRIPTIONS FOR INDIRECT PERSONNEL

Manufacturing Manager

Function:

Responsible for all manufacturing and production activities, including functional operations of each department.

Material Control Supervisor

Function:

Responsible for direction and coordination of production planning activities.

Duties:

Develop the master sales schedule based on approved marketing forecast. Establish and maintain material and finished-product inventory levels.

Material Planning Officer

Duties:

Coordinate dispatching of production orders and material supply requisitions with data processing records and buy cards. Forward buy cards to purchasing.

Purchasing Supervisor

Function:

Supervise purchasing personnel. Monitor performance of outside contractors. Survey new vendors and make periodic surveys of existing vendors.

Duties:

Supervise and coordinate all operations and procurement within assigned commodity areas. Maintain and improve existing methods; develop and recommend new concepts to increase efficiency.

Purchasing Expediter

Function:

Coordinate and expedite shipment and delivery of materials.

Duties:

Contact vendors by telephone to insure that materials and supplies are shipped and delivered on promised dates. Determine when deliveries may be delayed; coordinate with Purchasing and Manufacturing to expedite material requirements. Maintain records of purchases, received goods, returns of damaged items.

Clerk Typist

Duties:

Type purchase requisitions, mail out confirmation copies to vendors, maintain file on closed purchase orders.

Production Control Supervisor

Function:

Responsible for scheduling and monitoring the movement of material through production processes. Supervise material expediter.

Duties:

Monitor and schedule the movement of material. Subsidiary duties include determination of priority sequences, tracking line shortages, establising ship dates. Maintain all proper documentation on outbound shipments. Generate management reports on production, shipping, sales order, and assembly status. Provide coverage for material review board activities.

Expediter

Function:

Coordinate and expedite flow of material, kits parts, and assemblies within or between departments per production and shipping schedules.

Duties:

Monitor receipt of material, anticipate shortages, and alert purchasing department of priority requirements. Expedite materials for critical-path shortage items. Coordinate the flow of final assemblies through inspection, assembly, testing. Prepare shortage reports as necessary. Forward completed work orders to data processing personnel.

Receiving Clerk

Function:

Perform manual and clerical duties involved in receiving material, supplies, and equipment.

Duties:

Unpack and examine items received and verify completeness against bills of lading, invoices. Keep records of goods received. Reject damaged material and process necessary MRB paperwork. Process necessary paperwork for sending material to receiving inspection.

Stores Supervisor

Function:

Responsible for receipt, storage, and issue of material to support manufacturing activities. Supervise shipping, receiving, and stock clerks.

Duties:

Maintain accountability for material from receipt until disposition. Conduct required inventories and maintain inventory accuracy. Receive materials and stocks in accordance with warehousing techniques. Prepare kit materials pursuant to schedule. Establish backorders for material shortages and maintains files for same. Forward kit material and filled back-order lists to data processing.

Shipping Assistant

Function:

Perform manual and clerical duties involved in the preparation of material and supplies for shipment.

Duties:

Implement standard policies in preparing items for shipment. Verify and count material to be shipped. Prepare shipping instructions using standard shipping practices for transportation type and routes. Prepare bills of lading and other records pertinent to material being shipped.

ORT Processor (Operations Routing Traveler)

Duties:

Prepare ORT file along with a copy of the sales order. This file is made available for configuration instructions, inspection, shipping, and production control files.

Quality Control Section Manager

Functions:

Responsible for ensuring that the quality of workmanship meets the standards set by the product assurance department and that products manufactured by Creative Manufacturing Inc., and/or approved vendors adhere to engineering specifications. Responsible for reporting quality problems on a timely basis.

Duties:

Oversee all inspection activities, including receiving, in-process, final, shipping, and source inspection operations. Develop and improve quality control inspection methods and techniques. Provide for effective feedback of line rejects to receiving inspection. Control inspection budgets. Provide interface with Operations, Engineering, and Purchasing to meet production goals with minimum quality problems.

Inspection Supervisor

Function:

Supervise receiving inspection personnel. Ensure that parts/materials are manufactured in accordance with specifications and Creative Manufacturing, Inc.'s workmanship standards.

Duties:

Supervise inspection activities by scheduling work and assisting personnel on special quality problems. Establish in-process checks necessary to produce quality units. Report quality problems to Quality and Reliability Engineering. Ensure that proper inspection techniques are applied. Review quality and special engineering documentation.

Receiving Inspector

Function:

Inspect purchased parts and materials for conformity to specification and workmanship standards.

Duties:

Inspect parts and materials for proper identity and dimensions, using such measuring devices as micrometers, gauges, calipers, and component testers. Visually inspect for obvious defects, verify specification using POs, blueprints, and checklists. Maintain records of accepted and rejected items. Place accepted material in a specific location to be forwarded to stores.

Manufacturing Engineer

Function:

Translate completed product design into the facilities, tooling, processing, and documentation required to implement and support manufacturing.

Duties:

Develop manufacturing procedures and establish production processes. Evaluate existing methods and devise improvements for increased efficiency and cost reduction.

Perform project management of new product introduction into production phase by preparing manufacturing plans and facilities layouts and by participating in design reviews. Select manufacturing tooling and justify capital equipment.

Investigate manufacturing and process problems. Write procedure reports as required.

Direct Labor

	Months after startup												1st Yr Total	Quarters				2nd Yr Total
	1	2	3	4	5	6	7	8	9	10	11	12		1	2	3	4	
Widget II output—units							2	4	8	16	32	50	112	180	216	259	311	966
Direct standard hours Assy	27				54	108	162	324	405	675	756	756		1134	1539	2430	3240	
Test	10				20	40	60	120	150	250	290	290		420	570	900	1200	
Inspection	3				6	12	18	36	45	75	87	87		126	171	270	360	
Direct manpower:																		
Based on Assy					1	3	3	4	5	6	7	7		11	14	22	29	
112 hours Test					1	1	2	2	2	3	3	3		4	6	9	11	
per person Inspection							1	1	1	1	1	1		2	2	3	4	
per month																		

FIGURE 7.9. Direct labor

Indirect Labor Manpower

	Monthly Salary ($000)	Months after startup												1st Yr Total	Quarters				2nd Yr Total
		1	2	3	4	5	6	7	8	9	10	11	12		1	2	3	4	
Widget output units								2	4	8	16	32	50	112	180	216	259	311	966
VP operations	4.17	1	1	1	1	1	1	1	1	1	1	1	1		1	1	1	1	
Secretary	1.0						1	1	1	1	1	1	1		1	1	1	1	
Manager purchasing	2.5	1	1	1	1	1	1	1	1	1	1	1	1		1	1	1	1	
Buyer	1.73															1	1	1	
Receptionist	.92	1	1	1	1	1	1	1	1	1	1	1	1		1	1	1	1	
Clerk/typist	.83																1	1	
Materials planner	1.34																1	1	
Receiving clerk	.9			1	1	1	1	1	1	1	1	1	1		1	1	1	1	
Shipping clerk	.9															1	1	1	
Stock clerk	.9															1	1	2	
Manager production	2.92								1	1	1	1	1		1	1	1	1	
Supervisor assembly	1.6												1		1	1	1	1	
Supervisor test	1.9								1	1	1	1	1		1	1	1	1	
Manager quality control	2.5				1	1	1	1	1	1	1	1	1		1	1	1	1	
Quality engineer	1.9				1	1	1	1	1	1	1	1	1		1	1	1	1	
Receiving inspector	1.2											1	2		2	2	2	2	
Quality assurance technician	1.09						1	1	1	1	1	1	1		1	1	1	1	
Manager manufacturing engineering	2.08		1	1	1	1	1	1	1	1	1	1	1		1	1	1	1	
Test engineering	1.9			1	1	1	1	1	1	1	1	1	1		1	1	1	1	
Maintenance, mechanical	1.09					1	1	1	1	1	1	1	1		1	1	1	1	
Total		3	4	6	8	9	11	11	13	13	13	14	15		16	19	21	22	

FIGURE 7.10. Indirect labor manpower

Occupancy, Communications, & Data Processing Costs: Manufacturing Department Expenses

	Months after startup												1st Yr Total	Quarters				2nd Yr Total
	1	2	3	4	5	6	7	8	9	10	11	12		1	2	3	4	
Occupancy costs:																		
Rent 20K @s.30/ft²	6000	6000	6000	6000	6000	6000	6000	6000	6000	6000	6000	6000	72000	18000	18000	18000	18000	72000
Landscaping	200	200	200	200	200	200	200	200	200	200	200	200	2400	600	600	600	600	2400
Guard service	–	–	–	–	–	200	200	200	200	200	200	200	1400	600	600	600	600	2400
Cleaning	100	100	100	100	100	100	600	600	600	600	600	600	4200	1800	1800	1800	1800	7200
Garbage	50	50	50	100	100	100	100	100	100	150	150	150	1200	500	700	800	1000	3000
Electricity	200	200	200	300	300	300	300	400	400	400	500	500	4000	1500	2000	2500	2500	8500
Gas	50	50	50	100	100	100	100	100	100	200	200	200	1400	600	600	600	600	2400
Water	50	50	50	50	50	50	50	50	50	50	50	50	600	150	150	150	150	600
Miscellaneous	100	100	100	100	100	100	100	100	100	100	100	100	1200	300	300	300	300	1200
Maintenance	200	200	200	200	200	200	200	200	200	200	200	200	2400	600	600	600	600	2400
Total																		
Communications																		
Postage	50	50	50	50	50	50	100	100	100	100	100	100	900	400	500	600	700	2200
Telex	50	50	50	50	50	50	100	100	100	100	100	100	900	400	500	600	700	2200
Telephone	1000	1000	1000	1000	1000	1000	1500	1500	1500	1500	1500	1500	15000	5000	6000	7000	8000	24000
Data processing				200	200	200	300	300	300	400	400	400	2700	3000	4000	5000	6000	18000
Total	8050	8050	8050	8450	8450	8650	9850	9950	9950	10200	10300	10300	110300	33450	36550	39350	41750	151100
Total																		

FIGURE 7.11. Occupancy, communications, & data processing costs: Manufacturing department expenses

Manufacturing Department Operating Expenses($000)

	Months after startup												1st Yr Total	Quarters				2nd Yr Total
	1	2	3	4	5	6	7	8	9	10	11	12		1	2	3	4	
Equipment rental							.2	.2	.2	.5	.5	.5	2.1	2.0	2.0	3.0	3.0	
Equipment calibration							.2	.2	.2	.2	.2	.2	1.2	1.0	1.0	2.0	2.0	
Material scrap							.2	.2	.2	.5	.5	.5	2.1	1.5	2.0	2.5	3.0	
Develop material							.2	.2	.2	.2	.2	.2	1.2	0.5	.5	.5	.5	
Small tools						1.0	.5	.5	.4	.4	.3	.3	3.4	1.0	1.0	1.0	1.0	
Shop supplies	2.0					5.0	.5	.5	.5	5.0	1.0	1.0	13.5	3.0	3.0	4.0	5.0	
Office supplies	1.0	.5	.5	.4		.4	.3	.3	.3	.3	.3	.3	6.	1.0	1.5	2.0	3.0	
Furn & equip (<$100)		.5	.5	.5	.2	.5	.5	.5	.5	.5	.5	.5	6.5	2.0	2.0	2.0	2.0	
Forms			.2	.2		.2	.5	.5	.5	.7	.7	.7	4.4	2.0	2.0	3.0	3.0	
Rework material		.2	.2	.2	.2	.2	.5	.5	.5	1.0	1.0	1.0	4.5	3.0	3.0	4.0	4.0	
Outside repro				.2	.2	.2	.3	.3	.3	.3	.3	.3	2.8	1.0	1.0	1.0	1.0	
Outside services		.2	.5	1.0	1.5	1.5	1.5	1.5	2.0	2.0	2.5	2.5	1.8	.7	.8	.9	1.0	
Freight in	.2	.1	.1	.1	.1	.1	.2	.2	.2	.2	.2	.2	18.5	7.0	8.0	9.0	10.0	
Freight out	.2	.2	.2	.4	.5	.5	.6	.6	.7	.7	1.0	1.0	17.0	.9	1.0	1.2	2.0	
Employee travel	1.0	1.0	1.0	1.0	1.0	1.0	.5	.5	.5	.5	.5	.5	6.8	3.0	3.0	3.0	3.0	
Recruiting	.1	.1	.1	.1	.1	.1	.2	.2	.2	.3	.3	.3	5.0			–		
Shipping supplies						.5	.5	.5	.5	.5	.5	.5	3.5	2.0	3.0	4.0	6.0	
Janitorial supplies	.1	.1	.1	.1	.1	.1	.2	.2	.2	.3	.3	.3	2.1	1.0	1.5	2.0	2.5	
Equipment maintenance											.5	.5	1.0	1.0	1.0	1.0	1.0	
Total	4.3	2.8	3.4	4.1	4.7	11.2	7.1	7.1	7.6	13.5	10.7	10.7	87.2	33.5	37.3	46.1	53.	169.9

FIGURE 7.12. Manufacturing department operating expenses ($000)

Manufacturing Indirect Summary ($000)

	Months after startup													Quarters				
	1	2	3	4	5	6	7	8	9	10	11	12		1	2	3	4	
Indirect labor	7.59	9.49	11.48	15.18	15.88	19.35	22.15	22.15	22.15	22.15	23.49	24.69	215.75	84.81	103.17	110.97	113.85	412.8
Occupancy, Comm & D.P.	8.05	8.05	8.05	8.45	8.45	8.65	9.85	9.95	9.95	10.2	10.3	10.3	110.25	33.45	36.55	39.35	41.75	151.1
Operating expense	4.3	2.8	3.4	4.1	4.7	11.2	7.1	7.1	7.6	13.5	10.7	10.7	87.2	33.5	37.3	46.1	53	169.9
Total	19.94	20.34	22.93	27.73	29.03	39.2	39.1	39.2	39.7	45.85	44.49	45.69	413.2	151.76	177.02	196.42	208.6	733.8

FIGURE 7.13. Manufacturing indirect summary ($000)

Production Equipment—PWD Assembly & Test ($000 Omitted)

Page _____ of _____
Date _____

	Months after startup												1st Yr Total	Quarters				2nd Yr Total
	1	2	3	4	5	6	7	8	9	10	11	12		1	2	3	4	
Assembly																		
Work benches, stools, racks				2.0					2.0				4					
Board & racks				2.0					2.0				4					
Mark V lead preparation				3.0									3					
Hedco transfer preparation				2.0									2					
Amistar dip inserter													14	14				14
Semi-auto inserter													15	15				15
Flow solder & cleaner													15	15				15
Carts				.5						.5			1	.5				.5
Test																		
Signal generator							4.0		4.0				8		4.0			4
Scopes				2.5			2.5						5		2.5	2.5		5
Digital volt meters				.5			.5						1	.5	.5			1
Bendix test system				30.0									30					
Bed of nails fixture				5.0									5					
Test programs				10.0									10					
Vacuum pump & installation				2.0									2					
Exerciser				1.0			1.0						2					
				60.5			8		8	.5			77	47.5	7			54.5

FIGURE 7.14. Production equipment—PWD assembly & test ($000 omitted)

Production Equipment, Final Assy & Test ($000)

	Months after startup												1st Yr Total	Quarters				2nd Yr Total
	1	2	3	4	5	6	7	8	9	10	11	12		1	2	3	4	
Assembly:																		
Conveyor line				10.0									10.0	10.0				10.
Racks				.5					1.0				1.5		1.0			1
Carts				1.0					1.0				2			1.0		1
Holding fixtures				5.0								5.0	10		5.0			5
Burn-in racks					5.0								5			5.0		5
Benches, stools				1.5			.5			.5			2.5		2.0		2.0	4
Unit fork lift					6.0								6					
Shipping hoist						4.0							4					
Miscellaneous assembly tooling					5.0				5.0				10					
Test:																		
Scope				2.5		5.0				2.5			10	2.5		7.5	5.0	15
Exerciser				1.0		2.0				1.0			4	1.0		3.0	2.0	6
Computer test system																		
Burn-in box				2.0									2					
Total				23.5	16	11	.5	0	7	4	0	5	67	13.5	8	16.5	9	46.5

FIGURE 7.15. Production equipment, final assy & test ($000)

Production Equipment, Receiving Inspections ($000)

	Months after startup												1st Yr Total	Quarters				2nd Yr Total
	1	2	3	4	5	6	7	8	9	10	11	12		1	2	3	4	
Benches, stools & racks		1.0						1.0					2					
Desk		.5											.5					
Scopes			2.5										2.5					
Exerciser			1.0										1					
DVM			.5										.5					
Instruments-elect.			1.0				1.0				1.0		3					
Surface plate			1.0						1.0				2	1.0				1.0
Measuring tools			5.0					2.0				2.0	9					
Total		1.5	11.0	0	0	0	1	3	1	0	1	2	20.5	1	0	0	0	1.0

FIGURE 7.16. Production equipment, receiving inspections ($000)

Production Equipment, Receiving, Stockroom, & Shipping ($000)

	Months after startup												1st Yr Total	Quarters				2nd Yr Total
	1	2	3	4	5	6	7	8	9	10	11	12		1	2	3	4	
Receiving:																		
Desk & chair	.3												.3					
File cabinet	.2												.2					
Bench	.1												.1					
Stockroom:																		
Benches & stools	.6												.6	.3				.3
Cabinet	.2												.2	.1				.1
12″ wide racks		2.0				2.0			2.0				6	2.0				2
Bulk racks				3.0						3.0			6			3.0		3
Scale			1.5										1.5		1.5			1.5
Carts				.5			.5			.5			1.5				1.0	1
Stockroom tractor						5.0							5					
Shipping:																		
Desk & chair							.3						.3					
File cabinet							.2						.2					
Bench							.1						.1					
Total	1.4	2	1.5	3.5	0	7	1.1	0	2	3.5	0	0	22	2.4	1.5	3	1	7.9

FIGURE 7.17. Production equipment, receiving, stockroom, & shipping ($000)

Production Equipment—Subassembly ($000)

	Months after startup												1st Yr Total	Quarters				
	1	2	3	4	5	6	7	8	9	10	11	12		1	2	3	4	
Work benches, stools, etc.				2.0		2.0		2.0					6					
Carts				1.0		1.0		1.0					3		2.0			2
Racks				3.0		2.0							5	2.0				2
Conveyor line													—	25.0				25
Eubanks wire stripper							7.0						7					
Harness board rack									2.0				2					
Miscellaneous tooling				5.0					5.0				10					
P/S tester					7.0								7					
Total	0	0	0	11	7	5	7	3	7	0	0	0	40	27	2	0	0	29

FIGURE 7.18. Production equipment—subassembly ($000)

Production Equipment—Clean Room ($000)

	Months after startup												1st Yr Total	Quarters				2nd Yr Total
	1	2	3	4	5	6	7	8	9	10	11	12		1	2	3	4	
Pre-clean room:																		
Benches, stools & racks		.7											.7					
Vapo kleen degreaser		3.0											3					
Ultra sonic cleaner		2.0											2					
Carts		.3											.3					
Clean room:																		
Clean bench with nitrogen purge		4.5											4.5					
Clean room bench (std .4)		6.0											6			3.0		3
Mechanical certifier		55.0											55					
Counter (2 sets)		8.5											8.5			8.5		8.5
Head loading fixture		25.0											25					
Servo writer		150.0											150					
Stools (6) cabinets (2)		.8											.8					
Benches (3)		.6											.6					
Total		256.4											256.4			11.5		11.5

FIGURE 7.19. Production equipment—clean room ($000).

Production Facilities Improvement ($000)

Page _____ of _____
Date _____

	Months after startup												1st Yr Total	Quarters				
	1	2	3	4	5	6	7	8	9	10	11	12		1	2	3	4	
Clean room—28' × 24'								35.					35					
Electrical			10.0			10.0			10.0				30					
Factory A/C				5.0			35.0						35					
Miscellaneous changes								5.0			5.0		15					
Total	0	0	10	5	0	10	35	40	10	0	5	0	115	15	10	15	10	50

FIGURE 7.20. Production facilities improvement ($000)

Office Furniture Required

		Months after startup													Quarters				
		1	2	3	4	5	6	7	8	9	10	11	12		1	2	3	4	
Desk	$250	3	1		1		2	1				1			1	2	2		
Desk Chair	$100	3	1		1		2	1				1			1	2	2		
Side chair	$ 50	10	1		1		2	1											
Ref table	$ 50	2	1		1		2					1			1	2	2		
Typewriter	$965	1					1										1		
File cabinet	$150	3	1		1		2	1				1			1	2	2		
Bookcase	100	2	1		1		2								1	2	2		
Conference table	$500	1																	
Total $		3765	700	0	700	0	2365	550	0	0	0	600		8680	700	1400	2165		4265

FIGURE 7.21. Office furniture required

MARKETING/SALES PLAN AND BUDGET
(SELLING AND FIELD SERVICE DEPARTMENT)

Charter

To penetrate the OEM markets for the Widget II and Widget III with a goal of capturing at least seven percent of each market within three years of start for each product.

Organize an efficient and lean field sales force capable of selling widgets to high-volume (above $50,000/yr.) OEM accounts.

Organize a network of distributors to sell to low-volume systems houses and single-quantity customers.

Provide service/engineering support at three levels: evaluation phase, contract start-up, and contract monitoring (technical).

Analyze market trends and prepare plans for pricing and market positioning of products.

Develop and implement an advertising plan for each product.

Provide administrative support to sales for prime and spares equipment, including processing of orders from new prospect review through shipment; monitoring backlog, order rate, and shipments; and providing reports to division and corporate management.

Organization

The selling and field service department will include the following functions:

National sales management

Direct sales force.

Distributor network.

Product planning.

Advertising.

Administration.

Sales engineering (field service).

Descriptions of the major functions within the organization are included in this section.

Budget

The budgets for fiscal years 1 and 2 are shown below. The detailed budget for each year is also presented in this section.

Selling and Field Service as a Percentage of Revenue
($M)

	Year 1	Year 2
Revenue	.46	4.88
Selling and field service	.15	.36
Percentage of revenue	33.0%	7.4%

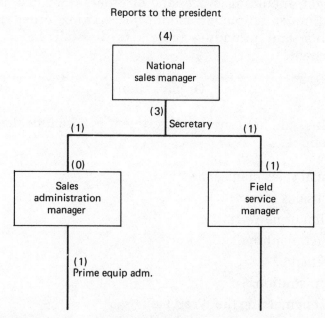

FIGURE 7.22.   Creative Manufacturing: Selling & Field Service Organization, Year 1

MARKETING/SALES DEPARTMENT JOB DESCRIPTIONS

National Sales Managers

Functions:

Regional sales.
Sales contracts administration.
Field service.
Advertising.

Duties:

Administer corporate marketing/sales goals and policies in the United States.
Staffing of organization.

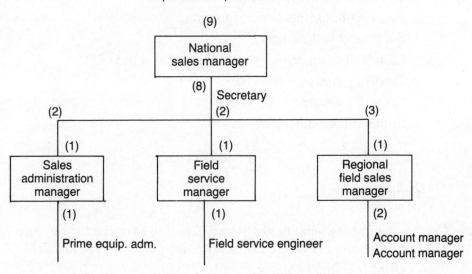

FIGURE 7.23. Creative Manufacturing: Selling & Field Service Organization, Year 2

Territory definition.

Quota assignment.

Sales planning.

Sales training.

Establish low-volume OEM distributors.

New prospect analysis.

Regional Field Sales Staff

Duties:

Manage OEM accounts.

Pursue volume OEM contracts.

Manage selling expenses.

Host regional trade shows.

Maintain customer files.

Qualify new prospects.

Forecast bookings and shipments.

Sales lead follow-up.

Maintain competitive product price and data file.

Territory analysis reports.

Growth planning.

Subordinate management.

Field Service

Duties:

Liason between customer and Creative Manufacturing, Inc., operations Provide OEM service support when required.

OEM technical support (applications).

Product presentations, in-plant/customer site.

Customer/prospect evaluation hardware support; evaluation unit status.

Regional trade show support.

Major OEM proposals.

Salesmen training.

Development and maintenance of competitive data file.

Customer CE training.

Marketing Manager

Functions:

Marketing administration.
  Field administration training.
  Financial analysis.
  Coordination with corporate MIS system.
  Order administration.
  Policies and procedures (MKT).
  Product scheduling.
Marketing services.
  Advertising.
  Customer training.
  Sales promotion.
  Sales training.
Marketing strategies.
  Competitive analysis.
  Product marketing.
  Plans and programs.
  Systems support.
Marketing plans and programs.
  Market planning.

Sales Administration

Duties:

Audit OEM agreements.

Audit and process all orders.

Obtain corporate credit approvals.

Follow-up with field sales on new account administrative package.

Return executed documents for distribution.

Furnish bookings, backlog, nonaccepted order information.

Advise field of order-related problems.

Prepare sales orders for issuance of credit memos by Accounting.

Prepare export documents for International.

Prepare manufacturers' affidavits for imports.

Advertising

Functions:

Advertising.

Sales promotion.

Trade shows.

Duties:

Advertising.
   Space advertising.
   Press releases/PR.
   Trade shows.
Sales promotion.

Direct-mail campaign.

Technical publications.

Sales brochures.

Inquiry handling.

Corporate publications (manuals).

FINANCE AND ADMINISTRATION
(General & Administrative)

Charter

Provide financial reporting required by corporate management.

Provide general accounting.

Monitor prices paid for parts and services, assembly costs, and variances to standard.

Assist corporate management in the preparation of annual financial plans and quarterly updates.

Conduct financial reviews that will enable management to assess trends and initiate corrective actions.

Analyze major contracts for profit and return on investment.

Budget

Finance and Administration (G&A) Budget as a Percentage of Revenues.
($M)

	Year 1	Year 2
Revenue	.46	4.88
G&A	.251	.342
Percentage of revenue	54.6%	7%

Selling & Field Service Personnel Requirements

	Months after startup												1st Yr Total	Quarters				2nd Yr Total
	1	2	3	4	5	6	7	8	9	10	11	12		1	2	3	4	
National sales manager	1	1	1	1	1	1	1	1	1	1	1	1		1	1	1	1	
Regional field sales account manager	–	–	–	–	–	–	–	–	–	–	–	1		1	1	1	1	
Account manager	–	–	–	–	–	–	–	–	–	–	–	–		1	1	–	2	
Secretary	1	1	1	1	1	1	1	1	1	1	1	1		1	1	1	1	
Sales administration manager	–	–	–	–	–	–	–	–								1	1	
Prime equipment administrator	–	–	–	–	1	1	1	1	1	1	1	1		1	1	1	1	
Spare parts administrator	–	–	–	–	–	–	–	–	–	–	–	–						
Field service manager	–	–	–	1	1	1	1	1	1	1	1	1		1	1	1	1	
Field service engineer	–	–	–	–	–	–	–											
Reference data																		
Unit shipment	–	–	–	–	–	–	2	4	9	16	32	50	112	180	216	259	311	966

FIGURE 7.24. Selling & field service personnel requirements

Selling & Field Service Labor Costs ($000)

Note: Monthly salary costs incl. commissions salary where applicable.	Mo salary	Months after startup												1st Yr Total	Quarters				2nd Yr Total
		1	2	3	4	5	6	7	8	9	10	11	12		1	2	3	4	
Internal sales manager	3.3/5.42	3.3	3.3	3.3	3.3	3.3	3.3	3.3	5.42	5.42	5.42	5.42	5.42	50.2	17.4	17.4	17.4	17.4	69.6
Reg field service	2.5/5	–	–	–	–	–	–	–	–	–	–	–	–		7.5	15	15	15	52.5
Account manager	2/3.6	–	–	–	–	–	–	–	–	–	–	–	–			–	–	12.84	12.84
Secretary	.9	.9	.9	.9	.9	.9	.9	.9	.9	.9	.9	.9	.9	10.8	2.9	2.9	2.9	2.9	11.6
Sales administration manager	2.1	–	–	–	–	–	–	–	–	–	–	–	–				6.74	6.74	13.48
Prime equipment administrator	1.0	–	–	–	1.0	1.0	1.0	1.0	1.0	1.0	1.0	1.0	1.0	9.0	3.21	3.21	3.21	3.21	12.84
Spare parts administrator	1.0	–	–	–	–	–	–	–	–	–	–	–	–						
Field service manager	2.1	–	–	–	2.1	2.1	2.1	2.1	2.1	2.1	2.1	2.1	2.1	18.9	6.74	6.74	6.74	6.74	26.96
Field service engineer	1.60	–	–	–	–	–	–	–							5.33	5.33	5.33	5.33	21.32
Total		4.2	4.2	4.2	7.3	7.3	7.3	7.3	9.42	9.42	9.42	9.42	9.42	85	43	51	57	70	221
Reference data:																			
Unit shipment								2	4	8	16	32	50	112	180	216	259	311	966

FIGURE 7.25. Selling & field service labor costs

Selling & Field Service Furniture & Test Equipment, Capital Equipment Costs

Page _____ of _____

Date _____

	Cost Each	Months after startup													Quarters				
		1	2	3	4	5	6	7	8	9	10	11	12		1	2	3	4	
Sales manager office set	$1450	1450												1450					
Executive sec'y desk	$ 350	350												350					
Executive sec'y chair	$ 100	100												100					
Executive sec'y file cab.	$ 225	225												225					
Desk	$ 250				500									500	750		250	500	1500
Chair	$ 100				200									200	300		100	200	600
Bookcase	$ 100				200									200	300		100	200	600
Table	$ 50				100									100	150		50	100	300
Small chair	$ 50				100									100	200		100	150	450
File cab	$ 150				300									300	450		150	300	900
Typewriter	$ 965	965			965									1930					
Calculator	$ 100	100			200									300					
Portable scope	$2200				2200									2200	4400			2200	6600
Scope accessories	$ 300				300									300	600			300	900
Tool kit	$ 400				400									400	800			400	1200
Widget exerciser	$2500				2500									2500	5000			2500	7500
Parts cabinet	$ 120				120									120				120	120
Bench lab	$ 200				200									200	400			200	600
Bench (clean)	$2000				2000									2000	2000			2000	2000
Stool	$ 80				80									80	160			80	240
Lamp	$ 40				40									40	80			40	120
Widgets	$3100			12200	9300	9300								31000					
Total $		3190	0	12200	19705	9300	0	0	0	0	0	0	0	44395	15590	0	750	9290	25630

FIGURE 7.26. Selling & field service furniture & test equipment, capital equipment costs

Selling & Field Service Department Expense ($000)

	Months after startup												1st Yr Total	Quarters				2nd Yr Total
	1	2	3	4	5	6	7	8	9	10	11	12		1	2	3	4	
Regular pay	4	4	4	7	7	7	7	9	9	9	9	9	85	43	51	57	70	221
Commissions (Included in reg. pay)	–	–	–	–	–	–	–	–	–	–	–	–	–	–	–	–	–	–
Vacations (3.4%)	–	–	–	–	–	–	–	–	–	–	–	–	–	2	2	3	3	10
Payroll taxes (6.7%)	–	–	–	1	1	1	1	1	1	1	1	1	9	4	5	5	7	21
Group insurance (1.5%)	–	–	–	1	–	–	–	–	1	–	–	–	2	1	1	1	2	5
Telephone	–	–	–	1	–	1	–	1	–	–	–	1	3	2	2	2	2	8
Stationery supplies	–	–	1	–	–	1	–	1	–	–	–	–	3	1	1	2	1	4
Expense reports	1	1	1	1	1	1	1	1	1	1	–	1	11	6	6	9	10	31
Other travel	1	1	1	1	1	2	2	2	2	2	2	2	19	12	12	12	12	48
Media advertising	–	–	2	–	1	–	4	4	4	1	4	5	20	–	4	2	2	8
Product literature	–	–	2	–	–	–	–	–	–	–	–	–	2	5	–	–	–	5
Representative comm	–	–	–	–	–	–	–	–	–	–	–	–	–					
Total	5	6	9	12	11	12	15	15	19	14	17	19	154	76	84	92	109	361
Head count																		
Sales	2	2	2	3	3	3	3	3	3	3	3	3		4	4	5	7	
Field service	–	–	–	1	1	1	1	1	1	1	1	1		2	2	2	2	

FIGURE 7.27. Selling & field service department expense

Administrative and Accounting Personnel Requirements

	Months after startup												1st Yr Total	Quarters				2nd Yr Total
	1	2	3	4	5	6	7	8	9	10	11	12		1	2	3	4	
President/G.M.	1	1	1	1	1	1	1	1	1	1	1	1		1	1	1	1	
Executive secretary	1	1	1	1	1	1	1	1	1	1	1	1		1	1	1	1	
VP finance/controller	1	1	1	1	1	1	1	1	1	1	1	1		1	1	1	1	
Payroll clerk	1	1	1	1	1	1	1	1	1	1	1	1		1	1	1	1	
Accounts record clerk	–	–	–	–	–	–	–	–	–	–	–	–			1	1	1	
Accounts payable clerk	–	1	1	1	1	1	1	1	1	1	1	1		1	1	1	1	
Collections clerk			–	–	–	–	–	–	–	–	–	–						
Posting clerk			–	–	–	–	–											
Clerk typist			–	–	–	–	–											
Personnel clerk								–	–	–	–							
Total	4	5	5	5	5	5	5	5	5	5	5	5	5	5	6	6	6	

FIGURE 7.28. Administrative and accounting personnel requirements

Administrative and Accounting Personnel Costs ($000)

	Mo. sal.	Months after startup												1st Yr Total	Quarters				2nd Yr Total
		1	2	3	4	5	6	7	8	9	10	11	12		1	2	3	4	
President/G.M.	5.0	5.0	5.0	5.0	5.0	5.0	5.0	5.0	5.0	5.0	5.0	5.0	5.0	60	16.05	16.05	16.05	16.05	64.20
Executive secretary	1.13	1.13	1.13	1.13	1.13	1.13	1.13	1.13	1.13	1.13	1.13	1.13	1.13	13.56	3.63	3.63	3.63	3.63	14.52
VP finance/cont	3.5	3.50	3.50	3.50	3.50	3.50	3.50	3.50	3.50	3.50	3.50	3.50	3.50	42.00	11.24	11.24	11.24	11.24	44.94
Payroll clerk	.9	.9	.9	.9	.9	.9	.9	.9	.9	.9	.9	.9	.9	10.8	2.89	2.89	2.89	2.89	11.56
Accounts receivable clerk	.9	–	–	–	–	–	–	–	–	–	–	–	–			2.89	2.89	2.89	11.56
Accounts payable clerk	.9	–	.9	.9	.9	.9	.9	.9	.9	.9	.9	.9	.9	9.9	2.89	2.89	2.89	2.89	11.56
Collections clerk	.9	–	–	–	–	–	–	–	–	–	–	–	–						11.56
Posting clerk	.8	–	–	–	–	–	–	–	–	–	–	–	–						
Clerk typist	.7	–	–	–	–	–	–	–	.7	.7	.7	.7	.7	3.5	2.25	2.25	2.25	2.25	9.0
Personnel clerk	1	–	–	–	–	–	–	–	–	–	–	–	–						
Total		11	12	11	12	11	12	11	12	11	12	11	12	138	39	42	42	42	165

FIGURE 7.29. Administrative and accounting personnel costs

Administrative and Accounting Furniture Plan Units Purchased

		Months after startup												1st Yr Total	Quarters				2nd Yr Total
		1	2	3	4	5	6	7	8	9	10	11	12		1	2	3	4	
Pres/VP finance office		2																		
Set—desk, chair																				
2 side chairs, bookcase																				
File cabinets set $1450																				
Executive secretary desk $350		1																		
Executive secretary chair $110		1																		
Executive secretary file cabinet $225		1																		
Desk $280/400		1	1					1									1			
Chair $100		1	1					1									1			
Bookcase $50		1	1					1									1			
Table $50		1	1					1									1			
Small chair $40		8															1			
File cabinet $150		1	1					1									1			
Typewriter $965		2	1														1			
Conference table $169		1																		
Calculator $100		1	1					1									1			

FIGURE 7.30. Administrative and accounting furniture plan units purchased

Administrative and Accounting Departments
Furniture Plan Estimated Costs ($)

	Months after startup												1st Yr Total	Quarters				2nd Yr Total
	1	2	3	4	5	6	7	8	9	10	11	12		1	2	3	4	
Pres & VP fin. office set	2900												2900					
Executive secretary desk	350												350					
Executive secretary chair	110												110					
Executive file cabinet	225												225					
Desk	400	400											800	—	400			400
Chair	100	100											200		100			100
Bookcase	50	50											100		50			50
Table	50	50											100		50			50
Small chairs	320												320	—				—
File cabinet		150											150		150			150
Typewriter	1930	965											2895		965			965
Conference table	167												167					
Calculator	100	100											200		100			100
Total	6702	1815											8517		1815			1815

FIGURE 7.31. Administrative and accounting departments furniture plan estimated costs

Administrative and Accounting Department Expense ($000)

	Months after startup												1st Yr Total	Quarters				2nd Yr Total
	1	2	3	4	5	6	7	8	9	10	11	12		1	2	3	4	
Regular pay	11	12	11	12	11	12	11	12	11	12	11	12	138	37	42	42	42	163
Vacation (3.6%)	–	–	–	–	–	–	–	–	–	–	–	–	–	2	2	2	2	8
Payroll taxes (6.2%)	1	1	1	1	1	1	1	1	1	1	1	1	12	3	4	3	4	14
Group insurance (2.6%)	1	–	–	1	–	–	1	–	–	1	–	–	4	1	2	1	2	6
Telephone	4	4	4	4	4	4	4	4	4	4	4	4	48	12	12	12	12	48
Stationery/supplies	1	1	1	1	1	1	2	1	1	2	2	1	15	6	6	6	6	24
Postage	–	–	–	1	–	–	–	1	–	–	–	1	3	1	1	1	1	4
Petty cash	–	–	1	–	–	1	–	–	1	–	–	1	4	–	2	2	2	6
Other supplies	–	–	–	–	–	–	1	–	1	–	–	1	3	–	1	2	2	5
Expense reports	–	–	–	1	–	–	–	1	–	–	–	1	3	1	2	2	2	7
Travel	–	–	1	–	–	1	–	–	1	–	–	1	4	1	1	1	2	5
Recruiting	–	–	–	–	–	–	–	–	1	1	1	1	3	1	3	4	4	12
Professional fees	1	1	1	1	2	2	1	1	1	1	1	1	14	10	10	10	10	40
Total	19	19	20	22	19	22	21	21	21	22	20	25	251	75	88	88	91	342
Reference data																		
Head count																		
Administration	2	2	2	2	2	2	2	2	2	2	2	2	–	2	2	2	2	
Finance	2	3	3	3	3	3	3	3	3	3	3	3	–	3	4	4	4	
Total	4	5	5	5	5	5	5	5	5	5	5	5	–	5	6	6	6	6

FIGURE 7.32. Administrative and accounting Department expense

Capital Equipment Requirements (Summary—All Departments) ($000)

	Months after startup												1st Yr Total	Quarters				2nd Yr Total
	1	2	3	4	5	6	7	8	9	10	11	12		1	2	3	4	
Engineering	35.6	13.7	3.7	.5	3.5	.2	0	0	.2	0	0	0	65.4	19.	1.5	0	0	20.5
Manufacturing																		
PWB assembly & test	0	0	0	65.4	0	0	8	0.1	8	0.5	0	0	82	47.5	7	0	54.5	
Final assembly & test	0	0	0	23.5	16	11	.5	0	7	4	0	5	67	13	8	16.5	9	46.5
Receiving inspection	0	1.5	11	0	0	0	1.0	3	1	0	1	2	20.5	1	0	0	0	1
Receiving, stock room, shipping	1.4	2.0	1.5	3.5	0	7	1.1	0	2	3.5	0	0	22	2.4	1.5	3	1	7.9
Sub-assembly	0	0	0	11	7	5	7	3	7	0	0	0	40	27	2	0	0	29
Clean room	0	256.4	0	0	0	0	0	40	0	0	0	0	256.4	0	0	11.5	0	11.5
Facilities imp	0	0	10	5	0	10	35	40	10	0	5	0	115	15	10	15	10	50
Office furniture	3.8	.7	0	0	0	2.4	.6	0	0	0	.6	0	8.1	.7	1.4	2.2	0	4.3
Sub total	5.2	260.6	22.5	100.5	23.0	35.4	53.2	46.0	35.0	8.0	6.6	7.0	611.0	106.6	29.9	48.2	20	204.7
Administrative & acctg	6.7	1.8	0	0	0	0	0	0	0	0	0	0	8.5	1.8	1.8	0	0	3.6
Selling & field service	3.2	0	12.2	19.7	9.3	0	0	0	0	0	0	0	44.4	15.6	0	.75	9.3	25.6
Total all depts	51	276	38	129	36	44	53	46	35	8	7	7	730	143	33	49	29	254

FIGURE 7.33. Capital equipment requirements (summary—all departments)

8

FINANCIAL REPORTS: DEVELOPMENT AND ANALYSIS

This chapter is a study of the key financial reports for your corporation and how they are developed. The examination makes use of a very productive tool: ratio analysis.

Your key financial reports include an income statement, cash flow statement, depreciation schedule, provision for income tax, and a balance sheet. Creative Manufacturing's versions of these financial reports will be used to show, on a step-by-step basis, the rationale behind the development of each. A discussion of ratio analysis and its application will conclude the chapter.

Financial reports are really the key to any business plan. They will tell you if it is worthwhile to proceed, to stop and reevaluate your situation, or cease operations altogether.

INCOME STATEMENT

As stated earlier, the income statement is the score card of your business and is probably one of the most useful reports for you and your investors. It provides you with a status check of your company's financial health, its revenue sources, where revenue was spent, and what remains as profit. More simply stated, the income statement reveals how much your company makes or loses during the year.

For a business plan, these figures are generally shown on a

monthly basis for the first year, quarterly for the second, and annually for all others. Table 8.1 is Creative Manufacturing's pro-forma income statement for its first five years of operation.

An income statement shows the money received from selling goods, services, and other income-producing items. By comparing these figures against all the costs of operating the company, it points up the net result: a profit or a loss for the year. Costs usually include material, direct labor, manufacturing overhead, engineering, marketing, and G&A. Total costs are then subtracted from the revenue (usually sales), with the difference being either your profit before taxes or a loss for the period under consideration.

Each of the income statement items is discussed below.

Revenue, Operating Revenue or Net Sales

The most important source of revenue is usually the first item of an income statement. Creative Manufacturing has chosen to call it *revenue*, though other companies may call it *net sales* and a utility company may call it *operating revenues*. Whatever it is named, it represents the primary source of money received by your company from its customers for goods sold or services rendered.

Creative Manufacturing has chosen to show the total worldwide market in units and value for its reference, as well as its product models, quantity sold, and the income received from the sales. This format is typical for a company's internal business plan but would not generally appear in a formal statement to its stockholders.

Creative Manufacturing's share of revenue was obtained from its sale of widget products and spare parts. The Widget II product was a primary source of revenue until the fourth year of operation, when Widget III became the dominant revenue source.

During the first year, 112 Widget II units were to be sold. This increased to 966 during the second year and 1788 in the third year. A further increase to 1,900 occurred in the fourth year. The fifth year saw a decrease to 1712 units, owing to the availability of the more cost-effective Widget III.

Widget III shipments, which numbered 112 units in the third

TABLE 8.1 Creative Manufacturing, Inc., Proforma Income Statement ($000), Widget II & Widget III Products

	Year 1													Year 2					Year Number		
	Month 1	Month 2	Month 3	Month 4	Month 5	Month 6	Month 7	Month 8	Month 9	Month 10	Month 11	Month 12	Total	Q1	Q2	Q3	Q4	Total	3	4	5
Total world wide Market (units)													9782					19780	27090	35212	45782
Total world wide market ($M)													33.2					63.3	84	109.2	142
Widget II units	0	0	0	0	0	0	2	4	8	16	32	50	112	180	216	259	311	966	1788	1900	1712
Widget III units	0	0	0	0	0	0	0	0	0	0	0	0	0	0	0	0	0	0	112	1900	5138
Revenue																					
Widget II products	0	0	0	0	0	0	0	0	0	75	150	235	460	828	994	1191	1431	4444	8046	8360	7362
Widget III products	0	0	0	0	0	0	0	0	0	0	0	0	0	0	0	0	0	0	666	11020	29030
Spare parts products	0	0	0	0	0	0	0	0	0	0	0	0	0	83	99	119	143	444	871	1938	3639
Total Revenue	0	0	0	0	0	0	0	0	0	75	150	235	460	911	1093	1310	1574	4888	9583	21318	40031
Cost of Goods																					
Material widgets	0	0	0	0	0	0	4	8	15	30	61	95	213	342	410	492	591	1835	3663	8123	15456
Material spare parts	0	0	0	0	0	0	0	0	0	0	0	0	0	12	15	18	22	67	131	291	546
Subtotal	0	0	0	0	0	0	4	8	15	30	61	95	213	334	425	510	613	1902	3794	8414	16002

Labor widgets	0	0	0	0	3	3	3	4	5	11	17	17	63	66	79	94	113	352	740	1583	3054
Labor spare parts	0	0	0	0	0	0	0	0	0	0	0	0	0	12	15	18	22	67	131	291	546
Subtotal	0	0	0	0	3	3	3	4	5	11	17	17	63	78	94	112	135	419	871	1874	3600
Total labor and material	0	0	0	0	3	3	7	12	20	41	78	112	276	432	519	622	748	2321	4665	10288	19602
Overhead	20	20	23	28	29	39	39	39	40	46	45	46	414	123	149	177	213	662	1376	2960	5688
Total cost of goods	20	20	23	28	32	42	46	51	60	87	123	158	690	555	668	799	961	2983	6041	13248	25290
Gross Margin ($000)	−20	−20	−23	−28	−32	−42	−46	−51	−60	−12	27	77	−230	356	425	511	613	1905	3542	8070	14741
Gross Margin (%)										−16	18	33	−50	39	39	39	39	39	37	38	37
Expense																					
Engineering	39	21	22	26	25	40	34	37	37	35	38	39	393	101	109	117	123	450	671	1492	2802
Marketing	5	6	9	12	11	12	15	15	19	14	17	19	154	76	84	92	109	361	862	1919	3603
General & Administrative	19	19	20	22	19	22	21	21	21	22	20	25	251	75	88	88	91	342	383	853	1601
Total expense	63	46	51	60	55	74	70	73	77	71	75	83	798	252	281	297	323	1153	1916	4264	8006
Profit(loss = −) before taxes	−83	−66	−74	−88	−87	−116	−116	−124	−137	−83	−48	−6	−1028	104	144	214	290	752	1626	3806	6735
Profit(loss = −) before tax %										−111	−32	−3	−223	11	13	16	18	15	17	18	17
Cum PBT(loss = −) before taxes	−83	−149	−223	−311	−398	−514	−630	−754	−891	−974	−1022	−1028	−1028	−924	−780	−566	−276	−276	1350	5156	11891

year, increased to 1900 in the fourth year and 5138 in the fifth year.

The total of Widget II and III units was based on a worldwide widget market share capture of 1 percent for the first year, 5 percent for the second, 7 percent for the third, 10 percent for the fourth, and 15 percent for the fifth year of operation.

Shipments of Model II Widgets during months seven, eight, and nine of the first year did not provide any revenue as they were loaned to prospects as evaluation units. Prospects use evaluation units for a period of 30 to 90 days, so they can insure that the widget will work in their systems before they buy large numbers of them. Evaluation units that are not sold to the prospect are eventually returned.

The average price for Model II Widgets was $4700 during the first year, $4600 during the second year, $4500 during the third, $4400 for the fourth, and $4300 for the fifth.

Model III Widgets were an advanced product that provided twice the performance of Model IIs and therefore commanded a higher price. Model III Widgets' average unit price was $5950 during the third year, $5800 during the fourth year, and $5650 during the fifth year. Contrary to trends in many industries, widget product prices have traditionally decreased with time, owing in part to rapidly advancing technology that provides more capability per unit. Widget Models II and III revenue for each year is the product of the number of units multiplied by the average unit price.

Spare-parts revenue is a valuable source of income and can represent 10 to 15 percent of gross sales in the widget industry. Creative Manufacturing achieved spare-parts revenue of 10 percent of sales during the first through the fifth years. There is often a one-year delay from the time prime equipment is shipped to the time customers order spare parts. The figures represent the revenue that was expected after taking into consideration returned goods and allowances for price reductions.

Cost of Goods

In a manufacturing firm, cost of goods represents all factory costs to convert raw materials into finished products. These costs include raw materials, direct labor, and factory overhead items, such as supervision, rent, electricity, supplies, maintenance, and repairs.

Creative Manufacturing chose to show the widget material and spare-parts material separately. Model II Widgets have a material cost of $1900 per unit, and Model III Widgets have a material cost of $2375. Material costs in the widget industry have a historical tendency to remain constant throughout a product's life, mainly because of cost reduction programs that tend to keep material prices in line with inflation. From past experience, spare-parts material costs were estimated at 15 percent of the sales price.

Direct-labor standards for each widget product were estimated at 27 hours for assembly, 10 for test, and 3 for inspection, for a total of 40 hours. Standard hours are based on the total hours that are actually required to assemble, test, and inspect a unit. They do not include employee fringe benefits, such as holidays, insurance plans, employer-paid social security taxes, or employee absenteeism benefits. These, of course, must be included in overall costs.

Excluding the first year, Creative Manufacturing used a direct-labor estimate of 144 percent of standard. This means that the 40 hours that it allocated for building a unit would actually cost 50.7 hours.

In accordance with past experience, direct labor for spare-parts assembly was estimated at 15 percent of the sales price. Labor rates, like all things, continue to increase with inflation. Creative Manufacturing based its plan on labor rates that were expected to increase by 7 percent annually. The company's direct labor rates during the first year of operation were $5.91 per hour. The estimated increases were to $6.32 in the second year, $6.76 in the third, $7.23 in the fourth, and $7.74 for the fifth.

Creative Manufacturing's overhead costs are the sum of indirect labor, occupancy, communications, data processing, and operating expenses (see Chapter 7 under the manufacturing department's plans and budgets). Total costs of goods is the sum of all material, direct labor, and overhead. Total cost of goods subtracted from sales provides gross margin. Gross margin is what is left to be divided between operating expenses and profit and is often expressed as a percentage of sales. It is calculated by dividing total cost of goods by sales, subtracting the quotent from 1 and multiplying the result by 100.

At the end of the second year, Creative Manufacturing had a 39 percent gross margin, which means that 39 cents of each sales dollar remains after paying for material, labor, and overhead.

One significant item that Creative Manufacturing did not include in its income statement is depreciation. Depreciation is the decline in the useful value of an asset because of wear and tear. Each year's decline in value of a machine used in the manufacturing process is an additional cost or a loss to be borne. Creative Manufacturing did develop a depreciation schedule for income tax calculations.

Depreciation is often shown as a line item following, and added to, operating expenses (those of Engineering, Marketing, and G&A). Creative chose to show depreciation as a line item on its "Provision for Federal Income Tax" statement (Table 8.4). Depreciation was subtracted from profit before taxes, which produces the same net effect as adding this item to the operating expenses on the income statement. It is more typical, however, to show depreciation on the income statement. Depreciation has the net effect of either adding to a company's losses for a given year or subtracting from its gains (profits).

Expenses

Engineering, Marketing, and General and Administrative (G&A) are often grouped separately from the cost of goods line. Product Development Engineering in a manufacturing industry can, and usually does, cost a substantial percentage of sales. In Marketing, salesmen's salaries and commissions, advertising and promotion, travel and entertainment are usually the significant cost items. G&A expenses usually include executive salaries, office payroll, and office expenses.

The engineering department's plans (see Chapter 7) represent 85 percent of each sales dollar during the first year. Though not unusual for a start-up widget manufacturing company, this figure was reduced to a more respectable, but still too high, 9 percent of sales in the second year. A further reduction to 7 percent occurred in the third year, a more typical level which was subsequently maintained.

Engineering costs of 9 percent during the second year were subtracted directly from the available gross margin of 39 percent, which left 30 percent to be distributed over the remaining expenses and profit.

Creative Manufacturing's marketing costs were 34 percent of each sales dollar during the first year, which is also typical for a start-up company. Personnel had to be hired and trained. Advertising and promotional material were prepared and had to precede the actual product. Travel and entertainment costs were incurred to sell the product, even before it was available.

Marketing costs decreased to 7 percent of each sales dollar during the second year, which was on the low side of average but manageable. They increased to 9 percent in subsequent years, which is more typical for a widget manufacturing firm.

During the second year, marketing costs of 7 percent were subtracted directly from the remaining 30 percent gross margin to leave 23 percent to be distributed over G&A and gross profit.

G&A was 55 percent of each sales dollar during the first year of operation, high for the industry but necessary in the opinion of Creative Manufacturing's management. This share dropped to a more typical 7 percent during the second year and was reduced to an even lower 4 percent in subsequent years. Four percent is on the very low side of average, whereas 7 percent is average for the widget industry.

When added together using arithmetic rounding, the three expense items during the second year amount to 24 percent of revenue, which leaves 15 percent for pretax profit. This improved in subsequent years to a high of 18 percent, a very respectable figure for a start-up company, considering that the 1978 U.S. average profit for business was approximately 10 percent pretax and 5 percent after tax.

Astute readers who add up the costs for the first year will discover correctly that the sum is greater than total sales. Creative Manufacturing's expenses exceeded income by $1,028,000, but as mentioned earlier, this was expected for a start-up company in the widget industry.

Other items that can appear on an income statement, but that do not appear on Creative Manufacturing's, have to do with additional sources of revenue, interest expenses, and federal income taxes. *Additional sources of revenue* come from dividends and interest received by a company from its holdings in stocks, bonds, real estate, and other investments. This income would be listed separately under an item called *other* or *miscellaneous income*. Total income would therefore be the sum of operating profit and other or miscellaneous income.

Interest expense, the money paid to bond holders for the use of their money, is sometimes called a fixed expense, in that interest must be paid year after year whether the company is making or losing money. Interest expense differs from dividends paid to shareholders, which are payable only if the board of directors declares them.

As a cost of doing business, interest expense is deductible from earnings to arrive at a base for the payment of income tax. The federal income tax rates in effect at the time Creative Manufacturing planned this business late in 1979 were 20 percent of the first $25,000 of income, 22 percent of the second $25,000, and 48 percent of all profits above $50,000. Creative Manufacturing's federal income taxes are shown on a separate schedule.

Creative Manufacturing's income statement did not show any other income or interest expenses because it did not have them. Start-up companies do not generally have sources of income other than sales. Creative Manufacturing did not have any interest expense because their investors provided all of the start-up capital.

Net profit is what remains after all income items have been added together and all expenses deducted from the total. Net profit, of course, is what business and free enterprise are all about.

CASH FLOW STATEMENT

The cash flow statement, a critical planning tool for your business, basically shows how much money your business needs to meet its obligations, when it needs it, and where it is coming from. Cash must flow into your business at the proper time if bills are to be paid and if you are to realize a profit at the end of the year.

The idea of cash flow follows from this general train of events: An order placed with your firm will generally require the purchase of *raw materials* in one form or another. The purchase of raw materials in turn generates an *accounts payable* for your firm, because, naturally, you must pay for these materials. As labor is applied to your raw materials, the *work-in-process inventory* will increase, and the *labor* to convert the raw materials must also be paid. As goods are completed, they move into *finished-goods inventory*. Finished-goods inventory is then sold. If you are a manufacturing firm, sales will probably be on credit. If your firm has sold on credit, it has not yet received any cash for its finished-goods inventory. Rather, it has created an *accounts receivable*. This point in the cycle represents the peak in your capital resource requirements. Thus far there has been no inflow of cash, only outflows. As your accounts receivable are paid and become cash, short-term obligations can be met.

Table 8.2 is Creative Manufacturing's proforma cash flow statement for the first five years of operation. It was developed along lines parallel to the train of events described above.

Creative's manufacturing cycle is 90 days, which means that it requires 90 days from the receipt of raw materials to the shipment of a completed widget. Raw materials must therefore be received 90 days *before* any planned shipments. Since a raw materials supplier may require 30 to 180 days to fill an order, materials must be ordered with this lead time in mind.

Creative Manufacturing purchased its raw materials on a 30 day credit account from its suppliers. The widget industry typically pays a 30 day credit account in 60 days. This practice essentially requires widget industry suppliers to finance their raw materials for 30 days. Though Creative Manufacturing used this practice at the outset of its planning cycle, it is *not* a recommended practice to follow. An established firm with a solid credit rating may be able to get away with this practice for a short time, but it will eventually catch up with it. Suppliers will increase prices to compensate for the additional finance charges they incur and will deliver to faster-paying customers first.

TABLE 8.2 Creative Manufacturing, Inc., Proforma Cash Flow Statement ($000), Widget II & Widget III Products

| | Year 1 | | | | | | | | | | | | | Year 2 | | | | | Year Number | | |
	Month 1	Month 2	Month 3	Month 4	Month 5	Month 6	Month 7	Month 8	Month 9	Month 10	Month 11	Month 12	Total	Q1	Q2	Q3	Q4	Total	3	4	5
Cash In																					
Accounts receivable																					
Drives/spares	0	0	0	0	0	0	0	0	0	0	0	75	75	689	972	1165	1398	4224	9035	19362	36912
Cash Out																					
Accounts payable																					
Material	0	0	0	0	0	4	8	15	30	61	95	118	331	377	452	544	725	2098	4179	9047	14688
Direct labor	0	0	0	0	3	3	3	4	5	11	17	17	63	78	94	112	135	419	871	1874	3600
Overhead	20	20	23	28	29	39	39	39	40	46	45	46	414	123	149	177	213	662	1376	2960	5688
Subtotal	20	20	23	28	32	42	42	43	45	57	62	63	477	201	243	289	348	1081	2247	4834	9288
Engineering	39	21	22	26	25	40	34	37	37	35	38	39	393	101	109	117	123	450	671	1492	2802
Marketing/sales	5	6	9	12	11	12	15	15	19	14	17	19	154	76	84	92	109	361	862	1919	3603
G&A	19	19	20	22	19	22	21	21	21	22	20	25	251	75	88	88	91	342	383	853	1601
Subtotal	63	46	51	60	55	74	70	73	77	71	75	83	798	252	281	297	323	1153	1916	4264	8006
Capital equipment & facilities imprv	51	276	38	129	36	44	53	46	35	8	7	7	730	143	33	49	29	254	479	1066	2002
Total cash out	134	342	112	217	123	164	173	177	187	197	239	271	2336	973	1009	1179	1425	4586	8821	19211	33964
Net cash flow	-134	-342	-112	-217	-123	-164	-173	-177	-187	-197	-239	-196	-2261	-284	-37	-14	-27	-362	214	151	2948
Cum cash out	-134	-476	-588	-805	-928	-1092	-1265	-1442	-1629	-1826	-2065	-2261		-2545	-2582	-2596	-2623	-2623	-2409	-2258	690

Conditions: Product is paid for 60 days after shipment.
    Material is brought in 90 days before shipment.
    Material is paid for 60 days after receipt.

Note: Year 6 has $6672 in receivables carried over from year 5.

Creative Manufacturing's customers were on a 30 day commercial credit account. To provide a safety factor for their cash needs, Creative Manufacturing planned to be paid 60 days after delivery of their widget products.

Creative Manufacturing paid for its direct labor, salaries, expenses, and capital equipment in the month they were incurred.

Creative's cash flow statement begins with sources of cash or "cash-in" and is followed by uses of cash, or "cash-out." For Creative Manufacturing, the only source of cash is accounts receivable, which result from shipping widgets to customers.

The 14 widgets shipped during the seventh, eighth, and ninth months (see Table 8.1) were nonrevenue units used by the marketing department as sales demonstration and customer evaluation units. These can be considered as capital equipment and treated as such, or sold later. The 16 widgets shipped during the tenth month and valued at $75,000 were Creative's first revenue shipments. They are shown as cash-in during the twelfth month since Creative expected to be paid in 60 days on its 30 day accounts.

Cash-out begins with material cost. Even though the widget shipments made in the seventh, eighth and ninth months were not revenue producing, their material content still had to be paid for. Since material had to be received 90 days before a unit shipment, material for the 7th-month shipment had to be received by the fourth month. Since Creative Manufacturing planned to pay its suppliers in 60 days, the first material had to be paid for in the sixth month.

Direct labor, manufacturing overhead, engineering, marketing/sales, and G&A costs were paid during the same month they were incurred. Even though there were no product shipments or income during the early months of the first year, department expenses were still incurred and they had to be paid.

Capital equipment purchased on 30 day commercial credit was paid for during the month payment was due. Since it was purchased on 30 day commercial credit, it could have been paid 30 days later than shown. (Capital equipment for an established firm is often financed with debt capital. Creative Manufacturing was financed through private venture capital money.)

The sum of all cash-out items for any period subtracted from the cash-in for the same period is the cash flow. If it is negative, noted in Table 8.2 by a minus sign, it means that this amount of cash must be provided for, either by investors (equity financing) or through debt financing.

Equity financing is money provided by investors who buy ownership and as such is a claim against future earnings. Equity also refers to the net value of a business. Thus, the equity, in this sense, is what is left when liabilities are subtracted from assets.

Debt financing is money lent to a business for a fee (interest). Although there may be a claim against certain assets (collateral) in case of default, the debt does not represent ownership. The holder of the debt does not participate in future earnings. Usually, to secure a loan, a business must have sufficient equity in plant, equity, or inventory to pledge as collateral.

Creative Manufacturing was financed totally through equity financing. Its investors therefore had to provide a cumulative total of $2,261,000 through its first year of operation; $2,623,000 through its second; $2,409,000 through its third; and $2,258,000 in its fourth. The investors finally saw the company generate a positive cash flow of $690,000 during the fifth year of operation.

Cash flow should not be confused with profit. A company like Creative Manufacturing can be profitable, which it was in the first quarter of the second year, but can still have a negative cash flow, as it did through its fourth year. The unprofitable first year and its resulting cash requirements had to be paid for out of future net earnings. It took the earnings of the second, third, and fourth years to pay for the cash requirements of the first one and one quarter unprofitable years.

DEPRECIATION SCHEDULE

As stated earlier, depreciation is the decline in the useful value of an asset due to wear and tear. It must therefore be considered as an expense chargeable against production and as a tax deduction. There are five principal methods of depreciation: (1) straight line, (2) sum-of-the-year's digits, (3) double declining balance, (4) units of production, and (5) accelerated cost recovery system (ACRS).

The *straight-line* figure is arrived at simply by dividing the asset's economic life (usually 10 years) into its total cost minus the estimated salvage value.

The *double declining balance* method of accelerated depreciation requires the application of a constant rate of depreciation each year to the undepreciated value of the asset at the close of the previous year. Since the straight-line rate is 10 percent per year, the double declining rate would be 20 percent per year. This rate during the first year is applied to the full purchase price of the asset, not to the cost less salvage value. During the second and subsequent years, it is applied to the undepreciated value of the asset.

Under the *sum-of-the-year's digits* method, the yearly allowance is determined as follows: (1) calculate the sum of the year's digits. In 10 years, the digits total 55: $1+2+3+4+5+6+7+8+9+10 = 55$. (2) Divide the remaining years by the year's digits, that is, 10/55, 9/55, . . . ,1/55, and multiply this fraction by the depreciable cost (total cost minus the salvage value) of the asset.

Under the *units of production* method, the expected useful life (in thousands of hours) is divided into the depreciable cost (purchase price minus salvage value) to arrive at an hourly depreciation rate. This rate is then applied to the number of hours the asset is used in each year to arrive at the annual depreciation value.

According to the *accelerated cost recovery system* (ACRS), assets are depreciated over 3-year, 5-year, 10-year, or 15-year periods, depending on the type of property. Typically, 3-year property includes such items as automobiles, tractors, light-duty trucks, and certain special manufacturing tools, 5-year property includes such items as most equipment, office furniture and fixtures, 10-year property includes public utility property, theme park structures, and manufactured and mobile homes; the 15-year class of assets includes all real property, such as buildings.

Depreciation under ACRS is figured by multiplying your "unadjusted basis" in the recovery property by a certain percentage. This percentage varies from year to year during the recovery period. The percentages for 3-, 5-, and 10-year property are shown below.

3-Year Property	
year 1	25%
year 2	38%
year 3	37%
5-Year Property	
year 1	15%
year 2	22%
year 3 through 5	21%
10-Year Property	
year 1	8%
year 2	14%
year 3	12%
year 4 through 6	10%
year 7 through 10	9%

The percentage for 15-year property depends on when it was placed in service during the year and on the year in question. It will vary from 1 to 12 percent. Your tax consultant will be able to advise you of the latest percentages as they may affect your property.

The expected salvage value is not subtracted from its basis when figuring your deduction under this form of depreciation.

The resulting depreciation figures, when used in the income statement, add to the total cost of goods and therefore decrease net income. As noted earlier Creative Manufacturing did not include this item on its income statement but did so on its "Provision For Federal Income Tax" schedule.

Depreciation is also used in the calculation of cash flow. *The classic formulation for cash flow* is that it is equal to net income plus depreciation. There is a common usage that states that depreciation is a "source of funds." In reality, this is a misnomer. Depreciation as such does not create any funds. It is only an accounting entry. However, to the extent it has reduced net income, it must be recognized and reversed. Common practice has led to labeling depreciation as an income source, when in fact net income merely has to be restored to its prewrite-off level.

Depreciation is also used to calculate income taxes. As noted above, depreciation is subtracted from gross income (profit before taxes) to reduce a company's total taxable income.

Table 8.3 is Creative Manufacturing's depreciation schedule. The company chose to use the straight-line method and an asset life of 10 years. The capital equipment requirements and expenditures were determined in the previous chapter's department plans and are shown in the left column of Table 8.3. Creative calculated the annual depreciation value by first applying 10 percent of an asset's value to each of 10 subsequent years beginning with the year that the asset was purchased. It did so for the five years after the assets were purchased. The depreciation values were summed to arrive at a total for the year in question. Creative assumed that there would not be any salvage value at the end of the 10 year period.

PROVISION FOR INCOME TAXES

Rather than provide a primer on the complex subject of income tax—a matter better left to the experts—this section merely attempts to show how depreciation and capital losses reduce total taxable income and how tax rates are applied to that income. The tax rates shown in these examples were in effect at the time Creative Manufacturing prepared its plan in 1979. You should check with the Internal Revenue Service for the most recent tax laws when you prepare your own business plan.

Corporate taxable income consists of two components: profit from the sale of capital assets and all other income defined as "ordinary income."

TABLE 8.3 Creative Manufacturing, Inc., Depreciation Schedule, Straight line, 10 Year
(Assumes 0 Salvage Value)
($000)

	Year 1	Year 2	Year 3	Year 4	Year 5	Year 6	Year 7	Year 8	Year 9	Year 10	Year 11	Year 12	Year 13
	73	73	73	73	73	73	73	73	73	73	0	0	0
	0	25.4	25.4	25.4	25.4	25.4	25.4	25.4	25.4	25.4	25.4	0	0
	0	0	47.9	47.9	47.9	47.9	47.9	47.9	47.9	47.9	47.9	47.9	0
	0	0	0	106.6	106.6	106.6	106.6	106.6	106.6	106.6	106.6	106.6	106.6
	0	0	0	0	200.2	200.2	200.2	200.2	200.2	200.2	200.2	200.2	200.2
Total	73	98	146	253	453	453	453	453	453	453	380	355	307

Capital assets, such as security investments, are defined as assets not bought or sold in the ordinary course of a firm's business. Gains and losses on the sale of capital assets are defined as capital gains and losses, and under special circumstances they receive special tax treatment. Real and depreciable property used in business are not defined as capital assets, but will be treated as such in the event of a net gain. In the event of a net loss on real and depreciable property used in the business, the full amount may be deducted from ordinary income.

At the time that Creative Manufacturing prepared its business plan in 1979, the tax laws stated that the sale of a capital asset held for six months or less gave rise to a short-term gain or loss. Its disposal, when held for more than six months, produced a long-term gain or loss. Short-term capital gains less short-term capital losses equal net short-term gains. Net short-term gains are added to the firms's ordinary income and taxed at regular corporate income tax rates. For net long-term capital gains, (long-term gains less long-term losses), the tax was limited to 30 percent.

Depreciable assets, such as a machine tool, are subject to depreciation. Their tax cost is defined as the original purchase price less accumulated depreciation. If a company sells a machine for more than its book value, it may incur either a capital gain or ordinary income for tax purposes. The sale of a depreciable asset is subject to the capital gains tax when the gain exceeds the amount of depreciation taken.

Any ordinary corporate operating loss can be carried back three years and forward five. In 1979, the law stated that the loss must be carried back to the earliest year, the remainder applied to the second earliest year, and so on. For example, an operating loss in 1977 could be used to reduce taxable income in 1974, 1975, 1976, 1978, 1979, 1980, 1981, and 1982. This sequence must be followed.

When Creative Manufacturing's plan was written in 1979, the first $25,000 of corporate taxable income was taxed at a 20 percent rate. The next $25,000 was taxed at a 22 percent rate. And all income over $50,000 was taxed at a 48 percent rate. Therefore, if a firm's taxable income were $100,000, for example, the tax would be computed as follows:

$$20\% \times 25{,}000 = \$5{,}000$$
$$22\% \times 25{,}000 = \$5{,}500$$
$$48\% \times 50{,}000 = \$24{,}000$$
$$\text{Total} = \$34{,}500$$

This relatively simple tax structure has wide implications for business planning. Because the tax rate more than doubles when corporate income rises above $50,000, it clearly would pay to break moderately sized companies into two or more separate corporations to hold the income of each unit under $50,000 and thus keep the tax rate at 22 percent. This was in fact done for many years by several firms, with some groups (retail chains, small loan companies) having literally thousands of separate corporations. However, the Tax Reform Act of 1969 eliminated the advantages of multiple corporations. If a group of firms having common ownership files separate returns for each company, then only one firm will be taxed at the low initial rates.

Table 8.4 is Creative Manufacturing's proforma five year income tax schedule. It was developed along the lines discussed in this chapter. The first entry shows Creative Manufacturing's pretax earnings (losses) during the first five years of operation. Note that there was a $1,028,000 operating loss during the first year of operation. Depreciation was subtracted from earnings to reduce the gross taxable income.

Since the first year had an operating loss, subtracting depreciation from "profit (loss) before taxes" increased the deduction for subsequent years to $1,101,000. This $1,101,000 was carried into the second and third years to reduced the net taxable income for those years. This reduced the net taxable income for the second year to zero and reduced the third year by $477,000.

The standard income tax rates of 20 percent on the first $25,000, 22 percent on the second $25,000, and 48 percent above $50,000 were applied to the net taxable income in the third, fourth, and fifth years. The result was Creative Manufacturing's net profit (loss).

Creative Manufacturing and all other firms must estimate taxable income for the current year and pay one fourth of the estimated tax on January 15, April 15, June 15, and September 15.

TABLE 8.4   Creative Manufacturing, Inc., Provision For Federal Income Tax ($000)

	Year 1	Year 2	Year 3	Year 4	Year 5
Profit (loss = −) before taxes	−1028	752	1626	3806	6735
Depreciation	73	98	146	253	453
Gross taxable income	−1101	654	1480	3553	6382
Tax loss carry forward	0	−654	−447	0	0
Net taxable income	0	0	1033	3553	6282
Tax 1st $25K at 20%	0	0	5	5	5
Tax 2d $25K at 22%	0	0	5.5	5.5	5.5
Tax above $50K at 48%	0	0	472	1681	2991
Total tax due	0	0	482	1692	3002
Net profit (loss = −)	−1028	752	1158	2114	3733
Cum profit (loss = −)	−1028	−276	868	2982	6715

The estimated taxes paid must be at least 80 percent of actual taxes, or the firm will be subject to penalties.

BALANCE SHEET

A balance sheet represents a company's financial picture as it is on one particular day of the year, as though the wheels of the company were momentarily at a standstill.

The balance sheet is divided in two. On the left (or at the top) are assets, on the right (or at the bottom), the liabilities and stockholders' equity. Both sides are always in balance. In the assets column are listed all the goods and property owned as well as uncollected claims against other parties.

The assets are arranged from top to bottom in order of decreasing liquidity. That is, assets toward the top of the column can be converted to cash sooner than those toward the bottom of the column. The top group of assets constitutes current assets—cash, marketable securities, accounts receivable, and inventories, which are expected to be converted into cash within one year.

The right side of the balance sheet is arranged similarly and lists all debts due. Those items toward the top of the claims column will mature and must be paid off relatively soon. Those further down the column are due in the more-distant future. Current liabilities must be paid off in one year.

Stockholders' equity is the amount of stockholder interest in the company, the amount for which the company is accountable to its stockholders. Because the firm never has to "pay off" common stockholders, common stock and retained earnings represent "permanent" capital.

Table 8.5 is Creative Manufacturing's proforma five year balance sheet. Its arrangement is slightly different from the norm because it shows five years instead of one. Because of this, the

TABLE 8.5   Creative Manufacturing, Inc., Balance Sheet (Proforma), Month 12 / Month End ($000)

	Year 1	Year 2	Year 3	Year 4	Year 5
Assets					
Cash	389	27	241	392	3,340
Receivables	385	1,050	1,598	3,553	6,672
Inventories	354	948	2,103	4,002	5,042
Total current assets	1,128	2,025	3,942	7,947	15,054
Gross plant & equipment	730	984	1,463	2,529	4,531
Less depreciation	73	98	146	253	453
Net plant & equipment	657	886	1,317	2,276	4,078
Total assets	1,785	2,911	5,259	10,223	19,132
Claims on Assets					
Accounts payable	213	520	1,017	2,034	2,543
Federal income tax	0	0	483	1,692	3,002
Total current liabilities	213	520	1,500	3,726	5,545
Stockholders interest	1,572	2,391	3,759	6,497	13,587
Total claims on assets	1,785	2,911	5,259	10,223	19,132

1. Assumes initial capitalization of $1,785.

2. Year 6 assumes a 25% growth-sales increase to $60,039.

top half under "assets" is actually the left side of the balance sheet. The bottom half under "claims on assets" is actually the right side of the balance sheet.

Creative Manufacturing started operation with a first-year capitalization of $1,785,000. All of it was supplied by its investors since it had no bank debt. Each item on the balance sheet will be discussed as to what it means and how it works.

Current assets include cash and those assets in the normal course of business that will be turned into cash in the reasonably near future, usually within one year from the date of the balance sheet.

Cash is what the name implies: bills and silver in the petty cash fund and money on deposit in the bank, plus short-term U.S. government securities.

Marketable securities is an item that would normally be listed under cash. This asset represents temporary investment of excess or idle cash that is not needed immediately. It is usually invested in commercial paper and government securities. Because these funds may be needed on short notice, it is essential that the securities be readily marketable and subject to a minimum of price fluctuation. The general practice is to show marketable securities at cost, with the market value listed parenthetically.

Creative Manufacturing does not own any marketable securities because as a new company, all of its money is needed to make its business grow.

Accounts receivable or receivables represent the amount not yet collected from customers to whom goods were shipped. Creative Manufacturing's customers are on a 30 day commercial account. However, as discussed earlier, the company does not expect payment for 60 days. Normally a company would have a provision for bad debts, to be subtracted from the uncollectable receivables. Bad debts, of course, are receivables that are not paid by customers, perhaps because of some financial difficulties befalling their own businesses.

A manufacturer's inventory is composed of three items: raw materials to be used in the product, partially finished goods in process of manufacture, and finished goods ready for shipment to customers. The generally accepted method of valuation of the inventory is at cost or market, whichever is lower.

The total current assets item includes, primarily, cash, marketable securities, accounts receivable, and inventories.

Fixed assets, also called property, plant and equipment, represents those assets not intended for sale that are used over and over again to manufacture the product, display it, warehouse it, and transport it. Included are land, buildings, machinery, equipment, furniture, automobiles, and trucks. A generally accepted and approved method for valuation is cost minus the depreciation accumulated by the date of the balance sheet.

Depreciation has been defined for accounting purposes as the decline in useful value of a fixed asset due to wear and tear from use and passage of time, or even, when not in use, by reason of action of the elements. Fixed assets can also suffer a decline in useful value from obsolescence, because new inventions and more-advanced techniques that come to light make the present equipment out of date. The cost incurred to acquire property, plant, and equipment must be spread over each asset's useful life. Four principal methods of depreciation were discussed earlier in this chapter.

Creative Manufacturing chose to use the straight-line method to depreciate its assets over a 10 year period. The amount of depreciation was subtracted from gross plant and equipment to arrive at net plant and equipment. For balance sheet purposes, this is the valuation in property, plant, and equipment. Therefore, fixed assets generally consist of the cost of the various assets in this classification, diminished by the depreciation accumulated to the date of the financial statement.

Prepayments, deferred charges, and intangibles (goodwill, patents, trademarks) are assets that also must be included when applicable. A new company like Creative Manufacturing, not having had time to accumulate them, would not carry them on its balance sheet.

Prepayments can arise, for instance, by paying off a three year fire insurance policy in a single year or by paying for leased equipment for two years in advance. At the balance sheet date, there exists an unused or unspent item that will be use in future years. In these situations, two years' worth of insurance premiums are still unused and one years' rental value of the leased equipment is still unused at the end of the first year. If advance payments had not been made, the company would have more cash in the bank.

Deferred charges represent a type of asset similar to prepayments. As an example, a manufacturer may have spent a large sum of money for introducing a new product, for research and development, or for moving a plant and personnel to a new location. The benefits will be spread over several years. Therefore, management does not feel that it is reasonable to charge off the full expenditure in the year it was spent. Instead it will be written off over several years according to approved accounting principles.

Intangibles are defined as assets having no physical existence yet having substantial value to the company. The common example is goodwill. Practices for assigning value to this asset vary considerably.

All of the asset items—total current assets, net plant and equipment, and where applicable, prepayments, deferred charges, and intangibles—when added together, constitute the balance sheet item called total assets.

Claims on assets include current liabilities, long-term liabilities, and stockholders' equity.

Current liabilities include all debts that must be paid within the coming year. This category is a companion to current assets because these assets are the source from which payments are made on current debts.

Accounts payable is the first item of the current-liabilities section of Creative Manufacturing's balance sheet. It represents the amount that the company owes to its regular business creditors from whom it has bought goods on an open account.

When applicable, notes payable and accrued expenses payable would be in this category. Creative Manufacturing had neither of these expenses. Notes payable is the money owed to a bank or other lender. Accrued expenses payable represents money owed for salaries and wages to employees, interest on funds borrowed from banks and from bond holders, fees to attorneys, insurance premiums, pensions, and similar items. To the extent that the accounts accrued are unpaid at the date of the balance sheet, they are grouped as a total under accrued expenses payable.

Federal income tax is the debt due to the Internal Revenue Service and is the same type of liability as any other item under accrued expenses payable. Because of its amount and importance, it is generally stated separately.

All of the current liability items—accounts payable, federal income taxes, and where applicable, notes payable, and accrued expenses payable—when added together, constitute the balance sheet item called total current liabilities.

Long-term liabilities is a debt that Creative Manufacturing was fortunate not to have incurred. It should however, be mentioned here that long-term liabilities are debts due after one year from the date of the financial report. Examples would be long-term mortgage loans or bonds.

Stockholders' equity is the total equity interest that all stockholders have in a corporation. It is the corporation's net worth after subtracting all liabilities. Creative Manufacturing's balance sheet shows this item only as stockholders' interest. However stockholders' equity is generally separated into three categories: capital stock, capital surplus, and accumulated retained earnings.

Capital stock represents shares in the proprietary interest in the company. These shares are represented by stock certificates issued by the corporation to its shareholders. Preferred stock certificates have preference over other shares in receiving dividends or assets in case of liquidation, or both. Additionally, preferred stock dividends are usually limited to some maximum value, a percentage of the stock's par value. Common stock has no maximum limit on dividends, which are payable in each year that the board of directors declares a dividend. In prosperous times when company earnings are high, dividends may also be high. And when earnings drop, so may common-stock dividends.

Capital surplus is the amount paid in by shareholders over the par or legal value of each share. If a company's common stock has a par value of $5.00 and is sold for $7.00 per share, then $2.00 would be shown in capital surplus.

Accumulated retained earnings are the profits left in the business after paying preferred- and common-stock dividends. This figure accumulates year after year.

All of the "claims on assets" items—accounts payable; when applicable, notes payable and accrued expenses payable; federal income taxes; and stockholders' equity—when added together, constitute the balance sheet item known as "total claims on assets." Total assets and total claims on assets must always be equal.

RATIO ANALYSIS

Ratio analysis is a tool that relates balance sheet and income statement items on one another. By permitting the charting of a firm's history and the evaluation of its present position, such analysis allows a financial manager to anticipate the reactions of investors and creditors and thus gives him an insight into how his attempts to acquire funds are likely to be received.

Ratios are classified into four basic types: liquidity, leverage, activity, and profitability. An explanation of each will be presented and the ratios will then be applied to Creative Manufacturing's proforma balance sheet and income statement for its first five years of operation. This example will illustrate the value of ratio analysis.

Liquidity Ratios

Examples of liquidity ratios include the current ratio, and the quick ratio also known as the acid test.

The *current ratio* is computed by dividing current assets by current liabilities. Current assets normally include cash, marketable securities, accounts receivable, and inventories. Current liabilities consist of accounts payable, short-term notes payable, current maturities of long-term debt, accrued income taxes, and other accrued expenses (principally wages).

The current ratio is the most commonly used measure of short-term solvency since it indicates the extent to which the claims of short-term creditors are covered by assets that are expected to be converted to cash in a period roughly corresponding to the maturity of the claims.

$$\text{Current ratio} = \frac{\text{Current assets}}{\text{Current liabilities}}$$

The Industry average for the current ratio is 2.5:1.

The following are the proforma current ratios for Creative Manufacturing's first five years of operation. Note: All dollars are in thousands.

$$\text{Year 1} = \frac{\$1128}{\$213} = 5.29$$

$$\text{Year 2} = \frac{\$2025}{\$520} = 3.89$$

$$\text{Year 3} = \frac{\$3942}{\$1500} = 2.63$$

$$\text{Year 4} = \frac{\$7947}{\$3726} = 2.13$$

$$\text{Year 5} = \frac{\$15054}{\$5545} = 2.72$$

The *quick ratio*, better known as the *acid test*, is calculated by deducting inventories from current assets and dividing the remainder by current liabilities. Inventories are typically the least liquid of a firm's current assets and the assets on which losses are most likely to occur upon liquidation. This measure of the firm's ability to pay off short-term obligations without relying solely on inventories is important.

$$\text{Quick (acid test) ratio} = \frac{\text{Current assets} - \text{inventories}}{\text{Current liabilities}}$$

The industry average for this ratio is 1:1.

The following are the proforma quick ratios for Creative Manufacturing's first five years of operation. Notes: All dollars are in thousands. Years 1 and 2 are distorted because Creative Manufacturing paid no income taxes in these years.

$$\text{Year 1} = \frac{\$1128 - \$354}{\$213} = 3.63$$

$$\text{Year 2} = \frac{\$2025 - \$948}{\$520} = 2.07$$

$$\text{Year 3} = \frac{\$3942 - \$2103}{\$1500} = 1.23$$

$$\text{Year 4} = \frac{\$7947 - \$4002}{\$3726} = 1.06$$

$$\text{Year 5} = \frac{\$15,054 - \$5042}{\$5545} = 1.81$$

Leverage Ratios

Leverage ratios measure the funds supplied by owners as compared with the financing provided by the firm's creditors. If owners have provided only a small portion of total financing, the risks of the enterprise are borne mainly by the creditors. By raising funds through debt, the owners gain the benefits of maintaining control of the firm with a limited investment. If the firm earns more on the borrowed funds than it pays in interest, the return to the owners is magnified.

Examples of leverage ratios include the debt ratio, times interest earned, and fixed-charge coverage ratios.

Debt ratio measures the percentage of total funds provided by the creditors. Debt includes current liabilities and all bonds.

$$\text{Debt ratio} = \frac{\text{Total debt}}{\text{Total assets}}$$

The industry average for this ratio is .33:1

Since Creative Manufacturing's investor owners provided all of the initial capitalization, and none was provided through debt financing, this ratio does not apply to them for the firm's first five years of operation.

The *times interest earned ratio* is calculated by dividing earnings, before interest and taxes, by the interest charges. The times interest earned ratio measures the extent to which earnings can decline without resultant financial embarrassment to the firm because of inability to meet annual interest costs.

$$\text{Times interest earned} = \frac{\text{Profit before taxes} + \text{interest charges}}{\text{Interest charges}}$$

The industry average for this ratio is 8:1

Since Creative Manufacturing did not have any bank debt and did not pay any interest charges, this ratio does not apply to it for the first five years of its operation.

The *fixed-charge coverage ratio* is somewhat more inclusive than the times interest earned ratio in that is recognizes that many firms lease assets and incur long-term obligations under lease contracts. As a result, this ratio is sometimes preferable to the times interest earned ratio for some financial analysis. *Fixed charges* are defined as interest plus annual long-term lease obligations.

$$\text{Fixed-charge coverage} = \frac{\text{Profit before taxes} + \text{interest charge} + \text{lease obligations}}{\text{Interest charges} + \text{lease obligations}}$$

The industry average for this ratio is 5.5:1.

Since Creative Manufacturing did not have any bank debt and did not pay any interest charges or have any lease obligation payments, this ratio does not apply to it for the five years of its operation.

Activity Ratios

Activity ratios measure how effectively the firm employs the resources at its command. These ratios involve comparisons between the level of sales and investment in various asset accounts. Examples of activity ratios include the inventory turnover ratio, fixed-assets ratio, and total assets turnover ratio.

The *inventory turnover ratio* is sales divided by inventories.

$$\text{Inventory turnover ratio} = \frac{\text{Sales}}{\text{Inventory}}$$

The industrial average for this ratio is 9:1.
The average for the OEM widget industry is 3 to 4:1.

The following are the proforma inventory turnover ratios for Creative Manufacturing for the first five years of its operation. Note: All dollars are in thousands.

$$\text{Year 1} = \frac{\$460}{\$354} = 1.3$$

$$\text{Year 2} = \frac{\$4888}{\$948} = 5.15$$

$$\text{Year 3} = \frac{\$9583}{\$2103} = 4.56$$

$$\text{Year 4} = \frac{\$21,318}{\$4002} = 5.33$$

$$\text{Year 5} = \frac{\$40,031}{\$5042} = 7.9$$

Fixed-asset turnover is the ratio of sales to fixed assets and measures the turnover of plant and equipment.

$$\text{Fixed-asset turnover ratio} = \frac{\text{Sales}}{\text{Net fixed assets}}$$

The industry average for this ratio is 5:1.

The following are the proforma fixed-asset turnover ratios for Creative Manufacturing for the first five years of its operation. Note: All dollars are in thousands.

$$\text{Year 1} = \frac{\$460}{\$657} = .7$$

$$\text{Year 2} = \frac{\$4888}{\$886} = 5.52$$

$$\text{Year 3} = \frac{\$9583}{\$1317} = 7.27$$

$$\text{Year 4} = \frac{\$21{,}318}{\$2276} = 9.4$$

$$\text{Year 5} = \frac{\$40{,}031}{\$4078} = 9.8$$

The *total assets turnover ratio* measures the turnover of all of the firm's assets and is calculated by dividing sales by total assets.

$$\text{Total assets turnover ratio} = \frac{\text{Sales}}{\text{Total assets}}$$

The industry average for this ratio is 2:1.

The following are the proforma total assets turnover ratios for Creative Manufacturing for the first five years of its operation. Note: Dollars are in thousands.

$$\text{Year 1} = \frac{\$460}{\$1785} = .26$$

$$\text{Year 2} = \frac{\$4888}{\$2911} = 1.68$$

$$\text{Year 3} = \frac{\$9583}{\$5259} = 1.8$$

$$\text{Year 4} = \frac{\$21,318}{\$10,223} = 2.09$$

$$\text{Year 5} = \frac{\$40,031}{\$19,132} = 2.09$$

Profitability Ratios

Profitability is the net result of many policies and decisions. The profitability ratios give final answers about how effectively the firm is being managed. Examples of profitability ratios include the profit margin or sales ratio and the return on total assets ratio, known as the return on investment ratio.

Profit margin or sales ratio is computed by dividing net profit after taxes by sales, which gives the profit per dollar of sales.

$$\text{Profit margin ratio} = \frac{\text{Net profit after taxes}}{\text{Sales}}$$

The 1977 industry average, including the widget industry, was 5 percent.

The following are the proforma profit margin ratios for Creative Manufacturing for their first five years of operation. Note: All dollars are in thousands.

$$\text{Year 1} = \frac{(\$1028) - 0}{\$460} = (224\%)$$

$$\text{Year 2} = \frac{\$752 - 0}{\$4888} = 15\%$$

$$\text{Year 3} = \frac{\$1626 - \$483}{\$9583} = 11.9\%$$

$$\text{Year 4} = \frac{\$3806 - \$1692}{\$21,318} = 9.9\%$$

$$\text{Year 5} = \frac{\$6375 - \$3002}{\$40,031} = 9.3\%$$

The return on total assets, which is the ratio of net profit to total assets, measures the return on total investment in the firm (ROI).

$$\text{Return on total assets ratio} = \frac{\text{Net profit after taxes}}{\text{Total assets}}$$

The industry average for this ratio is 10 percent.

The following are the proforma return on total assets ratios for Creative Manufacturing for the first five years of its operation. Note: All dollars are in thousands.

$$\text{Year 1} = \frac{(\$1028) - 0}{\$1785} = (58\%)$$

$$\text{Year 2} = \frac{\$752 - 0}{\$2911} = 25.8\%$$

$$\text{Year 3} = \frac{\$1626 - \$483}{\$5259} = 21.7\%$$

$$\text{Year 4} = \frac{\$3806 - \$1692}{\$10,233} = 20.6\%$$

$$\text{Year 5} = \frac{\$6735 - \$3002}{\$19,132} = 19.5\%$$

In summary, this chapter has reviewed the key financial statements of a company and showed with examples how they are developed. The review included Creative Manufacturing's income statement, cash flow statement, depreciation schedule, provision for income tax, and balance sheet.

As a conclusion, the chapter discussed ratio analysis, again using Creative Manufacturing's financial statements as an example. Ratio analysis illustrates how to tie the balance sheet and income statements together into meaningful relationships.

All of these financial statements and ratios indicate that Creative Manufacturing appeared to be a worthwhile and potentially profitable venture. The investors proceeded as planned.

9

PUTTING IT ALL TOGETHER: A SUMMARY

The preceding chapters have been a sequential development of the necessary elements for an effective business plan. This concluding chapter will illustrate how to summarize and arrange this data into the necessary and manageable components for an effective presentation. In so doing, it will use the summarized sections of Creative Manufacturing's business plan as an example.

YOUR AUDIENCE

Knowing *who* your audience is and what they expect, want to know, see, and hear from a business plan is a necessary prelude to an effective summary and organization.

If your audience is your department or general manager who will be reviewing your next year's plans, your summary will be different from one prepared for the corporate executive staff or the financial community.

There is one common thread woven through all plans regardless of your audience, namely, brevity. But it is brevity with all of the necessary facts to enable a decision. Busy executives and investors do not generally like or want to be deluged with a morass of detail. They usually want the meat or essence of a plan or program. Each plan section should be summarized into one page if possible, but no more than two or three at the most. The detailed, backup data can be included as an addendum or kept in reserve until asked for by the executives or their subordinates.

If your audience is a department manager or even a general manager of a small firm, your summary can include many specific details of the operation, including references to departments, personnel, equipment, and products and all interwoven with the working vocabulary of the operation or the industry. This type of audience is likely to demand more details than a plan prepared for an executive staff or financial community because of its familiarity with the organization's detail. It is best at the outset to find out what this audience wants and tailor the product (your plan) to fit its needs.

If your audience is the executive staff or the financial community, chances are they are not intimately familiar with the details of your operation. Because they are not, detailed references to personnel and equipment, certain specialized language should be omitted unless they add some special significance to the discussion. The examples that follow in this chapter were prepared with this in mind. Because Creative Manufacturing's products are technical in nature, not all of the specialized language has been eliminated—but it has been kept to a minimum.

Summarized plan sections should be prepared on easy-to-read white or soft-brown paper, typed double spaced with a pica font and presented in an appropriate folder or binder. Whoever the audience is, offering it an attractive, easy-to-read plan is the first step to a plan's acceptance. Its organization and appearance are a direct reflection of its author's thinking and provide an insight into its potential success or failure.

BUSINESS OPPORTUNITY SUMMARY

This section, the cornerstone of your summarized plan, is generally the first part of a plan reviewed by your audience. If this section is poorly written or provides insufficient or misleading facts, the audience may not read further. The business opportunity summary simply, clearly, and succinctly present the facts of the business opportunity in three pages or less.

It should begin with an opening paragraph identifying your product or service and the industry it will serve. These introductory remarks can be followed by a paragraph about the industry's size and growth rate. How large was the market last year and this year, and what are the expectations three years into the future? What is the percentage of growth this year over last? What is contributing to growth, and how long is it likely to be sustained? And why? This is important! Few people want to enter an industry that is not growing because its chances for success are reduced. If an industry is stagnating, it generally means that the companies already participating are probably fighting desperately with one another just to stay alive.

If an industry is growing at a moderate rate and if the growth is expected to be sustained for several years, it generally means that the market can support the growth of existing participants and new ones as well. The key words here are *sustained growth for several years*. It takes a number of years, usually three to five, just to recover an investment. Investors want to be assured of having a reasonably good chance to recover their initial investment and to realize a profit as well. Not too many investors would be willing to "back" the second generation hula hoop.

The business opportunity summary should include a few, short paragraphs about the company or program under discussion, its location and products, what market segment it will serve, when it can begin serving it, its expected profits, and when they will be realized.

A company's locations should be identified, along with the reason for its being there. Being in a particular location just because the proposed president lives there is generally not good enough. A location is generally chosen for its natural resources, proximity to its market, low labor rates, or other good reasons.

The product and market segment it is expected to serve should be described, not in glowing technological terms but in simple, down-to-earth language. Talk about what the product does and how it fits into the market picture. This segment should include a few clear-cut statements about why the product is as good as, or better than, current products on the market. If it is worse than existing competitive products, a statement should be included as to why it is expected to succeed.

If there are any special circumstances surrounding the product such as a license to build an already-successful device, such as Creative Manufacturing's widget system, these should be discussed as well.

A short statement about when the company will begin to serve the market should be included. This, along with previous statements about market size and growth rate, will indicate in what part of the product cycle, (introduction, rapid growth, or maturity) that the market will be served.

The most important statement to investors is the one about expected profits: how much and when. After all, this is what they are in it for. Profit is the basic reason for investing. The forecast should be short and factual and taken from the prepared income statement.

A concluding summary statement should state once again the business opportunity and the advantages that can be realized from its pursuit.

Figure 9.1 is the business opportunity summary taken from Creative Manufacturing's business plan. It is included because it demonstrates all of the points outlined in this discussion.

PRODUCT PLAN

This summary should be a brief, descriptive overview of the initial product offering in very general terms, basically identifying what it is and what it does. Operational details should be left to specifications or other documentation that should be included in an appendix. Any special features that will make it more marketable should be mentioned, also in general terms. If there is going to be a product enhancement or even a second-generation product, this should be noted.

The important point here is to keep things brief and informa-

The widget has been the primary element for widget systems for almost two decades and no technology is likely to replace it during the eighties.

In 1978, the estimated worldwide revenues generated by widgets were $3.3 billion. This represents a 17 percent increase over 1977. Forecasts through 1981 anticipate uninterrupted growth for the industry owing to a demand for on-line widgets that is accelerating faster than the rate of widget system installations. This situation has evolved because the widget capacity per installation is rapidly increasing. Worldwide revenues for 1981 are forecast as $4.75 billion, which represents an average annual growth rate of 14 percent.

This business plan proposes that a company be formed to enter a particular segment of the widget marketplace: The large-capacity widget marketplace!

The cornerstone of this plan is the availability of a marketing and manufacturing license from Diversified Manufacturing Corporation for its widget. This unit in its initial configuration is designed and is released. It is in pilot production and is currently entering full-scale production at the Orange facility of Diversified Manufacturing Corporation.

This product is, in many respects, a proven product. Its design is based on an earlier low-capacity widget. Diversified Manufacturing Corporation has installed over 1000 of these devices over the past three years.

It is expected that Diversified Manufacturing Corporation will be an equity participant in Creative Manufacturing, Inc., in exchange for its product license. There are a number of advantages that arise as a result of obtaining this license:

1. The product is proven from an engineering standpoint.
2. The product family is known in the marketplace and has a good reputation.
3. The product will become available at a time when the market segment is expected to expand rapidly because of acceptance of high-capacity widgets.
4. The investment in engineering required by Creative Manufacturing is low in comparison to similar start-up manufacturing concerns.

As a result of the licensing agreement, manufacturing activities can start immediately, and initial shipments will be made during the seventh month of operation.

In the period between start-up and shipments, the initial sales effort will be supported by a small quantity of widgets supplied by Diversified Manufacturing Corporation to be used for customer evaluation and demonstration. Estimated sales during the first year are $460,000, rising to $4.9 million and $9.6 in the second and third years, respectively.

Gross margin in the first quarter of the second year is calculated to be 39

FIGURE 9.1. Business, opportunity summary

percent and before-tax income at the end of the second year is forecast to be 18 percent.

The total required capital is estimated at $2.6 million, and positive cash flow is expected in the early part of the third year.

In summary, this plan identifies an opportunity to enter a rapidly expanding marketplace that has enormous potential for revenue and profit growth, using an already established product and an experienced and seasoned management team.

FIGURE 9.1. *Continued*

Widget II. Creative Manufacturing's initial product offering, Widget II, employ the latest technology and has a capacity of 158 operations per minute (as shown in the attached summary specifications). A detailed engineering product specification will be supplied by the company on request. Additional enhancements include compatibility with the industry standard widget interface/dual-port option, power sequencing, and additional information separators.

Intelligent Interface. An intelligent interface similar to that offered by Widget Technology Corporation will be offered as an additional product to reduce the amount of time necessary to integrate Widget II into a system. It will include a microcomputer-controller interface with error correction and a fast information buffer and international information mapping capabilities. It also will have a self-contained diagnostic tester that will help to reduce maintenance costs.

Widget III. The Widget II product will be followed by Widget III. This product will employ many features of the Widget II but will be enhanced by the prevailing technology, which will provide approximately four times the capacity with the same widget component configuration.

40 Percent Smaller Widgets. After completion of Widget III, Creative Manufacturing will design a 40 percent smaller widget. This product will be a compact, high-capacity widget and will be offered for low-cost widget systems.

The development of new products will be the result of a coordinated effort using market studies, sales, and engineering inputs.

With present and projected levels of development engineering capability, new products could be introduced at the rate of one per year.

FIGURE 9.2. Product plan

tive (which is sometimes difficult to do). Most entrepreneur's have a tendency to expound on the virtues of a product that is special to them. Once again, remember your audience and who they are. Your investors only care about what the product is and how it is going to make money for them. All other details are generally irrelevant. This may sound cruel and unsentimental, but these are the facts.

Figure 9.2 is the product plan summary for Creative Manufacturing's business plan, which succinctly describes its products in an acceptable manner and according to the above discussion.

MARKET OVERVIEW

The market summary should be no more than one or two pages in length. It should state what market segment the product offering will serve and the size of that market. Market figures in dollars should be included for several years to provide an overall growth perspective. Expected product prices should be included for these years to illustrate price increases or erosion. Some justification of a product's price may also be included, such as a competitor's advertised price, to demonstrate credibility.

Figure 9.3 is the market overview from Creative Manufacturing's business plan that illustrates this discussion.

COMPETITIVE SUMMARY

The competitive summary, while very brief, should completely state what other companies are offering for a similar product, their model numbers, and any other points that may highlight their products' strengths and weaknesses. Investors want to see at a glance what it is that they are up against and what may prevent them from earning a profit on their investment. Facts should not be hidden. This is not what someone wants, especially if they are about to invest a sizable amount of money.

Figure 9.4 is the competitive summary from Creative Manufacturing's business plan that illustrates these points.

The Widget II competes in the upper-capacity end of the 30 to 2000 DUPS fixed-widget market. The Widget II market is just beginning, with volume shipments expected to begin in late 1979.

The portion of the 30 to 200 DUPS fixed-widget market available to independent suppliers is expected to grow from $4.9 million in 1978 to $84 million in 1981. Most of the forecast shipments after 1980 will be greater than 80 DUPS capacity, as the lower end of the capacity range will be satisfied by the lower-cost and physically small widget products.

OEM Worldwide Shipments, 30–200 DUPS Fixed Widget

	1977	1978	1979	1980	1981
Market size ($million)	1.1	4.9	33.2	63.3	84.0
Average unit Price for 158 DUPS unit			4700	4600	4500
Widget Technology Corp.					
200 DUPS Model 4700					
Advertised Price, Qty. 100			4950		

Control Widget Data (CWD) unannounced but delivered 160 DUPS widget is reported to be competitively priced with Widget II.

FIGURE 9.3.   Market overview

SUGGESTED ORGANIZATION AND TABLE OF CONTENTS

Each of the elements for a successful business plan has been carefully developed in the preceeding chapters. In a successful plan, the individual elements must be organized in a logical sequence that will make sense to your audience. Enough information must be included to convey your intended message but not so much as to overwhelm and confuse. Remember, it is primarily facts that are of interest. Rhetoric, extolling the virtues of the

Major Competitors. Two companies have announced the latest widget products and a total of five companies are expected to be major competitors in the OEM widget market. These are shown below.

Major Competitors	Product Announced	Upgrade Planned
Control Widget Data	1630	Potential but no announced plans
InfoWid Corp.	393	
MemWid Co.	8300	
OK Widgets Co.	1500	Yes
Storage Widget Corp.	7600	Yes

Five companies offer versions of the older technology widgets that have maximum capacities near or above 80 DUPS. These are listed below.

Company	Model	Max. Capacity
Amwid Co.	100	87.8 DUPS
Control Widget Data	370	82.9 DUPS
Irish Widget Co.	5700	70.0 DUPS
MemWid Co.	409	75.0 DUPS
OK Widget Co.	7700	80.8 DUPS

Since the older-type widgets offered by the above companies are at the top of their DUPS capacity range, they are not expected to compete effectively with new-model widgets.

FIGURE 9.4. Competitive summary

product or company, is not what your potential investors want. They are interested in how much will be returned on their investment and when.

To secure their attention, keep your plan short and informative. Divide your plan into four or five sections. Your first section should provide an overview of the business opportunity, product plan, market overview, and competitive summary. These, of course, are all of the summaries discussed earlier in this chapter and provide an overview of the entire proposed company.

Contents

Section 1
  Business opportunity summary
  Product plan
  Market overview
  Competitive summary

Section 2
  Charter
  Organization
    Personal profiles
  Financial statements
    Income statement
    Cash flow analysis
    Depreciation schedule
    Provision for income tax
    Ratio analyses

Section 3
  Department plans
    Finance/Administration
    Marketing/Sales
    Engineering
    Manufacturing

Section 4
  Market studies
  Resumes key personnel
  Widget product specifications

FIGURE 9.5.   Creative Manufacturing, Inc. business plan

Your second section should provide more of the details pertinent to the company's operation and is the heart of the plan. It should include your charter, company organization, personnel profiles, and all of the proforma financial reports. The financial statements may be included as they were developed in Chapter 8. Specifically, these are the income statement, cash flow analysis, balance sheet, depreciation scehdule, income tax schedule, and ratio analyses.

Your third section should delve more into the operational details with a presentation of the department plans for Finance and Administration, Marketing, Engineering, and Manufacturing.

Your last section should be reserved for market studies, resumes of key personnel, and detailed product specifications.

Figure 9.5 is the table of contents for Creative Manufacturing's business plan that outlines the above business plan organization. This business plan organization offers another advantage in that it allows the plan to be tailored to the prospective audience. If investors are being approached for the first time, only the first section need be given to them. It provides enough information to let them know what is being attempted without "giving away the store." If they are still interested, give them section 2 during the next meeting. Further interest warrants giving them the remainder of the plan.

The above organization is by no means the optimum one. It is one that has been sucessful for this author. It is only through experience that the planner will learn what works best for a given industry and audience.

This author has attempted to provide many of the tools that are needed for writing an effective business plan. The lessons presented in these pages were learned through trial and error over many years because the writer could not locate any published works on this subject to smooth the way. It is his sincere desire that this book will provide some insight to other business planners about where to start and how to write effective business plans.

Good luck and best wishes for continued success!

APPENDIX

This Appendix includes two successful business plans that are shown exactly as they were presented to the investment community. Neither of these two plans were written by this author, however both exhibit many of the principles outlined in this book. The plan authors have graciously allowed us to reprint them in this book for the reader's use. Both companies were funded and are now in operation. The company names, as well as the participants, addresses, telephone numbers, schools, and places of employment, have been changed to protect their privacy.

The first of these two plans is a company which we have named Ministorage Corporation. They now manufacture cartridge disk drives, which are data storage devices used as the secondary memory for mini and personal computers. Even though the plan was written for a particular product and industry, the organization and principles around which it was written are sound and can be applied to any manufacturing firm.

The second plan is a fictitious company named Wiley Image, which was seeking a partially secured loan to enable it to pay franchise requirements to produce Olympic-Committee approved sport coins. These will be sold to Olympic Sponsors, U.S. Military Post Exchanges, and Swiss Sport Distribution. As with the first plan, the principles are sound and can be applied to other enterprises.

The author of this book, and the above business plans, wish you success in their use and application in your own enterprises!

BUSINESS PLAN

MINISTORAGE CORPORATION

BUSINESS PLAN
MINISTORAGE 5¼" CARTRIDGE DRIVE

Introduction and Summary
   Product Description
   Market Environment
      Technical Trends
      Competitive Companies
      Applications
   Assessment vs. Competition
   Marketing Strategy
   Development Milestones
   Product Cost Projections
   Organization and Staffing
   Financial Projections
   Resumes of Principals

INTRODUCTION AND SUMMARY

BUSINESS PLAN OF MINISTORAGE CORPORATION

Ministorage Corporation is a new business corporation whose primary activity is to design, manufacture, and sell, to OEM computer manufacturers, peripheral data storage devices known as a rigid disk drive.

Ministorage has essentially completed the mechanical design stage of its activity as a result of engineering development work by Carolyn Joseph, P.E., of Boston, Massachusetts. Ms. Joseph, one of the founders of Ministorage, has been an independent consulting engineer since 1974, specializing in disk drive design and servo mechanisms. Her major clients during that period have included BASF, Perkin-Elmer, Olivetti, and Memorex. Prior to entering independent consulting engineering practice, Ms. Joseph worked at Info Corporation (one year) and before that at Honeywell (five years) in the field of disk drive design.

Ministorage's first product rigid disk drive (known as FR 10 + 10) will be ready to enter the production and marketing stage 2Q82. To this end, an experienced team of management personnel in the disk drive field has been assembled (see attached resumes), and equity financing in the amount of $5 million is being sought. It is planned to complete the financing by the end of 1981 and to commence commercial production of the FR 10 + 10 by early 1983, approximately 6–12 months ahead of known competition. Twelve aspects of patent protection are being sought.

The FR 10 + 10 disk drive has a data storage capacity of 2 × 10 megabyte (= 2 × 10 million characters) of information, of which 10 megabytes are fixed within the drive and 10 megabytes are in a removable cartridge on which data may be stored "off-line" or "on the shelf." The drive is quite small (3¼" high by 5¾" wide by 8" deep). Projected manufacturing costs (see exhibit) indicate that it can be made profitably to sell in the relatively low price range of $1,000 to $1,500, to OEM purchasers. Because of its small size and low cost, it appears well-suited for use with the low-priced micro and mini computers sold to individuals and small businesses. Such small computers presently have limited internal memory capacity (usually 16K to 128K) and rely heavily on external disk drive storage (usually of the so-called "floppy" type) of up to 1 megabyte. Compared to the "floppys," the new FR 10 + 10 rigid cartridge disk drive represents:

1. A substantial increase in external storage capacity (10 fold or more).
2. Greater accuracy and durability.
3. Less handling.

Compared to 8" and 14" rigid disk drives, the FR 10 + 10 is smaller, less costly, and/or eliminates the need for a separate physical unit for the "back up" function. The FR 10 + 10 employs the standard ST506 controller interface, which will permit it to be attached in place of any of the existing 5¼" drives and some 8" drives.

The FR 10 + 10 is expected to have a product life cycle of about five years, commencing in early 1983. Given a six-month lead over competition, Ministorage's market share is projected to grow to 20% by 1986. Total market for this type of drive is estimated by industry consultants to start in 1983 with only 10,000 units and reach 165,000 units sold in 1985. These unit projections do not include similar levels of sales for 8" disk drives (30% more expensive) sold by Control Data now and under development by Perkin-Elmer, based on engineering originally provided to Perkin-Elmer by Carolyn Joseph as consultant. The remaining share of market in the 5¼" drives is expected to go mostly to a variety of small manufacturers also in a start up mode—including DMA System, Seagate Tech., Tandon Corporation and International Memories, Inc., and only later to "industry leaders." No smaller-size drives are known to be under development as yet.

The FR10 + 10 disk drive utilizes an aluminum disk with a magnetic coating. Ministorage will not manufacture disks. Instead, it will rely on their availability from a specialized manufacturer, such as Dysan Corporation of California. The fact that Dysan Corporation owns a significant but minority interest of a 5¼" competitor (Seagate Tech.) is not considered to be adverse to Ministorage.

Initial production of the FR10 + 10 is expected to take place in rented production facilities in New England using 20,000 square feet of space with 150 to 200 manufacturing employees. The initial marketing program will concentrate on creating top management personnel contacts with OEM computer manufacturers which will commence as soon as financing has been obtained.

It is the pattern within the disk drive industry to introduce a new product generation every 18–24 months. Ministorage's second generation product—the F40—will have a 40 megabyte fixed-only disk within the same size dimensions as the FR 10 + 10. Engineering on this generation is well underway and is believed to have a 6–12 month lead over competitors.

The competitive environment in the rigid disk drive market is changing very rapidly. Until 1979, Control Data Corporation had 42% of the revenues even though it sold only a 14" disk drive at a price of over $3,000 per unit. The first 8· disks appeared in 1979 produced by IMI were fixed. The Lark, a Control Data 8" cartridge, started volume shipments recently. In 1980, Seagate offered the first 5¼" disk drive (but without an integral back-up feature). The only other large corporations with possible plans to enter the 5¼" disk market are Texas Instruments and Xerox (through its Shugart subsidiary). Otherwise the competition will be among small businesses similar to Ministorage in size. Given a projected industry annual volume of 165,000 DD10 type units in 1985, and assuming an average selling price to OEM buyers of $1,300 per unit, these small businesses will be carving up some $200,000,000 of sales. Ministorage hopes to capture a 20% share based on lower cost and its engineering lead in providing integral back-up at this size and capacity.

To accomplish this goal, Ministorage has projected that $5M will take the company to a point where it can sustain itself on its own income (see attached financial exhibits). About $3M of this would be spent on operating expenses and capital equipment prior to volume production and the rest would finance the production ramp up.

Equity financing amounting to all of the $5 million is being sought during the last half of 1981. The form of such equity is flexible. No debt financing is planned in the current environment of high interest rates.

Management desires to retain a significant share of the equity. Present members of management include (see attached resumes):

James Brown	Chief Executive Officer	Honeywell
Linda Champion	Sales	Honeywell
Frank Edwards	Engineering	Wang
Carolyn Joseph	Research and Development	Various
Bill Diggins	Controller	

All of the above possess 15 to 20 years of experience in the disk drive industry. Mr. Brown has been a disk planner for Honeywell for nearly 10 years and as a result has intimate knowledge with the industry development. Ms. Champion has been in OEM sales of peripherals for 13 years and was personally responsible for the U.S. marketing of a 10 megabyte 10.5" drive for Honeywell over the last 5 years. Mr. Edwards has led disk developments for Data General and was hired to lead the in house development of disks by Wang. All are directors of Ministorage and will be full-time employees on completion of the financing. The exception to the foregoing is Carolyn Joseph, who will be placed on an exclusive consulting contract with Ministorage with regard to disk drives and related computer products, but will be permitted to continue her present consulting engineering activities in other fields, not to exceed one-third of her time.

Persons desiring to participate in the proposed financing or wishing further information, are invited to write or telephone

> Dr. Jack McLaughlin,
> MANAGEMENT CONSULTANT
> BUSINESS RESEARCH Consultants
> YARMOUTH, SAN JOSE, CA. 8000
> (408)888–8888

PRODUCT DESCRIPTION

DRIVE SPECIFICATIONS

Capacity 10 MB fixed, 10 MB removable

Average seek = 35M Sec.

Track-Track Seek = 5MSec.

Latency = 7.71M Sec.

Transfer rate = 5 Mbits/Sec.

BPI = 8000 (MFM)

Interface = ST506 compatible

\# Tracks = 566

Track Capacity = 8750 Bytes

Cap./Surf = 5 Mbytes

4235 RPM

Ri = 1.41"

Ro = 2.31"

Mechanical Drive Module
   Height   3.25"
   Width   5.75"
   Depth   8.0"

Electrical Module
   2 or 3 Boards = 8" × 5"
   Height   3.25"
   Width   5.75"
   Depth   8.0"

Cartridge Spec.
   "Club" Physical Standard
   10Mb capacity
   Height   7/8"
   Width   5 3/8"
   Depth   5.59"

Power Requirements
   5v ± 5%
   12v ± 10%
   25 watts

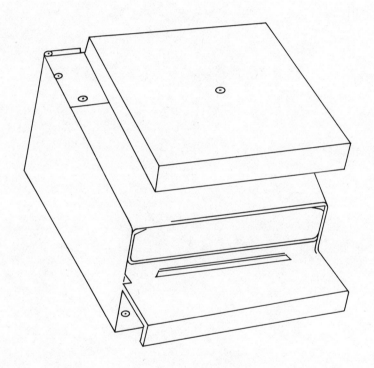

MARKET ENVIRONMENT

SMALL DISK MARKET

Partitioning of market by size:

14″ disks will be high capacity, high performance.
8″ fixed disks now 20–30MB increasing to 320MB by 1983.
8″ cartridges 16MB now increasing to 32–48 by 1983/4.
5¼″ fixed disks now 10MB increasing to 80MB by 1984.
5¼″ cartridges 8MB now increasing to 40MB by 1984.
3.5″ disks in 1982/3 5MB increasing to 20 MB by 1984/5.

Trend to lower cost:

Entry level at $500–$700 for 5–10MB.
$4000 for 100–200 MB.
$5000 for 600MB.

Trend to smaller size:

Smaller not always cheaper.
Packaging flexibility outweighs unit cost.
Small capacity units must be small physically.

Trend to fixed where back-up exists:

Media too easily damaged.
Environmental immunity.
Low absolute cost.
Higher capacity at one cost.
Packaging flexibility.
Back-up is offline.

Backup still a problem:

Floppies can support under 5MB.
GCR tape for 200MB and above.
Still no backup for 10–15MB.

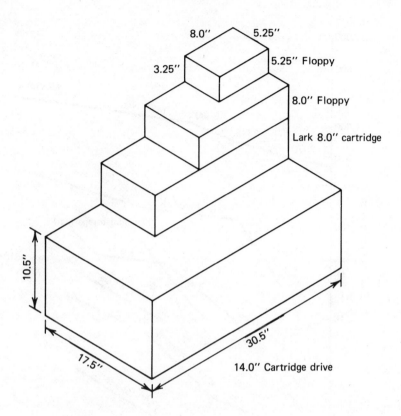

The Back-up Problem

Need for backup due to shift to fixed disk to save cost and greater environmental immunity.

Backup solution should not:

Degrade environmental immunity,

Cost more than difference between fixed and removable disk,

Require cumbersome operator procedures,

Take a long time to dump/restore,

Utilize costly media,

Contribute to the cabinetry space problem.

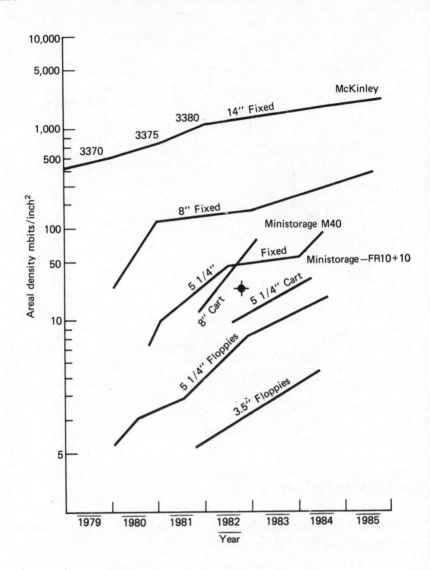

High end (above 200MB) GCR ½″ tape is good.
Low end (5MB) diskette back-up works.
In the middle range removable disk is still best.

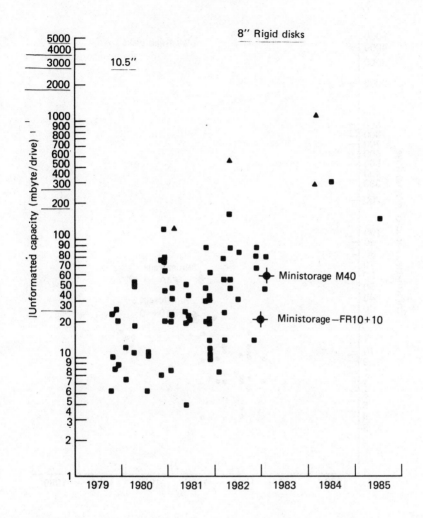

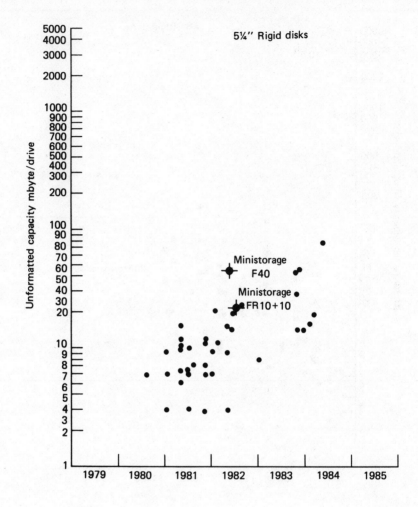

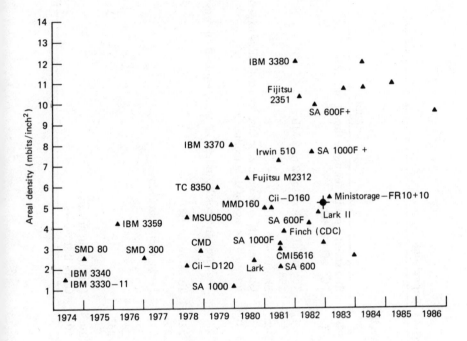

Backup Device Comparisons

Device	Media Capacity (MB)	Dump at full speed		Media cost	Considerations
		Per media (min.)	Per 10MB (min.)		
5¼"floppy	.655	2	15–20	3	Too small a media for more than 1 or 2 MB
	1.3MB	3	20	?	FCS 2Q 82, 4Q83
	2.0M	4			
8" floppy	1.3	2.1	19–20	4	Too small for less tha 2 or 3 MB
	2, 9, 18	?	?	?	1982, 83
Hifh perf. flopy	6–20	7–10	3–7	5–20	Short media life
Lark	6.7	.28	3	65–100	Good match to fixed media but for small files expensive for shelf storage of data exchange
5¼" cartridge	4–10MB	7–10	25–40		
IBM 8809 type	4.0	8.2	1	12	Too large and costly, unless ½" tape required anyway
¼" Cassettes					
3 M HCD 75	67	65	1	32	Too slow/costly
DEI	10	5	5	25	
	20	5	2.5	25	Large, costly, and slow
Tandberg	20	17	5	25	
	34	17	2.5	25	
CDC Sentinel	40	17	2.5	25	
DE-100 Cassettes					
TU58	.25	1.5	69–80	10	For commparison
Irwin	10	17	17	10	Good if it works

MARKET ENVIRONMENT

MARKET ENVIRONMENT

There are several major applications for this type of device:$6735 − $30021.   Small business system
2.   Small work station terminal
3.   Hobbyist (home market)
For the manufacturer there are several ways of reaching those users—all indirect:

1. Sales to CPU manufacturers who then incorporate the device into their units for hardware resale, usually to a system builder who adds software. Many of the companies in "2" also distribute in this manner in addition to their retail store outlet

2. Sales to large distributors via retail stores. Companies that run these are:

Tandy	Buys outside exclusively
Control data	Uses own disks
Digital Equipment	Uses own, CDC and ISS
IBM	Uses own but is buying 5¼ FDD
Data General	Uses own and others

3. Another mode of distribution is to the system builders who build software, buy hardware, and sell to the final users. They are generally small regional companies who vary in their ability to attach hardware. Many large companies have divisions that do system building for other divisions; examples are Ford, GM, and GE.

COMPETITION

Direct

New World Computers. Small company aimed at hobbyist market. Innovative design but the capacity is limited to 2MB. The drive is roughly competitive, but the removable cartridge is

$300. The combination of low capacity and high cartridge cost makes it noncompetitive.

CII-HB.   Large French company. Slow start with 10.5″ product, but now shipping product in U.S. and Europe. Future success better than past due to (1) Plans to offer 5¼″ technology gained from license with Seagate; (2) reorganization and expansion of U.S. sales force; (3) general broadening of product line. Will have 10MB removable plus 10MB fixed 5¼″ unit in 1983, 20MB removable plus 20MB fixed extension in 1984.

DMA Systems.   Brand new company with 5MB plus 5, 5¼″ product in 1982. Formed by a group of ex-Infomag people with $2 M of venture capital. Their drive specification of 5 fixed plus 5 removable is a marginal specification. Unless increased in capacity, it will be difficult to sell even at the estimated price of $1,200 to $1,300.

Seagate.   First in 5¼″ business, headed by previous founder of Shugart Associates. Very profitable due to issuance of licenses to two major firms. Shugart name and concept engenders trust by potential customers. Aggressive product roadmap including 5¼″ cartridge in 1983. Prognosis good.

Texas Instruments.   Gained U.S. license to Seagate product and has made improvements: Aggressive product roadmap plus massive company resources give good chance for success.

Control Data.   OEM industry leader in disks with greater than 46% of market. High overhead company with sales force of greater than 50 people. Product roadmap tends towards conservative and away from major emphasis on 5¼″ products. Success of 8″ Lark will force them into a protection mode though they have made inquiries about license of the Joseph drive.

Memorex.   Has announced 8″ cartridge, but problems ranging from financial to technical to general instability would indicate a poor prognosis for future and reduce any competitive concerns. Current takeover by Burroughs was preceded by cancellation of its low end OEM product line.

Shugart. Fixed only with no known plans to go to removable rigid drives. Shugart is a very powerful force in the floppy market and is expanding into fixed rigid drives and optical disk. Owned by Xerox, they can get the funding to support these ventures. They are very aggressive in their marketing.

Irwin International. A company started by Sam Irwin, the founder of Sycor. It has a 10 MB 5¼" disk with an embedded 10 MB tape cartridge. The concept is excellent, but the drive pushes technology quite far; 10,000 BPI and 900 TPI and 40 times the areal density of the nearest tape competitor. The drive is already well past the projected ship date. Funding is not a problem. In addition to over $4M in venture capital, Olivetti purchased 6% of the company. Prognosis unknown.

ASSESSMENT VERSUS COMPETITION

It has basic elements for entry into market:

SA506 interface (5¼" standard).

Standard "Club" cartridge.

5¼" floppy form factor.

Standard 5MBIT/SEC transfer rate.

Head tie down for shipment.

It has several major advantages:

Similar products are projected about one year later.

Most of market is concentrating on fixed.

The product is competitive against 5¼" fixed drives plus floppy both in device and media costs and offers better performance, reliability and simplicity as no other hardware does.

The 10MB cartridge sets it apart from all other 5¼" cartridges (5 to 6MB could be backed by diskette).

The large companies—CDC, Shugart—are not planning to compete with 5¼" cartridges.

The 8" competition is too big, too slow, too costly and has higher attachment costs. They must move up to higher capacity to survive.

If cost projections are met, margins in excess of 50% are possible.

It has one disadvantage:

All fixed media 5¼" drives fit in the space of one 5¼" floppy. This drive requires additional space, though the placement of electronics is flexible.

Ministorage Drive versus Competition

Parameter	Ministorage FR 10 + 10	14" Cartridges	8" Cartridges	5¼" Cartridges	8" fixed	5¼" Fixed
Capacity (MB)	10 + 10	5 + 5, 16 + 80	8 + 8 -16 + 16	5 + 5	20 - 80	10 - 40
Price (OEM$)	$1500 (1000 possible)	$3000	$2700 - 2000	$1200	$1500 - 3000	$1100 - 1800
Reliability (1000 hours)	8–10	2	6	8–10	8–10	8–10
Physical size (inches)	(3.25 × 5.75 × 8) (2)	10.5 × 17.5 × 30.5	4.6 × 8.6 × 15*	3.25 × 5.75 × 8	4.6 × 8.6 × 12	3.25 × 5.75 × 8
Power	+5 DC +12 DC	+5 DC +12 DC 120V AC	+5 DC +12 DC	+5 DC +12 DC	+5 DC +12 DC	+5 DC +12 DC
Interface	ST506	Diablo	SMD	ST506	SMD, AN511 ST506 Unique	ST506
Head Positioning Avg Time (MS)	35	30–40	30–60	30–40	30–60	20–170

* Approximate average.

MARKETING STRATEGY

MARKETING STRATEGY

Staffing

Primary sales force to be direct rather than rep's.

Initial staffing to be:

National sales manager—covers Northeast.

West coast salesperson.

East coast salesperson.

Technical support home office person.

Back-up from CEO and Engineering.

Further expansion determined by contracts.

Assume one salesperson can handle three major contracts, that is, three salespeople good for nine contracts (20K units/yr).

Compensation will be weighted toward commission to encourage performance.

Literature and Advertising

Use press release of company formation as first lead getter.

Handouts will be professional looking color brochures and data sheets.

Advertising primarily prior to National Computer Conference.

Representation at the National Computer Conference is mandatory.

National Computer Conference

Private suite.

Liberally distributed invitations.

Will show operating unit.

Preshow advertising.

PRICING STRATEGY

Initial pricing will be a balance between:

8″ cartridge competition.

5¼″ cartridge competition.

5¼″ fixed drive competition.

Need for market penetration.

Initially, margins are high enough not to be an issue.

Recognition that cost is the first decision factor.

Later pricing will be a balance of:

Margin, though current projections do not make this a limiter.

Market elasticity.

Production capacity.

Cost of expansion of production.

Competitive pressure.

Product demand.

The proposed pricing is:

Quantity	10 + 10 Unit	40MB Unit
1	2600	3000
100	2070	2160
500	1620	1910
1000	1612	1800
2500	1500	1675
5000	Quote	Quote

Licensing will be sought, especially overseas:

$500k + 3%

$300k + 3% + 2000 units

INITIAL CUSTOMER CONTACT

After working model can be shown.

Will be prepared to take orders for prototype evaluation models within 60 days.

Well-known qualified customer list will be contacted.

Large firms are a long shot—possible license.

Startup firms must be qualified or C.O.D.

Aim is customers who will use 1000 to 2000/yr.

Must be prepared to talk five-year product plan.

FORECAST ASSUMPTIONS

There should be any number of controllers existing that will accept the drive if it has the ST506 interface. These will interface the drive to most common micro computer buses.

There will be no other 5¼" 10 fixed plus 10 removable drive until at best mid 1983.

The lead time for system integration is minimized due to use of standard existing interface, physical dimensions, power and media.

12 to 18 months for a large user (2000/yr).

6 to 12 months for a smaller user (1000/yr).

Product life will be four to five years.

There will be a family of products with a new entry every 12 to 18 months.

Competitive Pricing Comparisons

Manufacturer	Product	Size	Capacity	Q = 1	Q = 100	Q = 500	Q = 1000	Q = 2600	Q = 5000	Q = 10000
CII-HB	D140	10.5	15F + 15R				2700			
CDC	Lark I	8	8F + 8R		2850		2700			
CDC	Lark II	8	16F + 16R		2850		2700			
P-E	Vanguard	8	17.6F + 17.6R	3000	2600	2600	2500	2400	2350	2200
Iomega	Alpha 10	8	10R				1200			
DMA		5.25	5F + 5R							
Newworld		5.25	4F + 4R		1296	1196	1300	1040		
Irwin	510	5.25	10F + 10 tape				1500			
CMI		5.25	6F	1350					Quote	Quote
		5.25	10F	2000	1300					
		5.25	40F				1800			
Ministorage	FR 10 + 10	5.25	10F + 10R	2600	2070	1620	1612	1500	Quote	Quote
	F40	5.25	40F	300	2160	1910	1800	1675		

Ministorage Drives Forecast by Quarter

Unit	1982				1983				1984				1985	1986
	1Q	2Q	3Q	4Q	1Q	2Q	3Q	4Q	1Q	2Q	3Q	4Q		
10 + 10	0	0	10	30	500	1000	2000	3600	4000	4200	4400	4800	20,000	20,000
40					10	30	50	500	1000	2500	4800	5200	25,000	30,000
20 + 20										20	50	200	10,000	20,000
80													200	15,000

Consecutive products will be complimentary not truncators.

The forecast will not be a major percentage of the total market for several years.

Forecast by Year

Unit	1982	1983	1984	1985	1986
10 + 10	40	7100	17,400	20,000	20,000
40	0	590	13,500	25,000	30,000
20 + 20	—	—	270	10,000	20,000
80	—	—	—	200	15,000

Revenue by Year
($M as shipped)

Unit	1982	1983	1984	1985	1986
FR10 + 10	.080	10.6	26.1	26	26
40	0	.9	22.6	40	45
FR20 + 20			.9	17	34
80					30
	.080	11.5	56.6	93	135

Total Market Forecasts

Hobbs*	USA (units × 1000)		All Rigid		WW = 1.25 USA	
		1981	1982	1983	1984	1985
	8″	70	125	210	315	430
	5¼″	40	100	190	300	440
	Total	110	225	300	615	870

Hobbs*	USA (units × 1000)		Removable			
	8″	12	30	65	110	165
	5¼″	0	10	35	95	165
		12	40	100	205	370

Dataquest*	WW (units × 1000)		5¼″	Rigid only		
	Total	50.5	139.6	246.2	370.7	487.8
	OEM only	48	121.3	196.7	282.5	356.1

Porter*	1980	WW	$M			
Cartridge 12MB						
	Total		473.3	346.5	255.8	
	OEM		202.7	159.6	122.6	
Cartridge 12MB						
	Total		548.8	748.3	915.3	
	OEM		219.8	323.3	411.7	
Rigid 30MB						
	Total		709.1	924.5	1088.1	
	OEM		169.4	243.5	314.0	

*Industry market reports.

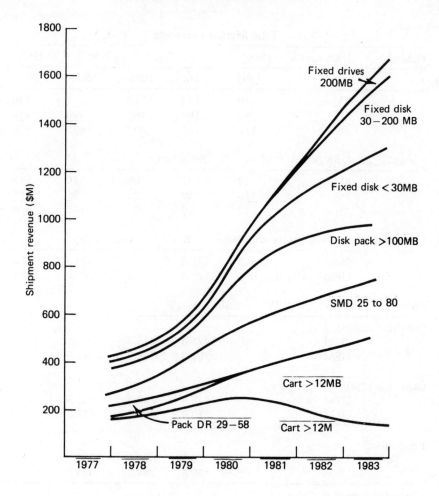

DEVELOPMENT MILESTONES

Major Milestones

Event	10 + 10 Cartridge	40MB Fixed
Specifications	Sept. 81	Sept. 81
Engineering model complete	March 82	Sept. 82
Prototype construction complete	May 82	Feb. 83
Prototype complete (3) (working with controller)	Aug. 82	March 83
Environmental test complete	Oct. 82	April 83
Prototype production—10 units	Sept. 82	April 83
Begin production ramp up	Dec. 82	July 83
Full scale production	Dec. 82	July 83
20 preproduction	Oct. 82	June 83
30 Preproduction	Nov. 82	July 83

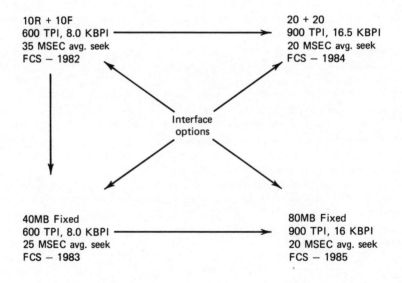

10R + 10F
600 TPI, 8.0 KBPI
35 MSEC avg. seek
FCS — 1982

20 + 20
900 TPI, 16.5 KBPI
20 MSEC avg. seek
FCS — 1984

Interface options

40MB Fixed
600 TPI, 8.0 KBPI
25 MSEC avg. seek
FCS — 1983

80MB Fixed
900 TPI, 16 KBPI
20 MSEC avg. seek
FCS — 1985

PRODUCT COST PROJECTIONS

Product Costs

Mech. Module MFG Cost	10 Mb Fixed 10 Mb Removable	40 Mb Fixed
Base assy.	70.80	70.00
Spindle assy.	41.50	121.50
Receiver assy.	16.92	—
Positioner assy.	136.10	204.10
Headloader assy.	18.00	
Subtotal	$283.32	$395.60
Elect. Module		
Box	20.00	20.00
Electronics	270.00	270.00
Fan	6.00	6.00
Subtotal	$296.00	$296.00
TOTAL	$579.32	$691.60
Labor 2.75 Hr. × $25./Hr.	68.75	68.75
MLB (1982)	$648.07	$760.35
MLB Goal (1985)	$500.00	$600.00

*Material–Labor–Burden (MLB)

ORGANIZATION AND STAFFING

OVERALL STRATEGY:
HIT THE TREADMILL RUNNING

Procure sufficient funding to last to positive cash flow.

    Provide minimum argument of stability necessary to attract large customers.

    Allow capital investment to save cost.

Staff to meet mid-1982 first shipments and year-end 1982 full production rate of 6,000–10,000 units per year.

Plan on one new product/year.

    Necessary to maintain market position.

    Necessary to make initial sale.

    Successive products must be complementary.

    Fixed units provide mainstream product. Competition is stiff but market is larger.

    Plan expenditures for moderate success, but have plan in place to shift to higher production should the opportunity present itself.

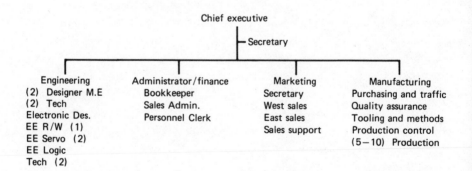

Headcount by Month

	1981			1982												1983		
	O	N	D	J	F	M	A	M	J	J	A	S	O	N	D	J	F	M
Chief executive	1																	
Secretary		1				1								1				
Administrator		1																
Bookkeeper					1													
Sales admin.														1				
Personnel clerk									1									
Finance									1								1	
Head marketeer		1																
Sales support	1																	
Salespeople							1				1				1			
Head engineer	1																	
M.E. design	1																	
EE		2	1	1	1													
Tech's		2	1	1	1													
Manufacturing		1					1											
Production control								1										
Purchasing and traffic									1									
Quality ass.								1										
Tooling and methods										1								
Production										1	2	2	2	2	2	2	2	2
Addirions	3	8	2	1	5	3	3	0	3	1	3	2	4	2	3	3	2	2
Cum. total	3	11	13	14	18	21	24	24	27	28	31	33	37	39	42	45	47	49

FINANCIAL PROJECTIONS

MONTHLY SPEND RATE ASSUMPTIONS

Benefits amount to 20% of salary.

Revenue arrives 60 days after shipment.

Material is brought in 30 days before shipment. Paid for in 45 days.

Rent is in advance, 1 month.

Capital equipment is shown as it is paid for.

Taxes are at 53% of net.

No income is assumed on cash reserve.

No fees for hiring expense.

No license was shown in the revenue, though a license sale would be sought.

Operating Expenses Outlay—by Periods
(in thousands)

	1981	1H82	2H82	1Q83	2Q83	3Q83	4Q83	1Q84	2Q84	3Q84	4Q94	1985	1986
Operating Expenses													
Salaries and fringe	104	495	696	414	426	435	444	450					
Travel and living	10	57	78	45	46	47	48	49					
Rent and utilities	15	30	85	48	48	48	48	50					
Tel. and tel. post.	3	29	48	27	27	27	28	28					
Sales literature	10	15	10	15	0	15	0	15					
Advertising	0	65	40	20	50	0	20	20					
Misc. legal and fin.	1	6	6	6	6	6	6	6					
Office supplies	3	29	48	27	27	27	28	28					
Total	146	727	1011	602	630	605	622	646	650	660	670	3300	3780
Capital Outlays													
Mfg. start-up	0	280	0	0	0	0	0	0	0				
Committed tooling	0	200	200	0	0	200	0	0	200				
Engineering equip.	176	176	0	0	0	100	0	0	100				
Office equip.	60	30	30	30	0	0	0	0	0				
Total	186	636	230	30	0	300	0	0	300	0	0	0	0
Depreciation													
Mfg start-up	0	19	18	10	9	10	9	10	9	10	9	37	36
Committed tooling	0	20	20	20	20	20	30	30	30	40	40	160	160
Engineering equip.	0	18	35	17	18	17	22	22	22	27	27	110	110
Office equip.	0	6	9	6	8	8	8	8	8	8	8	30	30
Total	0	63	82	53	55	55	69	70	69	85	84	337	336

Income Statement—by Periods
(in thousands)

	1H82	2H82	1Q83	2Q83	3Q83	4Q83	1Q84	2Q84	3Q84	4Q84	1985	1986
Sales	0	80	815	1545	3075	6065	7700	10540	14700	16260	83400	135000
Direct Cost of Sales												
Labor	0	8	36	73	143	278	345	467	639	709	3800	5845
Materials	0	72	295	600	1195	2435	3010	4172	5888	6490	34790	54250
TOTAL	0	80	331	673	1338	2713	3355	4639	6527	7199	38590	60095
Gross Margins	0	0	484	872	1737	3352	4345	5901	8173	9061	44810	74905
Operating Expenses	727	1011	602	630	605	622	646	650	660	670	3300	3780
Depreciation	63	82	53	55	55	69	70	69	85	84	337	336
Total Expenses	790	1093	665	685	660	691	716	719	745	754	3637	4116
Income Before Taxes	(790)	(1013)	(171)	187	1077	2661	3629	5182	7428	8307	41173	70789
Provision for Taxes	0	0	0	0	0	1034	1923	2746	3937	4403	21822	37518
Net Income	(790)	(1013)	(171)	187	1077	1627	1706	2436	3491	3904	19351	33271

Balance Sheets
(in thousands)

	12/31/81	12/31/82	12/31/83	12/31/84	12/31/85	12/31/86
Assets						
Cash	4668	2144	543	4961	22099	47106
Accounts Receivable	0	0	4223	11350	13900	22500
Raw Materials Inventory	0	113	1376	4213	6900	7500
Total Current Assets	4668	2257	6142	20524	42899	77106
Capital Equipment	186	1052	1382	1682	1682	1682
Less Accumulated Depreciation	0	145	377	685	1022	1358
	186	907	1005	997	660	324
Total Assets	4854	3164	7147	21521	43559	77430
Liabilities and Stockholders' Equity						
Accounts Payable	0	113	1376	4213	6900	7500
Stockholders' Equity						
Paid-in Capital	5000	5000	5000	5000	5000	5000
Retained Earnings	(146)	(1949)	771	12300	31659	64930
	4854	3051	5771	17308	36659	69930
Total Liabilities and Stockholders' Equity	4854	3164	7147	21521	43559	77430

Cash Flow—by Period
(in thousands)

	1981	1H82	2H82	1Q83	2Q83	3Q83	4Q83	1Q84	2Q84	3Q84	4Q84	1985	1986
Sources of Funds													
Beginning Cash	5000	4668	3305	2144	1373	1038	987	543	1092	1560	2350	4961	22099
Net Income	(146)	(790)	(1013)	(171)	187	1077	1627	1706	2436	3491	3904	19351	33271
Depreciation	0	63	82	53	55	55	69	70	69	85	84	337	336
Accounts Payable (45 days)													
Current	0	0	113	266	531	1152	1376	1895	2754	3001	4213	6900	7500
Prior	0	0	0	(113)	(266)	(531)	(1152)	(1376)	(1895)	(2754)	(3001)	(4213)	(6900)
	4854	3941	2487	2179	1880	2791	2908	2838	4456	5383	7550	27336	56306
Uses of Funds													
Raw Material Inv. (45 days)			113	153	265	622	223	521	857	248	1212	2687	600
Accounts Receivable (60 days)													
Current	0	0	0	623	1200	2382	4224	5449	7488	9973	11350	13900	22500
Prior	0	0	(0)	(623)	(1200)	(2382)	(4244)	(5449)	(7488)	(9973)	(11350)	(13900)	
	0	0	0	623	577	1182	1842	1225	2039	2485	1377	2550	8600
Capital Equipment	186	636	230	30	0	0	300	0	0	300	0	0	0
	186	636	343	606	842	1804	2365	1746	2896	3033	2589	5237	9200
Ending Cash	4668	3305	2144	1373	1038	987	543	1092	1560	2350	4961	22099	47106

Manufacturing Start-up

Conveyor (for 50,000/yr., 200/day, 25/hr.)	65,000
Benches	20,000
Board line stuffing and soldering	10,000
Wave solderer	15,000
System test (3 device exercisers)	30,000
Test jigs and fixtures (assembly 10)	40,000
Clean hoods	100,000
	280,000

Capital Equipment

Oscilloscopes	51K
Spectrum analyzer	20
Dynamic analysis system	50
Logic analyzer	15
Software development system	30
Displacement meas. equipment	12
Accelerometers	15
Particle counter	10
Vector impedance meter	6
Gaussmeter	3
Clean booths	10
Mech. hardware, gauges, etc.	20
Misc. electrical	20
	262K

Supplies

Mech. hardware	5
Electrical hardware	25
	30K

CPU and WP
(May be elsewhere if combined with
general Co. CPU)

	60K
352K	400K
	(48K to build
	several
	prototypes)

Committed Tooling

Servo writer	$200,000
Flexcable artwork	3,000
Board artwork	10,000
Magnet sinter die	2,000
Prototype carriage tool	5,000
Prototype base tool	15,000
Prototype door tool	2,000
Fixed disk cover die	5,000
Receiver die	10,000
Die	3,000

Magnet glue jig	1,000
Coil glue jig	1,000
H. L. base die	10,000
H. L. wire die	4,000
H. L. driver die	3,000
2 filters	4,000
Head arm die	2,000
	$279,000
Misc.	15,000
Permanent die castings base	80,000
Door	6,000
Carriage	20,000
Total tooling	$400,000

Resume
Carolyn Joseph, P.E.
187 South Street
Boston, MA 02000
617–000–0000
617–000–0001

EDUCATION: 1959–1960, 1 year study to an MSEE, University of Conn.
1954–1959, BSME, Northeastern University

EXPERIENCE: 11/74–Present Principal P.E.—Owner
Joseph Associates–Consulting Engineers

I founded Joseph Associates to provide consulting service to my clients in electro-mechanical and computer fields. Clients came to Joseph Associates from Massachusetts, Connecticut, Oklahoma, New Hampshire, New York, Florida, Colorado, California, Italy, Japan and Germany.

With Joseph Associates on new products, I have been handling product development, market surveys, product specifications, technology surveys, concept generation, configurations, feasibility, patent matters, prototype design, prototype development, testing, product design, cost reduction, pricing, tooling and business planning. On existing products I conducted design reviews, solved technical problems and contributed to cost reduction programs.

Types of projects included precision rotating machinery, positioning systems using electro-magnetic and electro-hydraulic servos, steppers, mechanisms, gearing, band drives, automatic transmissions and controls.

Some techniques used were simulation modeling of non-linear, multi degree-of-freedom systems and testing using advanced state-of-the-art instrumentation.

11/73–11/74 Chief Mechanical Engineer
Info Corporation, Bedrock, Mass.

Conceived, designed and built floppy disk in three months. Set up production line, developed vendors and designed all tooling.

11/68–11/73 Honeywell

Started in 1968 as Staff Engineer to Group Director of mass storage (disk drive) development. Responsible for design reliability—performed simulations of all mechanisms in drive to fix margins. Verified reliability with life testing.

In 1972 I took over the servo department and brought into production a 3330 type positioner with the fastest access time in the industry.

In 1973 I set up a department for evaluation of O.E.M. peripherals to be used in Honeywell's mini-computer. Screening reviews were conducted by specialists in various departments to assess risk levels and desirable features of each device. We then conducted extensive evaluation of devices before final selection.

6/59–10/68 Worked as an Engineer for consulting firms.

Gained broad background in product design, special machinery, mechanisms, structures and servo-mechanisms. Representative clients were I.B.M., Honeywell, Nortronics, Sylvania and Hamilton Standard.

PATENTS:
1. Dual Drive Mechanism U.S. Pat. 1010101
2. Fuel Flow Limiting Apparatus U.S. Pat. 0101010
3. Linear Stepper (Pending)
4. Damper (Pending)

PAPERS:　"Friction Relaxation Oscillations" Honeywell Journal

PERSONAL:　Married, 5 Children, U.S. Citizen, Veteran, Secret Clearance

PROFESSIONAL AFFILIATIONS:　Member N.S.P.E., P.E.P.P.
Society for Computer Simulation
Registered Professional Engineer Mass. #11001

James Brown
2000 Concord Street
Boston, Massachusetts 02000   Telephone: (617)000–0002

JOB OBJECTIVE

Management position in planning or marketing with potential for rapid advancement in return for results.

QUALIFICATIONS

Ten years of direct experience in market and product planning for computer peripherals. Two years of direct experience in marketing of OEM peripherals, and five years of experience in engineering-planning management in a field service home office environment.

EDUCATION

1961   BSSE (Science Engineering, University of Massachusetts

EXPERIENCE

Since 1961, I have worked for Honeywell in many capacities. All previous employment was part-time during college.

8/80 to present	*Manager Storage Peripherals*: This position has as its charter the responsibility for all magnetic or optial disk and tape storage devices. It includes specification and selection, and program management of such devices used on all mini computer and small, medium and large business systems. There are eight reporting positions including Product Planners and Program Managers, each responsible for portions of the product line.
1/77 to 8/80	*Manager of Peripheral Product Planning*: The position had reporting to it six Product Specialized Professional Planners who were responsible for improving and maintaining competitiveness and profitability for the product areas assigned to them. This included the definition, selection of the source, and gaining of program approval for new products as well as improvements to existing programs.
5/71 to 12/76	*Marketing Planning Manager*: The responsibilities of this position included the establishment of business strategies, specification of products, specifications for future products, the writing of the business plan and the gaining of management approval. Product responsibilities included all disk, mass storage subsystems, and magnetic tape subsystems.
2/69 to 4/71	*OEM Marketing Manager*: In this newly created position, I was responsible for all functions associated with the establishment of Honeywell as an OEM peripheral vendor. It was

run as a small business—eleven people at the largest—within the peripheral device operations. The job included all phases of the operations from engineering to administration and direct sales.

1/68 to 1/69

Manager of Systems and Planning—Field Services: Starting with six people growing to thirty within one year, I established four new groups: (1) Financial Planning—responsible for product business plan input for FED; (2) Systems—a liaison group which defined and supervised new data processing projects for FED use; (3) Performance Analysis—a group which administered to FED Labor reporting system; and (4) Organizational Research—a group formed to apply management science techniques to field service problems.

9/66 to 1/68

Manager of Logic and Communications: Managed two field service groups, each with its own supervisor. The groups were composed of home office hardware troubleshooters and design engineering liaison men. One group handled central processors and tape R/W systems; the other, digital communications units and terminals.

1/64 to 9/66

Logic Group Supervisor: Headed a group of home office troubleshooters and maintain-ability engineers. As a side project, I was instrumental in specifying and implementing the field performance reporting system.

7/61 to 1/64

Held various field engineering posts in the backup of central processors, memories and tape R/W systems.

RESUME

Linda Champion
35 Bay Road
Boston, MA 02000

Date of Birth: May 28, 1932
Marital Status: Married, 2 Children
U.S. Citizen

CAREER OBJECTIVE:

An executive position with P & L responsibilities and equity incentive.

I would consider a challenging position in general management, sales management or marketing management commensurate with my qualifications and having the potential to lead to my career objective within a reasonable time frame.

QUALIFICATIONS:

More than twenty years successful technical, sales and marketing experience with the last nine years in a management position.

Master degree with Honors in Business Administration (Marketing, Finance, Management).

My determination to achieve success and my dedication to the commitments I make and the responsibilities I accept.

MAJOR ACCOMPLISHMENTS:

Contributed directly to securing and supporting several multi-million dollar contracts with leading U.S. Original Data Processing Equipment Manufacturers. Built the U.S. OEM Marketing organization of Honeywell including its repair/depot and logistic support center in Massachusetts.

EXPERIENCE:

February, 1978 to present	*Honeywell, Waltham, MA.* Director, OEM Marketing North America.
	Responsible for the marketing of Honeywell's EDP products to Original Equipment Manufacturers in North America. Responsibilities include: recruiting, incentive compensation plan, goals and quotas achievement, departmental operating budget, direct sales, distributor sales, sales administration, contractual negotiations, advertising and trade shows, technical support.
January, 1972 to January, 1978	*Honeywell Information Systems, Inc., Wellesley, MA.* OEM Sales Manager.
	Responsible for OEM Sales in the U.S. and Canada of the complete line of computer peripherals manufactured by Honeywell Information Systems, Inc.
May, 1970 to December, 1971	*Honeywell Information Systems, Inc., New York.* OEM Account Manager.
	Responsible for OEM sales of computer peripherals and account management in an assigned territory in the U.S.

May, 1968 to April, 1970	*Honeywell Information Systems, Inc.*. OEM Sales Representative.
	Responsible for sales of computer peripherals and account management in an assigned territory in the U.S. and Canada.

November, 1963 to April, 1968	*Honeywell Information Systems, New York.* OEM Product Engineer.
	Product application engineering, customer training, consultation in maintenance and technical liaisons with manufacturing plants in Europe.

October, 1962 to October, 1963	*Burroughs Corporation, New York*, EDP Field Engineer.
	Responsible for the maintenance of several computer systems sites.

February, 1960 to September, 1962	*Saxon Laboratories, Inc., New York*, Electrical Engineer.
	Telecommunications and audio systems design including manufacturing engineering.

January, 1959 to January, 1960	*State Lab, Inc., New York* Laboratory Manager.
	Industrial testing and certification of electrical and electronic components to U.S. Military specifications.

EDUCATION:

MBA, Boston University (September, 1978).

Other formal complementary training in:

Electronic Engineering Technology
   Computer Operation, programing and maintenance
   Sales and executive skills

FOREIGN LANGUAGES:

Fluent French, academic Italian.

APPENDIX

B. S. Kanin
Wiley Image
42 Time Avenue
Las Vegas, Nevada 00010
Phone: 213/737–8420

Application

$200,000 partially secured term loan payable in 24 monthly installments of $9,840.00 including interest at sixteen and one-half (16½) percent per annum.

Purpose

To enable B. S. Kanin to pay franchise requirements for Las Vegas Olympic-Committee-approved sport coins. He will produce coins for sales to Olympic Sponsors, U.S. Military Pxs, and Swiss Sport distribution.

Use of Funds

The money required and uses of funds are as follows:

Working capital	$200,000
Total loan requested	$200,000

Ownership

Wiley Image, Inc., is a corporation with the following owner-ship:

Owner and Address	% Owned/Office
B. S. Kanin 1911 Fourth Avenue Las Vegas, Nevada 00010	100% / President

Repayment

The comparative and projected financial statements and foot-notes in Tables A.1-A.4 demonstrate Wiley Image, Inc.'s financial history.

WILEY IMAGE HISTORY AND KEY PERSONNEL

History

The following is the history of Wiley Image Company including the background, capabilities, and education of B. S. Kanin and other key personnel:

Wiley Image Company began operations in 1900 and now it is still in full-force under the direction of B. S. Kanin, president of Wiley Image. Kanin has a long record of expertise and experience in business. As he puts it, "when you know about management, you know about business and your business can't help but be successful." He has more than proved that concept by taking a business endeavor and making its figures grow to proportions that many enterprises never realize. He has a close-knit, warm, working relationship with his employees.

Key Personnel

Kanin has been a leading small businessman for over 15 years. He began his career in the banking industry as a loan officer for

TABLE A.1 Comparative Financial Statements for Wiley Image, Inc.

	12 Month 12/31/89 Inc. Tax ($)	12 Month 12/31/90 Inc. Tax ($)	12 Month 12/31/91 Inc. Tax ($)	6 Month 6/30/92 P & L ($)
Sales and other	821,412	606,517	526,740	91,262
Inventory, beginning	94,362	32,220	10,027	12,506
Raw materials purchase	352,363	226,521	233,629	15,544
Direct labor	218,588	116,623	112,383	31,951
Freight	20,357	11,608	16,804	2,566
Factory overhead	99,756	77,407	102,871	685
Inventory, ending	32,220	10,027	12,506	36,532
Cost of sales	753,296	453,992	463,208	26,720
Gross profit	68,206	152,525	63,532	64,542
Operating expenses:				
Auto	2,847	2,338	405	50
Bad debt	937	2,075	– 0 –	– 0 –
Commissions	9,247	9,348	1,849	262
Contributions/Penalties	7,726	8,572	1,472	1,737
Depreciation	591	987	1,474	– 0 –
Dues and subscriptions			3,143	175
Freight out	21,300	14,778	10,905	2,120
Gifts/samples	419	1,220	475	85
Insurance	3,459	2,553	2,482	– 0 –
Interest	24,364	37,749	– 0 –	617
Legal/accounting	8,938	19,415	9,291	650
Officer's salary	– 0 –	– 0 –	– 0 –	3,046
Other tax	308	– 0 –	– 0 –	951
Miscellaneous	116	7,698	5,822	362
Payroll tax	2,118	1,392	1,799	– 0 –
Rent	1,811	1,748	1,744	8,742
Repairs/maintenance	1,463	490	– 0 –	266
Supplies	8,519	5,536	13,464	5,337
Telephone	2,117	2,155	– 0 –	1,333
Travel/entertainment	4,796	7,747	3,771	1,550
Utilities	440	418	– 0 –	2,224
Wages	19,176	12,823	26,934	593
Total operating expenses	122,865	141,603	120,468	30,621
Net income	(54,659)	10,922	(56,946)	33,921

TABLE A.2   Projected Financial Statements for Wiley Image, Inc.

	12 Month Projected, Year 1 ($)	12 Month Projected, Year 2 ($)
Sales and other	2,640,000	6,454,000 [1]
Cost of sales	1,980,000	4,818,000 [2]
Gross profit	660,000	1,636,000
Operating expenses:		
Advertising	28,000	51,500
Auto	12,000	32,000
Bad debt	27,000	43,000
Commissions	39,120	95,600
Contributions	4,500	6,000
Depreciation	11,100	11,100 [3]
Dues and subscriptions	1,200	6,000
Freight out	28,950	44,000
Gifts/samples	4,800	6,000
Insurance	6,000	7,200
Interest	33,000	7,100 [3]
Licenses/tax	3,600	4,800
Miscellaneous	4,500	6,000
Professional services	49,000	106,000
Payroll	91,000	160,000
Payroll tax	16,300	28,800 [3]
Public relations	52,000	80,000
Rent	12,000	12,000 [3]
Repairs/maintenance	1,800	12,600
Supplies	4,800	30,800
Telephone	6,000	8,400
Travel/entertainment	12,000	21,500
Utilities	6,000	8,400
Total operating expenses	468,550	788,800 [3]
Net income	191,450	847,200

TABLE A.3 Monthly Income Projections for Wiley Image, Inc., Year 1

	Month 1	Month 2	Month 3	Month 4	Month 5	Month 6
Sales[1]	$ 44,000	44,000	88,000	88,000	132,000	132,000
Cost of sales[2]	33,00	33,00	66,000	66,000	99,000	99,000
Gross profit	11,000	11,000	22,000	22,000	33,000	33,000
Expenses[3]	39,046	39,046	39,046	39,046	39,046	39,046
Net profit	$ (28,046)	(28,046)	(17,046)	(17,046)	(6,046)	(6,046)

	Month 7	Month 8	Month 9	Month 10	Month 11	Month 12	Total
Sales	$264,000	264,000	352,000	352,000	440,000	440,000	2,640,000
Cost of sales	198,000	194,000	264,000	264,000	330,000	330,000	1,980,000
Gross profit	66,000	66,000	88,000	88,000	110,000	110,000	660,000
Expenses	39,046	39,046	39,046	39,046	39,046	39,046	468,550
Net profit	$26,954	26,954	48,954	48,953	70,952	70,952	191,450

TABLE A.4 Monthly Income Projections for Wiley Image, Inc., Year 2

	Month 1	Month 2	Month 3	Month 4	Month 5	Month 6
Sales[1]	$440,000	440,000	440,000	440,000	528,000	528,000
Cost of sales[2]	330,000	330,000	330,000	330,000	396,000	396,000
Gross profit	110,000	110,000	110,000	110,000	132,000	132,000
Expenses[3]	65,733	65,733	65,733	65,733	65,733	65,733
Net profit	$ 44,267	44,267	44,267	44,267	66,267	66,267

	Month 7	Month 8	Month 9	Month 10	Month 11	Month 12	Total
Sales	$528,000	616,000	616,000	616,000	616,000	616,000	6,454,000
Cost of sales	396,000	462,000	462,000	462,000	462,000	462,000	4,818,000
Gross profit	132,000	154,000	154,000	154,000	154,000	154,000	1,636,000
Expense	65,733	65,733	65,734	65,734	65,734	65,734	788,800
Net profit	$66,267	88,267	88,266	88,266	88,266	88,266	847,200

Notes on Projected Items for Tables A.1–A.4

1 Sales are based on expected income for the first year of operation.

2 Cost of Sales is based on 75 percent of sales, according to a cost study, Exhibit II. Items in cost of sales and their percentages are as follows:

Item	Percentage of Sales
Direct labor	10.0
Materials	47.00
Manufacturing overhead	2.0
Royalties	16.0

3 Operating expenses are based on historical and industry averages. Operating expenses are explained in more detail in the following footnotes.

3 Depreciation is based on historical averages.

3 Interest is for a $200,000 loan for 2 years at 16.5% per annum. Principal Loan Repayment represents $85,000 the first year.

3 Payroll tax abd Benefits are projected at 18 percent of salaries for federal, state, and local authorities.

2 Rent for the premises is expected to be $1,000 per month. The proposed lease is in Exhibit IV.

Personal Data The following is a personal financial statement of B. S. Kanin as of 1 October 1992

B. S. Kanin — Personal Financial Statement

Assets		Liabilities & Net Worth	
Cash	$ 150	Credit cards	$ 700
Deposits in excrow	– 0 –	Notes payable	37,000*
Autos	1,500	Installment, auto	450
Real estate	– 0 –	Total liabilities	$38,150
Personal property	3,500	Net Worth	(33,000)
Total assets	$5,150	Total liab. & net worth	5,150

*Notes payable include the following:

Note Holder	Amount	How Secured
Nevada Western Bank	$37,000	Tillie Wright
449 Throughfare Ave.		Edward Johnson
Las Vegas, Calif. 90018		

Pro Forma: **The following proforma and comparative balance sheet show Wiley Image, Inc., at disbursement.**

Proforma Balance Sheet

	6/30/82		At Disbursement	
Assets				
Cash	$ (14,335)		$185,665	
Accounts receivable	105,997		105,991	
Inventory	36,532		36,532	
Deposits: Royalty/addias	10,000		10,000	
Total current assets		138,194		338,194
Furniture and fixtures	2,090		2,090	
Machinery/equipment	222,233	(1)	222,233	
Office equipment	4,025		4,025	
Improvements/buildings	16,902		16,902	
Automobile	2,793		2,793	
Less: depreciation	(110,184)		(110,184)	
Total fixed assets		137,858		137,859
Deposits	4,548		4,548	
Total other assets		4,548		4,548
Total assets		$280,600		480,600
Liabilities and Net Worth				
Notes payable	$104,133		$104,133	
Short-term notes payable	(1,975)		(1,975)	
King Glove Transf. acct.	2,669		2,669	
Unearned income	30,485		30,485	
Accounts payable	32,982		32,982	
Accrued insurance	10,588		10,588	
Accrued taxes	12,061		12,061	
Accrued wages	7,116		7,116	
Accrued interest	129,790		129,790	
New $200,000 loan, current	– 0 –		$ 85,080	
Total current liabilities		327,849		412,929
Note payable	265,056		265,056	
New $200,000, long term	– 0 –		114,920	
Total long-term liabilities		265,056		379,976
Total Liabilities		592,905		792,905

	6/30/82		At Disbursement	
Common stock	41,960		41,960	
Preferred stock	50,000		50,000	
Retained earnings	(438,187)		(438,187)	
Profit	33,921		33,921	
Owner's Equity		(312,306)		(312,306)
Total Liab. and Equity		$280,600		$480,600

Bank of Gold, rose to the position of vice-president; he held the position of manager and director of the Blacks Bank; and lastly was manager of the Toms Beach office of United Coastal Bank. He was in on the beginnings of the Blacks Bank as an original officer and participated in the establishment and subsequent growth of the bank. His responsibilities included the implementation and execution of the total loan portfolio.

His education includes engineering school in Germany, graduation from Houston City College, and schooling at the American Institute of Banking. In his association with institutions of higher education, he serves as a member of the Board of Councilors at the USC Von Slow Center.

Right alongside B.S. Kanin is Marge Kanin, his sister, and John, his brother, who are as dedicated as Kanin in keeping Wiley Image company a full-service manufacturing establishment. Both Marge and John are top-notch business people, complementing Kanin's management with efficient administrative and production support.

Marge Kanin has a Masters Degree in Urban and Regional Planning from SMU, a B.A. from Texas State University in Education

WILEY IMAGE'S PRODUCTS AND FACILITIES

Wiley Image, Inc., currently specializes in manufacturing clothing and a large variety of sport and casual coins. This firm is an SBA 8(a) certified company.

The facilities are located in 20,000 square feet of leased space at 42 Time Avenue in Las Vegas. This includes adequate office, storage, plant, and loading facilities. There are at present 23 employees, and the firm is operating at about 30 percent of its total capacity.

Wiley Image has a letter of intent from Swiss Sport that would designate the company as a sublicensee. The consumation of this agreement would give the company tremendous potential for expansion of its sport coin marketing. It would give Wiley Image the exclusive right to produce a line of coins using the Olympic designs and mascot. The coins will be produced for sales and distribution to Swiss Sport throughout the eleven Western states and Canada, direct sales to U.S. PX establishments, direct sales to the official Olympic Sponsors, and sales to minority-owned wholesale and distribution firms.

Internally the company has well-established business systems that will allow this increase in activities to occur with no interruption or distortion. The company owns an Apple computer system that handles the accounting functions including accounts receivable, sales, invoicing, payroll, and general ledger.

BIBLIOGRAPHY

1. Abraham, Alfred B. *Analyze Your Records to Reduce Costs* (Washington, D.C.: S.B.A., 1978).
2. *Business Plan for Small Manufacturers* (Washington, D.C.: S.B.A., 1973).
3. Cohen, Jerome B., Edward D. Zinborg, and Arthur Zeikel. *Guide to Intelligent Investing* (Homewood, Ill.: Dow Jones-Irwin, 1977).
4. *Dun & Bradstreet Reference Book* (New York: Dun & Bradstreet Publishing Company).
5. *Electronic News Financial Fact Book & Directory* (New York: Fairchild Publications).
6. Feller, Jack H., Jr. *Keep Pointed Toward Profit* (Washington, D.C., S.B.A., 1978).
7. Fremgen, James J. *Accounting for Managerial Analysis*, 3d ed. (Homewood, Ill.: Irwin, 1972).
8. Goulet, Peter G. *Attacking Business Decision Problems with Breakeven Analysis* (Washington, D.C.: S.B.A., 1977).
9. *Guide to American Directories*, 9th ed. (New York: B. Klein Publications, 1975).
10. Hosmer, LaRue T. *A Venture Capital Primer for Small Business* (Washington, D.C.: S.B.A., 1978).
11. *How to Read a Financial Report* (New York: Merrill, Lynch, Pierce, Fenner & Smith, Inc.).
12. John, Webster H., and S. W. McFarland. *How to Use the Business Library: With Sources of Business Information*, 4th ed. (Cincinnati: Southwestern Publishing Co., 1957).
13. Matz, Adolph, and O. J. Curry. *Cost Accounting—Planning and Control* (Cincinnati: Southwestern, 1972).
14. Miller, Jeffrey G. *Manufacturing Management* (Washington, D.C., S.B.A., 1976).

15. Murphy, John F. *Sound Cash Management and Borrowing* (Washington, D.C.: S.B.A., 1978).

16. Smith, Ivan C. *Tips on Getting More for Your Marketing Dollar* (Washington, D.C.: S.B.A., 1978).

17. *Thomas Register of American Manufacturers* (New York: Thomas Publishing Company).

18. *U.S. Industrial Directory* (Boston: Cahners Publishing Co.).

19. Weston, Fred, and Brigham, Eugene F. *Essentials of Managerial Finance* (Hinsdale, Ill.: The Dryden Press, 1976).

20. *World's Who's Who in Finance and Industry* (Chicago: Who's Who, Inc.).

INDEX